VISUAL QUICKSTART GUIDE

MAYA 4.5

FOR WINDOWS AND MACINTOSH

Danny Riddell

D1411968

Peachpit Press

Visual QuickStart Guide
Maya 4.5 for Windows and Macintosh
Danny Riddell

Peachpit Press
1249 Eighth Street
Berkeley, CA 94710
510/524-2178
800/283-9444
510/524-2221 (fax)

Find us on the World Wide Web at: http://www.peachpit.com
To report errors, please send a note to errata@peachpit.com
Peachpit Press is a division of Pearson Education

Copyright © 2003 by Danny Riddell

Editor: Jill Marts Lodwig
Technical Editor: Andrew Britt, Eric Anderson, and Victor Gavenda
Production Coordinator: Lisa Brazieal
Copyeditor: Jill Simonsen
Compositor: Owen Wolfson
Indexer: Karin Arrigoni
Cover Design: The Visual Group
Cover Production: Nathalie Valette

ISBN 0-321-17239-6

9 8 7 6 5 4 3 2 1

Printed and bound in the United States of America

To my incredible wife, Yee-Ju, and family for inspiring me, believing in me, and challenging me. Without their love, dedication, and support, this book would not have been possible.

Acknowledgements

I'd especially like to thank the following people: Andrew Britt, for his writing and knowledgable technical review on the first edition; Jill Marts Lodwig, for her positive attitude and guidance throughout the project; Jill Simonsen, for steering my wordsmithing in the right direction; Marjorie Baer, for her constant encouragement and leadership; Lisa Brazieal and Owen Wolfson, for their production and design expertise; and Eric Anderson, for his technical contributions to this edition.

TABLE OF CONTENTS

INTRODUCTION

Figure i.1 This voracious prehistoric lizard is just one of the myriad creatures you can bring to life in Maya.

Welcome to *Maya: Visual QuickStart Guide*.

Alias|Wavefront's Maya is the high-end 3D program that has brought to life many of the three-dimensional people, animals, plants, cars, and machines you see in film, videos, and games. Whether you want to create pod races, realistic anatomy, or scenes with an artistic flair, Maya can help you achieve the desired look and feel. Maya's only restriction is your imagination; if you can think it up, you can create it in Maya, with precise control over the final imagery (**Figure i.1**).

Maya is an extremely powerful character-animation application. By offering tools for both cartoon and photo-realistic character animators, Maya has become the preferred 3D character animation program.

This book will introduce you to Maya's interface and features. You'll soon realize, though, that Maya has enough depth to keep you learning for years. What makes Maya spectacular is that the average user can learn enough to build incredible images relatively quickly. Maya offers ease of use for beginners and extreme depth for advanced users, propelling it to the top of the 3D software genre.

Who Is This Book For?

If you want to learn basic 3D concepts, or if you are familiar with other 3D software and want to learn Maya, this book is for you. You should be familiar with computers and other graphics software packages, but you don't need prior 3D knowledge (though it will make Maya easier to learn). This book will guide you through the expansive Maya interface and show you how to animate and render your 3D projects. If you work through this book from cover to cover, you'll end up with a solid Maya foundation—familiarity with the user interface and the capability to model, texture, and animate 3D content.

Once you've completed this book and mastered the Maya basics, you'll be ready to explore Maya's more advanced features—for example, particle and dynamic simulations (for creating fire, water, and other elements) and real-time rendering (for online and game development). Good resources for game links and tutorials are *www.upaxis.com* and *www.carboncollege.com*.

After exploring Maya modeling, rendering, and animation, you may find that you're better at one or the other. As you work through this book, think about which area interests you most. Using Maya could develop into a hobby or even a career in creating 3D content for movies, product ads, and interactive entertainment!

What You Will Need

For starters, of course, you'll need a copy of Maya for Macintosh or Windows installed on your computer. See Maya's documentation for instructions on installing the program.

In terms of hardware, Maya's incredible power comes at a price. Maya is the most resource-intensive software I know of, so I recommend beefing up your machine with as much RAM and processor power as you can manage—you'll definitely feel the difference. Also, be aware that Maya requires using a three-button mouse. Check out the Maya documentation for minimum system requirements, or visit Alias|Wavefront's Web site (*www.aliaswavefront.com*).

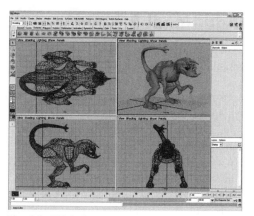

Figure i.2 This is the Maya 4.5 interface as it appears on Windows.

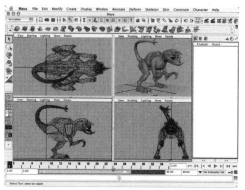

Figure i.3 Here's a look at the interface of Maya 4.5 for Mac OS X.

Maya Versions and Flavors

This book covers Maya 4.5 for Windows and Mac OS X (**Figures i.2** and **i.3**). With this version, there's very little difference between the two versions—at least in the features I cover. However, whenever there *is* a difference in functionality, we'll point it out.

One difference between the Maya interface in Windows and Mac versions is that the Mac version lets you tear off Hotbox menus. Another difference is that Maya 4.5 for Windows comes in three flavors: Builder, Complete, and Unlimited; whereas Maya 4.5 for Mac OS X comes in just one: Complete.

Let's take a closer look at the different flavors of Maya for Windows:

- **Maya Builder** is designed for low-polygon modeling and game production. It includes a full complement of polygon-modeling tools for developing real-time Web 3D and game-console content.

- **Maya Complete** includes all of the tools and features of Maya Builder with the addition of advanced character-animation tools, dynamics (the use of physics to simulate real-world forces), and effects.

- **Maya Unlimited** includes all of Maya Complete's tools and features, plus Maya Cloth, Maya Fur, Advanced Modeling Tools, Subdivision Surfaces, Matchmoving, and Maya Batch Renderer.

MAYA VERSIONS AND FLAVORS

Because this book is for beginning to inter-mediate users, I cover only those features and tools found in Maya Complete. However, I also cover fluid dynamics, which is a hot new capability in Maya Unlimited, even though it's not available in Maya Complete. And Maya's scripting language, MEL (Maya Embedded Language), which is a part of all versions of Maya, is not included because it's really beyond the scope of this book.

What's new in Maya 4.5?

Other than the coalescing of Windows and Mac versions of Maya in version 4.5, other notable enhancements in the new version, and to this book, include multiple additions to modeling tools like the smooth proxy, wedge, poke faces, and cut faces tools. There are also workflow enhancements which include new align and snapping tools.

In this book I've added two new chapters: one on deformers and one on dynamics. The Deformers chapter shows you how to deform geometry in new and exciting ways and speed workflow using the deformation tools. The Dynamics chapter shows you how to add real-world particle simulations to enhance dynamic effects. Also included in this chapter is the much-anticipated fluid dynamics capability , which you can use to create water and fluid-based effects.

Additional Resources

There are hundreds of Maya- and 3D-related resources on the Web. One of my favorites is *www.upaxis.com*. UpAxis offers tutorials, classes, and listservs to which many talented 3D artists contribute daily. UpAxis.com is operated by the online 3D animation school Carbon College of Design (*www.carboncollege.com*). Some other good 3D tutorial and informational sites include Highend 3D (*www.highend3d.com*), 3D Café (*www.3dcafe.com*), 3D Ark (*www.3dark.com*), and Animation World Network, or AWN (*www.awn.com*).

Maya Basics

Maya's layered user interface is very easy to use, yet it lets you access the application's great depth of functionality. This chapter introduces you to that interface and shows you how to set preferences, start a project, and access online help. First, though, it's a good idea to know something about the way Maya works.

About Maya

Maya is a node-based program. A *node* is a visual representation of an element, such as a surface, texture, or animation curve. Every element in Maya is represented by a node or several connected nodes (**Figure 1.1**). The nodes themselves are made up of many *attributes,* which are the information that defines the node, such as an object's position or size. You access nodes in the Outliner and Hypergraph (**Figure 1.2**) panels. The advantage of this node-based architecture is that it gives you precise control over which nodes get connected to or disconnected from other nodes—which in turn determines the behavior and look of the object. Maya lets you view all of a scene's connections from within the Hypergraph (**Figure 1.3**). The arrows and lines represent the connections. (The Hypergraph is covered in more detail later in this chapter.)

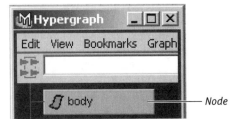

Figure 1.1 Nodes can be viewed in the Hypergraph or the Outliner. A new node is created for each object.

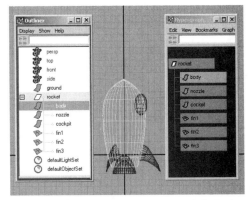

Figure 1.2 A Maya scene file can consist of a limited number of nodes and connections, or it can have thousands of nodes in more complex scene files.

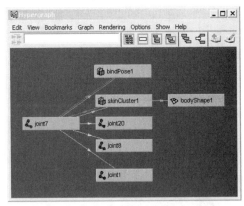

Figure 1.3 Node connections can be seen in the Hypergraph, with colored arrows showing the connections between the nodes and the directions of those connections.

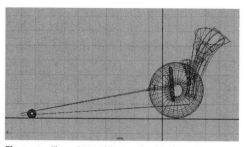

Figure 1.4 Flat, 2D graphics work with the *x* and *y* axes but lack a depth axis that enables images to become three-dimensional.

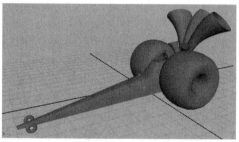

Figure 1.5 Adding another axis allows objects to become three-dimensional. These 3D models can now become accurately represented.

Maya's coordinate system

Traditional animation and graphics applications, like Adobe Photoshop, work with two axes, usually *x* and *y* (**Figure 1.4**). An *x* and *y* coordinate system provides height and width but lacks the depth to make objects appear three-dimensional. Maya adds a third axis, *z*, which gives objects depth (**Figure 1.5**). The addition of the third axis lets you create proportionally accurate models and animations.

Within the XYZ coordinate system are two kinds of coordinates, *world* and *local*. World coordinates start at the center of the scene in location 0, 0, 0, called the *origin* (**Figure 1.6**). Local coordinates are those around the area of the object.

Objects themselves have what's called *UV coordinate space*. A surface has a U direction and a V direction. In the simple example of a plane, the U direction goes from left to right, and the V direction goes from top to bottom (**Figure 1.7**). It's like latitude and longitude on a world map. Just as you can find a position on earth by its latitude and longitude, you can determine a position on a surface by its U and V coordinates. This becomes especially important when positioning textures on a surface.

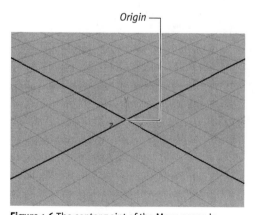

Origin

Figure 1.6 The center point of the Maya scene is called the *origin*. All directional values start at **0** from the origin.

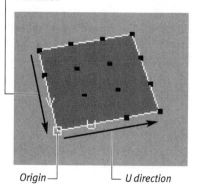

V direction

Origin — — U direction

Figure 1.7 Each surface is described with a U direction and a V direction. You can place curves on surfaces using U and V coordinates.

Maya's Interface

The Maya interface can appear daunting at first glance, but it's actually very organized and easy to get around once you're familiar with it (**Figure 1.8**). Along the top of the Maya interface is the main menu bar, which contains all the major Maya commands. Because Maya contains more menus than can fit in a window, you can't view all of them simultaneously in the menu bar. For this reason, Maya's menus are grouped into menu sets, arranged by tasks, which can be accessed from the menu at the far left of the status line.

The status line, located directly beneath the main menu bar, holds many important selection functions. Below the status line is the Shelf, which holds often-used tools. Along the left side of the interface is the toolbar, which holds Maya's manipulation tools. You use these tools to select, rotate, move, and scale objects or pieces of objects, called *components*.

The default Maya layout opens with four views: Front, Side, Top, and Perspective. The areas containing these views are called *panes*. The default layout has four panes. At the bottom of the interface are the *Range Slider* and *Time Slider*, which allow you to control your position in time for animation. At the right-hand side of the interface is the *Channel Box*, which holds shortcuts to object attributes.

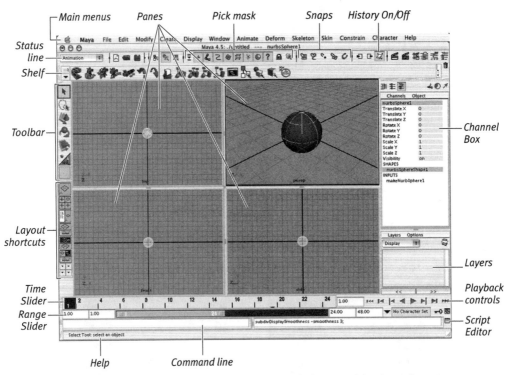

Figure 1.8 This is the Maya interface as it appears by default. Many of the elements seen here can be hidden or customized to suit the task at hand.

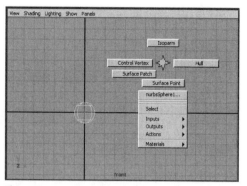

Figure 1.9 A Marking Menu holds additional shortcuts for turning different components on and off.

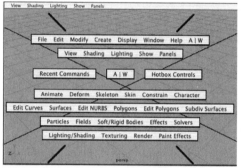

Figure 1.10 The Hotbox is a convenient way to access the program's menus and commands. It can be modified to suit a user's workflow in the Hotbox Controls menu.

In addition to the main menu bar, there are menus that can be accessed from within individual panes and through *Marking Menus* (**Figure 1.9**). Marking Menus represent a convenient way to quickly access tools or commands. They appear when you right-click an object or when you click in one of the five Hotbox regions (see "About the Hotbox," later in this chapter). Maya is full of menus, and it can take a significant amount of time to truly master them.

One of Maya's best features is the Hotbox (**Figure 1.10**). It holds all of Maya's menu sets and appears directly above the mouse pointer when you hold down the (Spacebar) (and then disappears again when you release the key). The Hotbox can be a great time-saver because you can access it from wherever your mouse is—without going up to the main menu bar and selecting a command.

To change an object's position, rotation, or scale (collectively known as *transforms*), you can type values in the Channel Box (**Figure 1.11**) or use Maya's *manipulators*, which allow you to change an object's value by clicking and dragging an interactive handle (**Figure 1.12**).

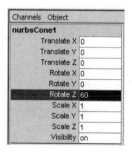

Figure 1.11 You can interactively change values by first selecting the attribute's name in the Channel Box, moving the mouse over a view pane, and then dragging the pointer back and forth in the view using the middle mouse button to alter the attribute numbers.

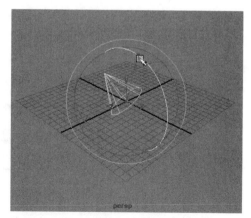

Figure 1.12 This cone is surrounded by a rotate manipulator. By clicking and dragging the circles, you can make the cone rotate.

Using the Shelf

The Shelf is where you can store often-used tools and commands. You can use multiple Shelf sets to organize your favorite and most frequently used tools. Maya 4.5 provides an extensive set of preset shelves (**Figure 1.13**). It is convenient to categorize items into individual Shelf sets. For instance, you could create one Shelf for all the modeling tools you frequently use and another Shelf for all your favorite rendering tools. You might even have a third Shelf that just holds your 10 or 15 most frequently used tools and commands.

In the Shelf you can add or delete items or choose from any of the preset Shelf commands. Although the Shelf is useful, it also takes up a lot of screen space. You can show and hide the Shelf when you need more screen space. To hide the Shelf, simply choose Display > UI Elements > Shelf (**Figure 1.14**).

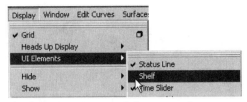

Figure 1.14 Maya's many windows can make screen space scarce. To save screen space, you can hide many interface elements by deselecting them in the Display > UI Elements submenu.

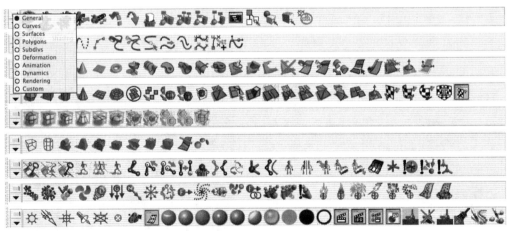

Figure 1.13 The Shelf holds tools and commands. You can customize it, or create additional Shelves, to contain frequently used commands and tools to suit the current task. All of the default shelf sets are shown (from top): General, Curves, Surfaces, Polygons, Subdivs, Deformation, Animation, Dynamics, Rendering.

MAYA'S INTERFACE

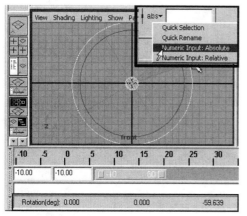

Figure 1.15 The Help Line shows important information about commands and translations. Here, at the bottom of the image, it is showing the rotation of a sphere in degrees.

The items you add to a Shelf retain their most recent settings—which means you can add the same tool to the Shelf twice but with different settings. For example, you could add two Create > Primitive > Sphere icons to the Shelf but adjust one's option to be a full 360 degrees and the other to less than 360 (for example, 240). You could then just click each of these icons to produce the sphere with the amount of degrees you want without having to go back into the options.

To add an object to the Shelf:

◆ Select the menu item you want to add to the Shelf while pressing (Ctrl)/(Control) and (Shift) at the same time.

The tool is added to the Shelf.

To remove an object from the Shelf:

◆ Using the middle mouse button, drag the icon from the Shelf to the trash.

The tool is removed from the Shelf.

About the Help Line

The Help Line provides information on object transformations and hints as to what your next step should be. When you move the mouse pointer over a menu item, text appears in the Help Line describing the steps needed to complete the command. If you rotate an object, the Help Line will reflect the change numerically (**Figure 1.15**).

The Numeric Input field to the right of the status line is where you can type precise values for the transformations. This can be useful when you need to have exact positioning for objects such as architectural buildings and product designs. Maya gives you the option to build things by eye or by entering exact position and size figures. When these changes are made, the new values appear in the Help Line.

MAYA'S INTERFACE

About the Channel Box

The Channel Box, which lists a selected object's *keyable* attributes, is located on the right side of the Maya interface (**Figure 1.16**). Keyable attributes are object properties that can be animated. You can change an attribute's value quickly in the Channel Box without having to open another full window (thus saving screen space). You can enter values in any attribute's field, or you can click on the attribute's name and interactively change its value by using the middle mouse button—to drag in any view pane.

Ten default attributes in the Channel Box display when an object is selected (**Figure 1.17**): Translate X, Translate Y, Translate Z, Rotate X, Rotate Y, Rotate Z, Scale X, Scale Y, Scale Z (known collectively as *transforms*), and Visibility. The values for these attributes can be typed in one at a time, in small sets, or all at once. More attributes can be added to the Channel Box list by using the Channel Control.

Below the transforms are the Shapes and Inputs nodes (**Figure 1.18**). The Shapes section lists the node name of every object that is defined by a node, and these node names collectively define the geometry. Take a close look, for example, at how the Shapes section lists pSphereShape every time you create a sphere. If more than one shape makes up an object, the nodes for those shapes will be listed under the shapes section. The Inputs section usually holds attributes that affect the construction history of the selected object. (See "About construction history," later in this chapter.)

If more than one object is selected, the Channel Box displays the last object selected; however, any value change to an attribute will affect all selected objects. You can click and drag across multiple values in the Channel Box to select them (**Figure 1.19**). With multiple attributes selected, one value change will change all the selected attributes' values.

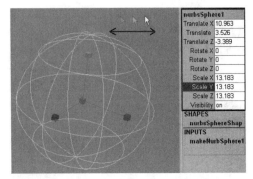

Figure 1.16 The Channel Box, at right, holds information about an object, including its position (Translate), scale and rotation.

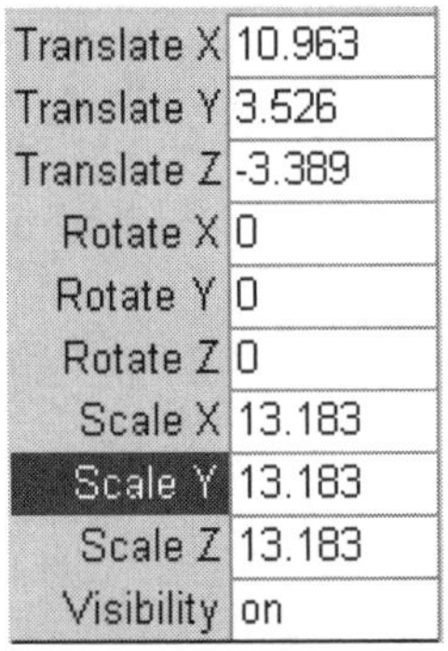

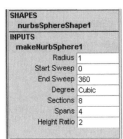

Figure 1.17 The Channel Box includes ten default attribute listings for an object; however, you can also add or change attributes.

Figure 1.18 Inputs node attributes can be adjusted to change a surface's attributes after it is created.

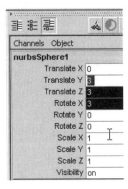

Figure 1.19 Once multiple attributes in the Channel Box are selected, they can be changed simultaneously.

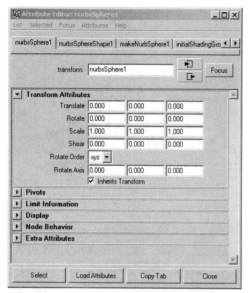

Figure 1.20 The Attribute Editor contains all of the information about a selected object (or objects).

About the Attribute Editor

The Attribute Editor is similar to the Channel Box in that it allows you to access attributes that can be changed. However, the Attribute Editor provides a much more detailed representation of the attributes (**Figure 1.20**). In addition to the attributes in the Channel Box, the Attribute Editor contains attributes that are not keyable (that is, they cannot be animated).

About the Hotbox

The Hotbox is a collection of menu sets you can access from anywhere your pointer is located, simply by holding down the [Spacebar]. The Hotbox is divided into five regions: North, South, East, West, and Center (**Figure 1.21**). Each of these regions has an associated Marking Menu.

continues on next page

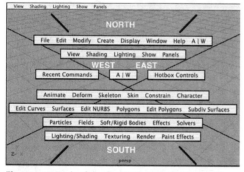

Figure 1.21 Each of the five Hotbox regions—North, South, East, West, and Center—holds a different Marking Menu. The center region is defined by the A/W symbol.

The default Marking Menu for the North region holds shortcuts to different interface layouts (for example, a Single Perspective window) (**Figure 1.22**). The South Marking Menu changes the contents of the selected pane (**Figure 1.23**)—for example, from a Perspective view to an Outliner (see "About the Outliner," below). The West Marking Menu holds preset selection masks (**Figure 1.24**), which filter the object types that can be selected. The East Marking Menu hides or displays specific user-interface elements (**Figure 1.25**)—for example, allowing you to hide the Shelf to create more screen space. The Center Marking Menu offers shortcuts for switching camera views (for example, from a front view to a perspective view). (**Figure 1.26**).

In addition to providing access to all of the Marking Menus, the Hotbox also provides access to all of Maya's menu sets. The top row of menus in the Hotbox includes the most commonly used commands (such as those for saving and opening scene files). The second row of menus includes those that you'll find at the top of each panel. In the third row are the Recent Commands and Hotbox Controls menus.

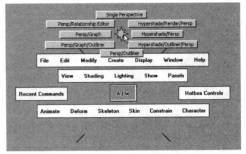

Figure 1.22 In the North region Marking Menu, you can select from different interface layouts.

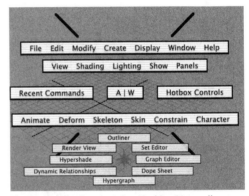

Figure 1.23 The South region Marking Menu allows you to change contents of panes.

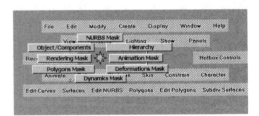

Figure 1.24 You can change object and component selection modes with the Hotbox's West region Marking Menu.

MAYA'S INTERFACE

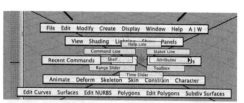

Figure 1.25 You can toggle interface elements on and off with the East region Marking Menu to make more room for modeling and animation.

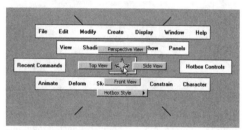

Figure 1.26 You can change views using the Hotbox's Center Marking Menu.

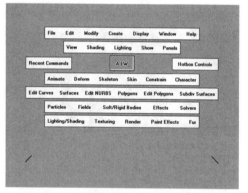

Figure 1.27 This is the Hotbox with all of the menus visible.

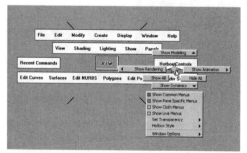

Figure 1.28 You can view one or all of the menu sets inside the Hotbox.

The Hotbox Controls allow you to hide or show rows of menus in the Hotbox. You can choose to show only the middle row of menus, or you can choose to make other, specific, menu sets visible. You can even display all of the rows of menus simultaneously (**Figure 1.27**).

To show all menu sets in the Hotbox:

1. Hold down the (Spacebar).

   The Hotbox will appear for as long as you hold down the (Spacebar).

2. Click Hotbox Controls.

   A Marking Menu appears over that button (**Figure 1.28**).

3. While still holding down the (Spacebar) and the mouse button, select Show All. Release the mouse button but continue to hold down the (Spacebar).

   All of the menus appear (Figure 1.27). If you have trouble finding a menu, this is a good way to make it easier.

MAYA'S INTERFACE

11

About the Hypergraph

The Hypergraph window shows how all the nodes in your Maya scene are organized and connected. These connections are very important to the quality of the final animation and rendering. Character setup and movement rely on proper node connections in order for character body parts to move naturally as one entity. This organization and connection of individual nodes is called a *hierarchy* (**Figure 1.29**). A scene's hierarchy is shown in the Hypergraph as well as in the Outliner and can be adjusted and deleted within these windows or from inside a pane.

Each Maya object type has an associated icon (**Figure 1.30**). Without these icons, each node would look exactly the same. As you get more familiar with Maya, you will begin to recognize each object type's icon. For example, a curve's icon is ▨, and a spotlight's icon is ▨. In the Hypergraph, you can view nodes by object type (**Figure 1.31**), or you can view all object types at once (**Figure 1.32**). In the Hypergraph, nonanimated nodes appear rectangular; animated nodes appear slanted (**Figure 1.33**).

To show the Hypergraph

◆ From the Window menu choose Hypergraph.

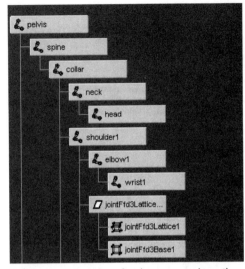

Figure 1.29 Any number of nodes connected together creates a hierarchy. The order of the hierarchy is shown in the Hypergraph and Outliner.

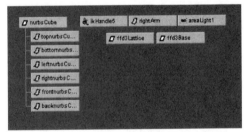

Figure 1.30 A small icon on each node reveals that node's object type. For example, a surface node has a small, blue icon that resembles a simple surface.

Figure 1.31 You can have the Hypergraph display just one type of node to make it easier to find and select specific objects. For modeling, for example, you might only want to see curves and surfaces. However, for animating, you might choose to see just joints and IK handles. Joints and IK handles are used to select and move portions of a character to simulate motion.

Figure 1.32 The default setting for the Hypergraph is Show All. This view helps illustrate how geometry is connected to a joint, and other hierarchy information.

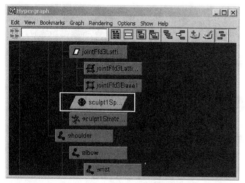

Figure 1.33 Animated nodes appear slanted, making it easy to isolate unwanted animation on an object.

Figure 1.34 The upstream and downstream graph of an object reveals additional dependencies of the object. Some of these dependencies may be shading groups, lights, or textures.

Dependencies

Each node in the Hypergraph has connected *dependencies,* which display additional nodes connected to the selected object. Say you were selecting a newly created sphere and showing its upstream and downstream connections in the Hypergraph (**Figure 1.34**). The sphere's Shape node, the default Shader node, and the connected makeNurbs Construction History node would all become visible. Arrows between the nodes show the directions of the connections. One way you can view a node's dependencies is to click the Show Upstream and Downstream Connections icon 🔺. When you've finished viewing these connections, you can click the Scene Hierarchy icon 🔺 to set the Hypergraph back to showing the scene hierarchy.

continues on next page

Connected nodes can be collapsed to shrink the number of simultaneously displayed nodes and then expanded again when needed. A red arrow appears on a collapsed node hierarchy (**Figure 1.35**). To collapse a hierarchy, double-click the topmost node. Double-clicking the top node of a collapsed hierarchy expands the hierarchy one node at a time (**Figure 1.36**). To expand the entire hierarchy, click the topmost node using the right mouse button and select Expand All from the pop-up menu (**Figure 1.37**).

The Hypergraph is one of the most heavily used windows in Maya. The ability to connect, disconnect, and move nodes around is essential to keeping your scene organized and functional.

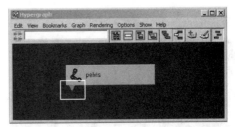

Figure 1.35 You can collapse a hierarchy to make more room in the Hypergraph. A collapsed hierarchy is indicated by a red arrow under the top node.

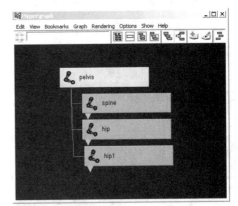

Figure 1.36 A collapsed hierarchy can be expanded one node at a time, which is often useful for temporarily showing a node and then collapsing it again.

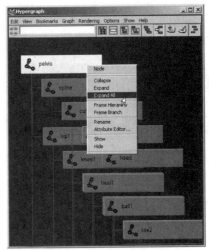

Figure 1.37 When you want to see the whole hierarchy again, you can click the top node using the right mouse button and select Expand All.

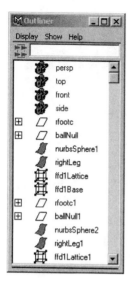

Figure 1.38 The Outliner appears in a slim window, which makes it easy to select and move objects.

Figure 1.39 In the Outliner, as in the Hypergraph, the user can control which objects are viewed.

Figure 1.40 The four default camera views appear in the Outliner.

About the Outliner

The Outliner is similar to the Hypergraph, but it displays the hierarchy in a small, vertical window (**Figure 1.38**), which makes it easier to find and select objects. The Outliner's menus contain functions for filtering out specific object types, thereby reducing the number of nodes displayed at one time (**Figure 1.39**). You can use the Outliner to change an object's position in the hierarchy as well as to quickly select objects deep down in the hierarchy.

When the Outliner is opened and before any new objects are created, you will see colored listings of the top, front, side, and perspective camera nodes in addition to the defaultLightSet and defaultObjectSet icons (**Figure 1.40**). As each new object is created, a new node becomes visible. Once connections are made and a hierarchy has been established, a plus sign appears next to the top object in the hierarchy; you click this to expand the list of objects within the hierarchy (**Figure 1.41**).

Its small size makes the Outliner a convenient tool for selecting objects. However, although the Outliner occupies much less screen space than the Hypergraph, it doesn't give the user as much flexibility in node placement.

Figure 1.41 To see which objects are connected to other objects, click the arrows to expand the hierarchy. Each object in the Outliner has its own icon to indicate its object type.

MAYA'S INTERFACE

15

About construction history

As you build surfaces in Maya, the software maintains connections to the original curves or surfaces used to create them. This connection is referred to as *construction history*. The construction history remembers the steps you used to create an object and allows you to change the final object's shape by altering the original curve or surface geometry. This is very useful when you want to tweak a surface without having to rebuild it. An example might be drawing a curve that defines the shape of the outside of a vase (**Figure 1.42**) and revolving it to complete the vase shape (**Figure 1.43**). Once the vase is created, the construction history remembers the curve's position and ties it to the shape of the final surface. When you want to change the shape of the vase, you can select part of the original curve and move it; the final surface will follow the changes of the curve (**Figure 1.44**).

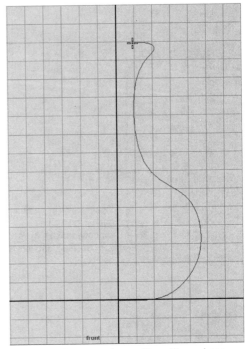

Figure 1.42 Curves can be used to outline a shape that can later be revolved to create a surface.

Figure 1.43 One curve can be revolved and then edited to affect the final surface shape after it"s created through the object's history.

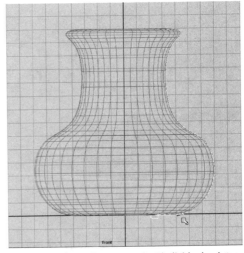

Figure 1.44 The entire curve or just individual points on it can be selected and moved to alter the surface shape. The surface is attached to the curve through history and must follow the curve's edits.

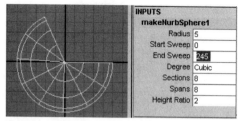

Figure 1.45 An object's primitive surface can be altered via its Inputs node, which contains multiple editable attributes specific to each object type.

Most of the *NURBS* (nonuniform rational B-splines) and polygon primitives have construction histories attached to their surfaces. The History nodes for the primitives appear in the Channel Box under the Inputs heading. These Inputs nodes are useful for altering common object attributes after the original object creation. An example of this is adjusting the End Sweep of a primitive sphere to take a slice out of the shape (**Figure 1.45**).

To turn the construction history on or off:

◆ Click the Construction History On/Off icon in the Status bar. ▨ is on, and ▨ is off.

✔ Tip

■ Once you've turned off the construction history, no objects that you create will include one. To include a construction history, you must rebuild the object.

To delete an object's construction history:

1. From the Create menu select NURBS Primitive > Sphere to create a sphere or select an object.

2. From the Edit menu select Delete by Type > History.

Beginning a Project

Because of Maya's complexity and the numerous files that may be produced for each project, you need to create a folder set that has multiple folders for specific types of files. You can use Maya's premade folder set, called a *project*, to quickly organize all the files you create (**Figure 1.46**).

Once you create a new project, you can tell Maya where you want your files to go by setting that project as the working project. When a project is set, Maya knows which folders to put your renders in and which folders to put your scene files in.

The Maya working file, called a *scene file,* should be saved in the Scenes folder. The best way to create a successful file structure is to first create a new project, set the project, create a new scene, and save the scene in the Scenes folder. The following section describes that process step by step.

To create a new project:

1. From the File menu select Project > New (**Figure 1.47**).

2. Enter a name for the project in the Name field at the top of the window.

3. Click Browse (next to the Location field) and select a folder in which to create the project folders (**Figure 1.48**).

4. Click Use Defaults to use preset folder names.

Figure 1.46 Keeping all the different files organized is essential for a steady workflow. You can either use Maya's preset folder set or create your own folders.

Figure 1.47 Creating a new project places a main project folder on your hard drive with multiple folders to organize images, renders, textures, and scene files.

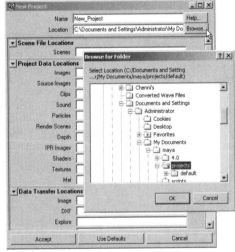

Figure 1.48 Browse to a folder where you want to consistently place new project files.

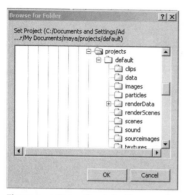

Figure 1.49 Using the default names for the folders helps maintain consistency among projects.

Figure 1.50 Once a project and its folders have been created, you can set the project as Current and Maya will place saved files into the correct folders—scene files into the Scenes folder, for instance.

Figure 1.51 Scene files can be used to create separate models or scenes to be imported or opened at a later date. The scene file stores information about textures, models, animation, particles, and all the user settings.

5. Click Accept.

A project folder is created at the specified location; it has multiple subfolders created with the default folder names (**Figure 1.49**).

For Maya to know which folder set you want to store your files in, you must set a project to be associated with your current working files. The final rendered files will go into the set project, so be careful to set the correct project before rendering. (Rendering is the process of turning your wireframe 3D scene into a final 2D image. For more on this topic, see Chapter 15.)

To set a project:

1. Create a project by following the steps in the previous section.

2. From the File menu select Project > Set (**Figure 1.50**).

3. Browse to and select the folder for the project you want to use.

4. Click OK to set the project.

A Maya working file is called a *scene file;* it can be saved, opened, and imported into other scene files.

To create a new scene:

◆ From the File menu select New Scene (**Figure 1.51**).

A blank Maya scene is created.

To save a scene:

1. From the File menu select Save Scene.
   The Save window appears the first time
   a file is saved.

2. Click the pop-up menu next to "Look in"
   to select a folder in which to save the file
   (**Figure 1.52**).

   If you have set the project correctly, the
   pop-up menu should already show the
   Scenes Folder inside the project folder
   you set.

3. Enter a name for the file in the "File
   name" field, and click Save (**Figure 1.53**).

   The scene is now saved in the Scenes
   folder.

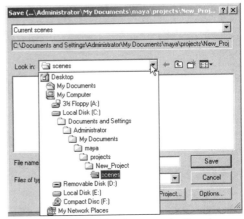

Figure 1.52 If a project has been set, the Save As
command will automatically open the scene folder
for the set projects, into which you can save the file.

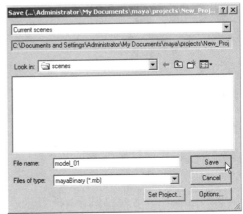

Figure 1.53 It's good practice to name your files in a
numbered sequence since projects often use multiple
scene files.

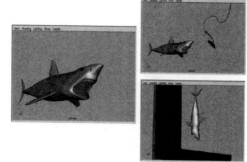

Figure 1.54 Referencing a file into multiple scenes allows the original scene file to be edited; the reference files will inherit the changes.

Importing, Exporting, and Referencing

There are two ways to bring files and geometry into a Maya scene: importing and referencing. When you import a file into Maya, you are permanently merging the file into the current scene. This is recommended if you're working with just one file.

Often, you'll want to use the same model in multiple scenes (**Figure 1.54**). You can use referencing to bring the same file into multiple scenes simultaneously. Referencing gives you a chance to edit the original file and have those revisions updated in all the scene files that use the reference. For instance, you can create a character in one file and then reference it into different files for each camera shot. If you later want to make changes to the character, you can open the original character file and make the changes, then save the file. The updates are automatically made to all files that reference the character (**Figure 1.55**).

Referencing can be particularly helpful when more than one person is working on the same project. In such cases, you can have the modeler create a low-resolution character for the animator to reference into a scene. This way, the modeler can continue making additions to the character while the animator is creating its motion. As the model is updated, the animator can see the changes as he or she works.

continues on next page

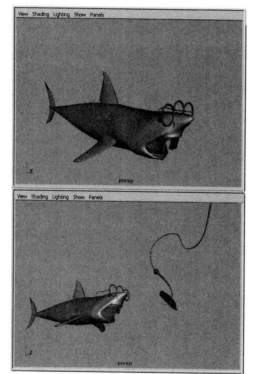

Figure 1.55 Changes made to a referenced file are automatically included in each scene in which the referenced file is used.

In addition to importing and referencing, you can also export objects out of a scene. There are two export options: Export All and Export Selection. The Export All command exports everything in the current scene to a new file. The Export Selection command exports currently selected objects. Be aware that Export All also exports the Orthographic and Perspective cameras. This means that the scenes into which the objects are imported will have two sets of Front, Top, Side, and Perspective cameras—cumbersome when selecting and rendering the cameras.

To export an entire scene:

1. From the File menu select Export All (**Figure 1.56**).
   The Export window opens.

2. Navigate to the folder in which you want to place the exported file.

3. Click Export.
   All the file components are exported.

To export selected objects:

1. Select the objects you want to export (**Figure 1.57**).

2. From the File menu select Export Selection (**Figure 1.58**).
   The Export window opens.

3. Navigate to the folder where you want to place the exported file.

4. Click Export.
   The selected objects are exported.

Figure 1.56 To export everything in the scene, use the Export All command.

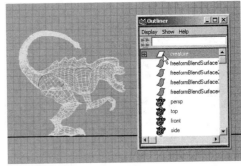

Figure 1.57 This creature is being selected in the Outliner so that it can be exported separately from the rest of the scene.

Figure 1.58 To export only the items that are selected in a scene, use the Export Selection command.

Figure 1.59 Importing a file into another scene combines the imported file with the open file.

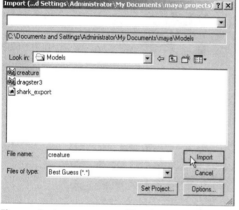

Figure 1.60 A creature scene file is being imported into the currently open scene.

Figure 1.61 Select File > Create Reference to bring a file into an existing scene.

To import a file:

1. From the File menu select Import (**Figure 1.59**).

   The Import window opens.

2. Navigate to the folder where the file you want to import is located.

3. Click the file you wish to import, and then click Import (**Figure 1.60**).

   The file is imported into the scene.

To reference a file:

1. From the File menu select Create Reference (**Figure 1.61**).

   The Reference window opens.

2. Navigate to the folder where the file you want to reference is located.

3. Click the file you want to reference, and then click Reference (**Figure 1.62**).

   The file is referenced into the scene.

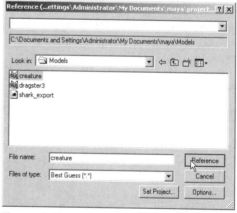

Figure 1.62 Browse to the file you want to reference and click Reference, or double-click the file name to use it as the reference file.

Setting Maya Preferences

Maya has multiple preferences that can be altered to suit your working style as well as your favorite color scheme. In this section, we'll look at just a few of the most essential preference settings. If you want to learn more about preferences, you can refer to the Maya help files.

You can set the number of "undos" that are allowed, determining the number of times you can back out of previous commands.

To change the number of undos:

1. From the Window menu select Settings/Preferences > Preferences (**Figure 1.63**).

   The Preferences window opens.

2. Click Undo under Categories to view the Undo preferences (**Figure 1.64**).

   The Preferences window opens.

3. The default number of undos is 10. Change the Queue setting to Infinite (**Figure 1.65**).

   Setting the Queue to Infinite allows you to back out of every command you've executed—up to the last saved version.

4. Click Save to lock in the changes.

   You now have an unlimited number of undos.

✔ Tip

■ Each saved undo takes up memory, which means your machine may run slowly if you have too many stored undos.

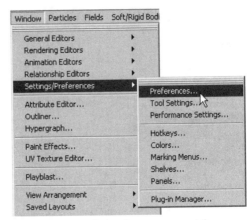

Figure 1.63 By setting preferences, you get the interface configuration you want each time you start the software.

Figure 1.64 In Preferences, Undo is selected to change the number of undos allowed.

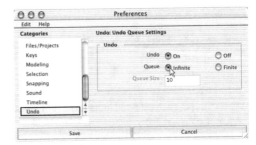

Figure 1.65 In most cases, you want your Undo Queue to be set to Infinite.

Figure 1.66 Under Manipulators in the Preferences window, you can change the size of the manipulators.

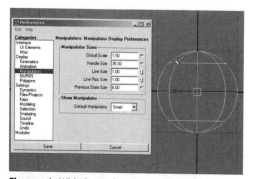

Figure 1.67 With the Preferences window still open, click the sphere to select it.

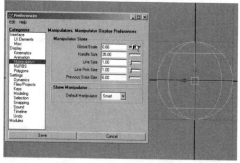

Figure 1.68 Global Scale changes the overall size of the manipulators. Here, they have been made smaller.

The manipulator settings control the look and size of the manipulators. Larger manipulators can often be easier to grab and move.

To change the size of a Maya manipulator:

1. From the Create menu select NURBS Primitive > Sphere.

   A sphere is created at the origin.

2. Select the Move tool by pressing w or clicking the Move icon in the toolbox.

3. From the Window menu select Settings/Preferences > Preferences.

   The Preferences window opens.

4. Select Manipulators in the Categories list (**Figure 1.66**).

   The Manipulator Display Preferences are displayed to the right.

5. Move the Preferences window so you can view the sphere. Click the sphere to make sure it's selected (**Figure 1.67**).

6. In the Manipulator Display Preferences move the Global Scale slider slowly to the left and right. Adjust it until the spacing of the manipulator is to your liking (**Figure 1.68**).

continues on next page

SETTING MAYA PREFERENCES

Watch the manipulator on the sphere while adjusting the slider. The overall scale of the manipulator is changed (**Figure 1.69**).

7. Adjust the Handle Size slider back and forth to a position of your liking (**Figure 1.70**).

   The handle icons for the manipulator get smaller when you move the slider left and larger when you move the slider right (**Figure 1.71**).

To set preferences back to the default set:

◆ In the Preferences window select Edit > Restore Default Settings (**Figure 1.72**). The default settings are restored.

✔ Tip

■ Remember to change your undos back to Unlimited after you restore the default settings.

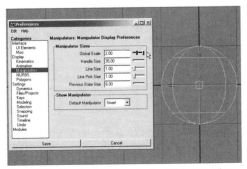

Figure 1.69 Moving the slider to the right scales the manipulator larger; moving the slider to the left shrinks the manipulator.

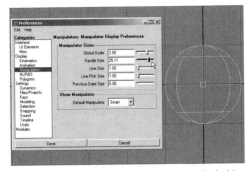

Figure 1.70 The Handle Size setting adjusts the bold part of the manipulators—the arrows, in the case of the Move tool.

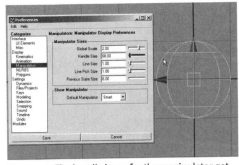

Figure 1.71 The handle icons for the manipulator get smaller when you move the slider left and larger when you move the slider right.

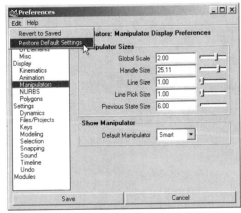

Figure 1.72 You can reset the options to defaults by selecting Edit > Restore Default Settings inside the Preferences window.

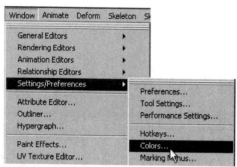

Figure 1.73 You can change the colors of many interface items using the Colors preference settings.

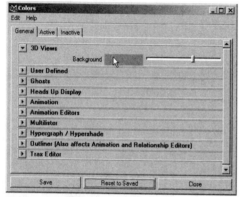

Figure 1.74 In the Colors window, click the color swatch next to Background to open the Color Chooser.

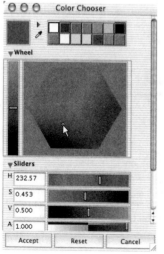

Figure 1.75 Click in the Wheel to pick a color for the background.

To alter your Maya color scheme:

1. From the Window menu select Settings/Preferences > Colors (**Figure 1.73**).
   The Colors window opens.

2. Click the 3D Views arrow ▼ 3D Views to view the Background color slider (**Figure 1.74**).

3. Click the color swatch next to Background to open the Color Chooser.

4. In the Wheel, click the color you would like for your Maya background (**Figure 1.75**).

5. Click Accept to lock in the color.
   Your Maya background becomes the color chosen.

✔ Tip

- You can follow the same steps to change any part of the interface color scheme.

Keyboard Shortcuts

Any function in Maya can have an associated keyboard shortcut, or *hotkey*. Hotkeys can be huge time-savers, because you can use them rather than go to the menu bar to select a function or command. Maya has many default hotkeys, which we recommend keeping until you become more adept with the interface. Later, you may find that you want to set up hotkeys for particular commands that you use regularly. The following describes how to create a new hotkey or view the currently set hotkeys.

To create a new hotkey:

1. From the Window menu select Settings/Preferences > Hotkeys (**Figure 1.76**).

   The Hotkey Editor opens.

2. In Categories, click the category name for the command you want to set (**Figure 1.77**).

   The category name is the same as the name of the menu the command is under.

3. Under Commands select the command name you want to create a hotkey for.

   If the command already had a hotkey assigned to it, you would see which key it was in the upper-right corner of the window.

4. In the Hotkey Editor under Assign New Hotkey, choose a Key and a Modifier for the command (**Figure 1.78**).

   You should remove any current hotkey currently assigned to the command before assigning a new hotkey.

5. Click Assign.

6. Close the Hotkey Editor window.

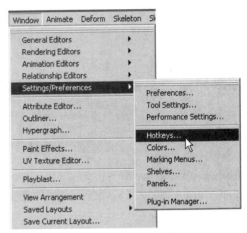

Figure 1.76 Hotkeys can be set to add keyboard shortcuts to nearly any command.

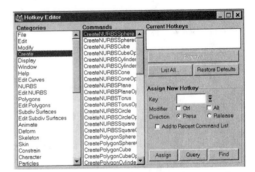

Figure 1.77 In the Hotkey Editor, select the name of the menu and the menu item in the Categories and Commands lists, respectively, to add a shortcut.

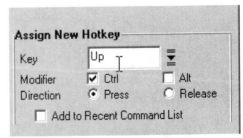

Figure 1.78 In the Assign New Hotkey portion of the Hotkey Editor, choose the key and modifier you want to use as a hotkey for the selected command.

KEYBOARD SHORTCUTS

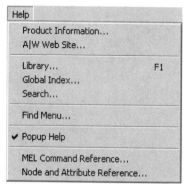

Figure 1.79 The Help menu provides ways to search and browse for information on specific topics.

Maya Help

Maya's manual comes preloaded in the help files. You can search these files by topic or browse through them page by page. The help files are a good resource when you want additional information about a specific topic.

Under the Help menu in the upper right-hand corner of the Maya interface are links to the Maya library, search functions (Windows only), a global index of topics and definitions, and a Find Menu feature in case you forget where a menu item is located (**Figure 1.79**).

The Maya library includes tutorials, definitions, and references that are easy to navigate, many of which offer step-by-step instructions.

The Search function (Windows only) allows you to type in a topic on which you would like more information and shows you a list of links categorized by the percentage of relevance to the topic you chose (**Figure 1.80**).

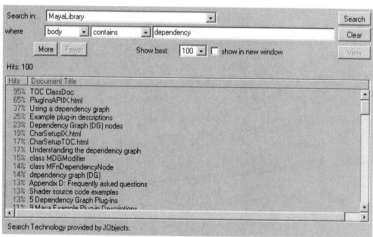

Figure 1.80 The Search window (Windows only) in the Help menu shows multiple listings for additional information on a specified topic.

MAYA HELP

Maya's Global Index is similar to an index in the back of a book. You pick the topic you want from an alphabetical listing, and Maya gives you a definition as well as relevant information on the topic (**Figure 1.81**).

The Find a Menu Item feature allows you to type in the name of a topic or function and get the item's menu and path (**Figure 1.82**). This can be particularly useful when you know what a function is called but can't remember on what menu it resides.

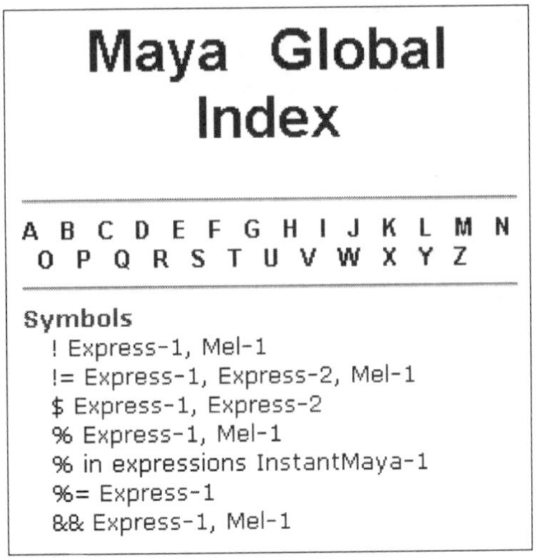

Maya Global Index
A B C D E F G H I J K L M N
O P Q R S T U V W X Y Z
Symbols
! Express-1, Mel-1
!= Express-1, Express-2, Mel-1
$ Express-1, Express-2
% Express-1, Mel-1
% in expressions InstantMaya-1
%= Express-1
&& Express-1, Mel-1

Figure 1.81 The Global Index contains command definitions and tutorials for all the Maya help files.

Find a Menu Item
Enter a string to search for:
parent
Use Case Sensitive Search
Edit->Parent
Edit->Unparent
Deform->Edit Wire->Parent Base Wire
Close

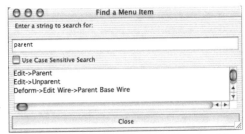

Figure 1.82 The Find a Menu Item feature is a quick way to find every menu in which any given command is located.

NAVIGATING AND CHANGING THE INTERFACE

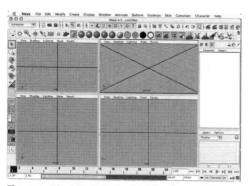

Figure 2.1 The Maya interface can be changed to suit each user.

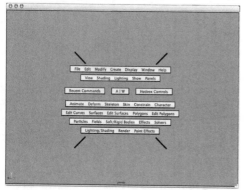

Figure 2.2 The Hotbox is a set of menus that appear where your mouse is when you hold down the Spacebar.

Maya's interface is fully customizable (**Figure 2.1**), which means you can alter its layout to suit your current project and workflow. For example, you can hide each menu and window until you're viewing only one pane—a panel or window in which to work—while the rest of the interface is hidden. However, even when menus are hidden, you can still access them via the Hotbox (**Figure 2.2**).

You can also hide and show specific object types in a pane using the Show menu. Once you're viewing the object types you want in the pane, you can *dolly*, *track*, and *tumble* around the objects (movie-industry terms for specific camera movements) to get a better, more three-dimensional view.

Maya provides many ways to accomplish the same task—another way it helps speed users' workflow. It includes hotkeys (keyboard shortcuts) for commonly used commands, and you can add hotkeys for just about any command you want.

In the pages that follow, I'll describe the ways you can change the interface and navigate the scene.

Dollying, Tracking, and Tumbling

Dollying, tracking, and tumbling allow you to change your view of a scene, controlling how far or near its objects appear. Since you're always looking through a camera, dollying, tracking, and tumbling provide ways to move that camera around the scene. These are some of the most important tools in Maya because you need to see objects from every direction and dimension. The point of view from which you're viewing your scene becomes important to the alignment and placement of objects.

Tracking a view moves that view up, down, or sideways. You might track a view to get a look at an object that's currently out of view.

To track a view:

1. Move the mouse over any pane.

2. Hold down Alt (⌘ on a Macintosh) and use the middle mouse button to drag the scene in the desired direction (**Figure 2.3**).

Dollying a view visually enlarges or shrinks the view, bringing objects closer (zooming in) or moving them farther away (zooming out).

To dolly a view:

1. Move the mouse over any pane.

2. Hold down Alt /⌘ plus the left and middle mouse buttons, dragging left to shrink the view and right to enlarge the view (**Figure 2.4**).

✔ Tip

■ You can marquee-zoom in by pressing Ctrl /Control and Alt /⌘ while dragging a marquee from upper left to lower right with the left mouse button. You can zoom out by dragging lower right to upper left. The smaller the square, the larger the zoom.

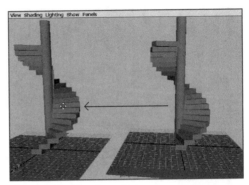

Figure 2.3 Tracking drags the scene up, down, or sideways.

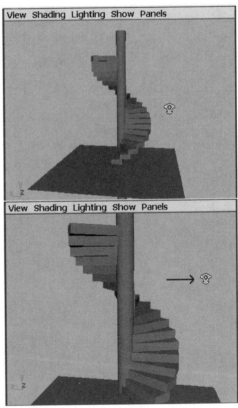

Figure 2.4 Dollying is used to zoom in and out of specific areas of the scene; dollying right (bottom) enlarges the view.

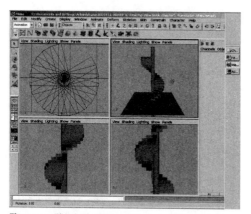

Figure 2.5 This is the Maya interface with four panes visible. Tumbling (which only works in the Perspective view) rotates the view around an object or scene.

Tumbling a view visually rotates it around the center of interest—useful for getting the full 3D effect of the objects and scene. For example, you could tumble around an object to get a view of its front, back, and sides from any angle.

To tumble the view:

1. Move the mouse over the Perspective view.

2. Hold down (Alt)/(⌘) and use the left mouse button to drag and rotate the scene in the direction desired (**Figure 2.5**).

✔ Tip

■ You can hold (Shift) while tumbling to constrain the tumble along a specific axis.

Changing the Layout

Maya has two windows that are easily confused because their names are so similar, *pane* and *panel*. A pane is conceptually the same as a window pane. If you look inside a window with panes, you might see something different in each pane. The same is true here. A pane can hold a Front, Top, Side, or Perspective view, or a panel.

A panel is a type of Maya window that helps with different Maya functions. For example, the Hypergraph and Outliner are panels that show all of the nodes in a scene, and the Graph Editor is a panel used to edit animation curves. Many of these panels can be opened in their own windows (**Figure 2.6**) or within a specific pane (**Figure 2.7**). One advantage to opening a panel inside a pane is the ability to then tap the Spacebar to minimize (**Figure 2.8**) or maximize (**Figure 2.9**) the pane. You can temporarily access the pane and then shrink it back down, gaining access to the other panes as well.

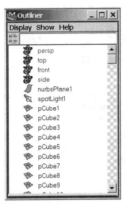

Figure 2.6 The Outliner is open in its own window.

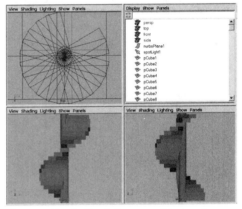

Figure 2.7 The Outliner is in one pane and can be enlarged and shrunk for convenience.

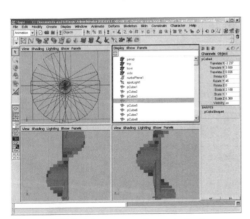

Figure 2.8 Minimizing a pane allows you to view multiple panes at once.

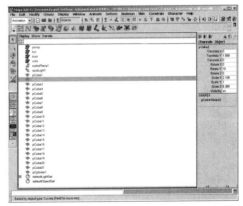

Figure 2.9 Maximizing a pane enlarges the view over any other panes, giving you more workspace within that pane.

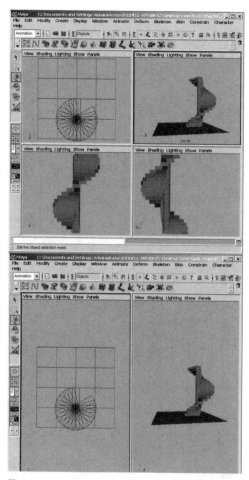

Maya's programmers understood that different users would want to work with Maya and its interface layout differently. With this in mind, they've provided many ways to change Maya's interface and layout. (When I talk about the *layout*, I'm referring to the number of panes the user is viewing and the specific panels and views that are placed within those panes, **Figure 2.10**).

Figure 2.10 Layouts can be sized, saved, and changed to accommodate the user's current needs. The top image is a four-pane layout; the bottom image is a two-pane (side-by-side) layout.

When you open Maya for the first time, you'll see that its default pane layout is set to four views: Top, Persp (Perspective), Front, and Side. The Front, Side, and Top views are orthographic, meaning they present a 2D view of the surfaces (**Figure 2.11**). This allows you to view the surfaces straight on from the selected view angle. Viewing the surfaces in this manner can be important for proper placement and alignment of objects. The three orthographic views combine to provide an accurate portrayal of the objects' placement relative to the rest of the scene. Users new to 3D often forget to check their objects in multiple views, which can cause placement problems for other objects. While the objects may look perfectly placed from the Front view, they could be completely off in the Side or Top view. The Perspective view gives you a full three-dimensional view of your scene (**Figure 2.12**). The combination of all of these views makes it possible for you to access your scene from virtually any angle.

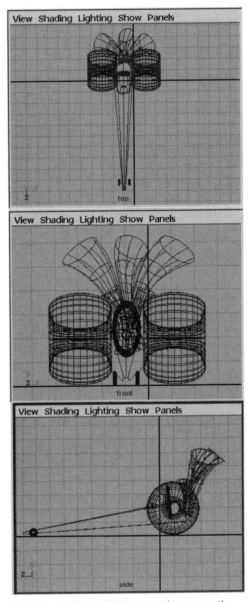

Figure 2.11 Orthographic views are the same as the views you would use when drafting with a pencil. You have three views that are from a straight-on camera, making editing and placement easier.

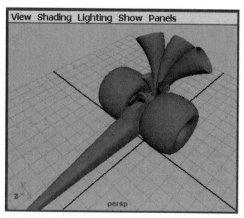

Figure 2.12 The Perspective view is the only view that allows you to tumble around the scene; it gives the user the full 3D effect.

Maya allows you to change the layout of the panes, save a new layout, or change just one panel. In this chapter, we'll show you how to perform each of these layout changes.

To change a pane into a Perspective view:

◆ From the Panels menu inside the pane you want to change, select Perspective > persp (**Figure 2.13**).

To change a pane into an orthographic view:

◆ From the Panels menu inside the pane you want to change, select Orthographic > front, side, or top (**Figure 2.14**).

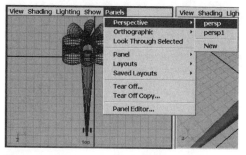

Figure 2.13 Any pane can be changed into a Perspective view by selecting Perspective > persp.

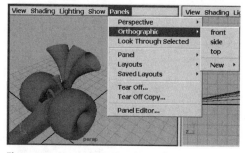

Figure 2.14 Any pane can be changed to any orthographic view (for example, Front or Top) by selecting the Orthographic menu.

CHANGING THE LAYOUT

Panes don't always have to be view panes like Front or Perspective; they can also be panels that provide access to other areas and windows within Maya. These panels are often animation windows, like the Graph Editor (see Chapter 1) (**Figure 2.15**), or node representations of your scene, like the Hypergraph (see Chapter 1) (**Figure 2.16**). As you learn more about Maya, you will learn what each of these panels does to help your workflow.

To change a pane into a nonview panel:

◆ From the Panels menu inside any pane select Panel, and choose the panel name you want—Outliner, for example—to change the pane into its respective view (**Figure 2.17**).

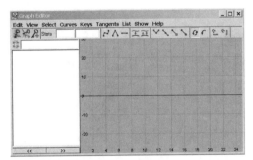

Figure 2.15 The Graph Editor holds all of the animation curves that can be edited. This panel can be embedded in a pane or opened in a window.

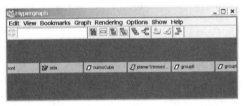

Figure 2.16 The Hypergraph holds visual representations of all the objects in the scene and can be embedded in a pane or opened in a window.

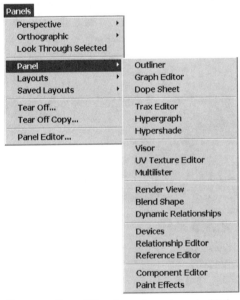

Figure 2.17 Many different panels can be embedded inside a pane.

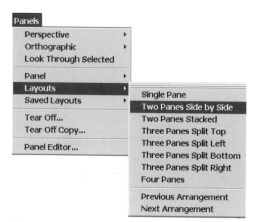

Figure 2.18 Preset layouts give you quick access to the number of panes visible and the panel sets that will go in them.

Figure 2.19 The layout icon shortcuts can be altered after being chosen by holding down the arrows at the bottom of the tool box. You could change a preset pane into a Perspective view with the arrows. The number of arrows varies with the layout selected.

To change the pane layout:

♦ From the Panels menu inside any pane select Layouts, and choose the preset layout name you want—two Panes Side by Side, for example (**Figure 2.18**).

If you select Two Panes Side by Side, you will have only two panels to work with, and they will be laid out adjacent to one another.

or

♦ Select the icon of the layout you want from the toolbar on the left side of Maya's interface (**Figure 2.19**).

To save a layout:

1. Set up the layout you would like to save and use later.

2. From the Window menu select Save Current Layout.

3. Enter a name for the layout and click OK.

To change your current layout to a saved layout:

♦ From the Panels menu inside any pane select Saved Layouts, and choose the name of the saved layout you would like to use.

To edit a layout:

1. From the Panels menu inside any pane select Saved Layouts > Edit Layouts.

2. Under the Layouts tab select the name of the layout you would like to edit (**Figure 2.20**).

3. Under the Edit Layouts tab change the Configuration pop-up menu to the new configuration you would like to use (**Figure 2.21**).

4. Pull any of the center dividers for the numbered blocks to adjust the blocks' size relative to the size of the other blocks (**Figure 2.22**).

5. Click the Close button to close the window.

   You can now access the new layout from the Panels > Saved Layouts menu.

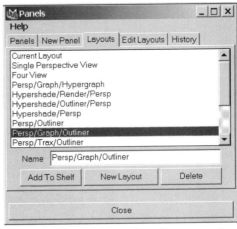

Figure 2.20 You can edit an existing layout or create a new layout under the Layouts tab.

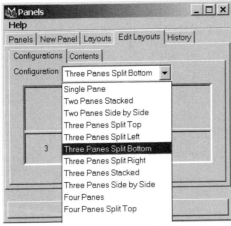

Figure 2.21 You can change the number of panes the layout uses by selecting Edit Layouts tab > Configuration tab > Configuration menu.

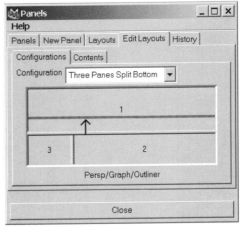

Figure 2.22 It can be helpful to resize the panes at this point to make the size of each one comparable to its use. For instance, you might want to make the Perspective pane larger so that you always have more working area in that view.

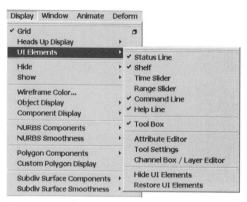

Figure 2.23 Each interface element or related section can be turned on and off to save screen space when the element is not needed.

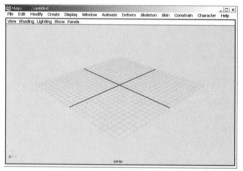

Figure 2.24 A quick way to gain more working space is to use the Hide UI Elements command.

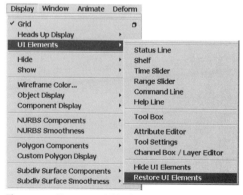

Figure 2.25 You can quickly show all interface elements when needed by using the Restore UI Elements command.

To hide or show a UI element:

◆ From the Display menu select UI Elements, and choose the UI elements you would like to hide or show (**Figure 2.23**).

Each UI element name toggles between hidden and shown. If it is hidden, selecting it will show it, and vice versa.

To hide all UI elements:

◆ From the Display menu select UI Elements > Hide UI Elements.

All elements become hidden except the main and pane menu bars and your current pane layout (**Figure 2.24**).

To show all UI elements:

◆ From the Display menu select UI Elements > Restore UI Elements (**Figure 2.25**).

All UI elements are shown.

CHANGING THE LAYOUT

To hide or show the main and pane menu bars:

◆ Hold down the ⌜Spacebar⌝ anywhere in a pane, and select Hotbox Controls > Window Options > Show Main Menubar (Windows only) or Show Pane Menubars (**Figure 2.26**).

Show Main Menubar and Show Pane Menubars are toggled on and off. If they're on, selecting them will turn them off, and vice versa.

Using the Show menu

The Show menu comes in handy when you want to isolate a particular type of object (and hide other types), such as curves or lights. It offers a convenient way to display only the object types you want, or to edit and hide all other object types. When animating, for example, you might want to show only the character's surface in one pane and only its bones in another (**Figure 2.27**).

The Show menu allows you to turn all types of objects on and off at once. It also lets you turn objects on and off individually. You may want to turn off all objects first, then turn back on just the object type you want to isolate (**Figure 2.28**).

The Show menu only visually hides or shows object types; it does not delete the objects. Object types turned off in the Show menu will still appear in the final render.

Figure 2.26 The main menu bar and the pane menus must be turned on and off individually.

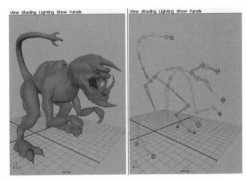

Figure 2.27 You can open two of the same panes, in this case Perspective views, and show different object types in each pane, making it easier to select and visualize objects.

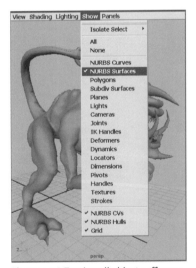

Figure 2.28 Turning all objects off or on in the Show menu helps you to quickly turn on only the relevant object types in the pane.

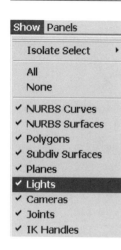

Isolate Select ▶

All
None

✓ NURBS Curves
✓ NURBS Surfaces
✓ Polygons
✓ Subdiv Surfaces
✓ Planes
✓ Lights
✓ Cameras
✓ Joints
✓ IK Handles

Figure 2.29 The Show menu hides and shows all objects of the chosen type. If you choose Lights, all lights in the view will be hidden.

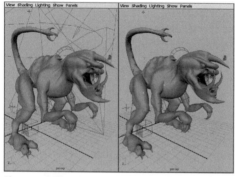

Figure 2.30 There's no way to see or select an object type in a pane while it's hidden through the Show menu. In the right pane, Lights have been turned off in the Show menu.

To hide object types with the Show menu:

◆ From the Show menu inside any pane select the object type you want to hide (**Figure 2.29**).

The object type selected is hidden from view (**Figure 2.30**).

To show hidden object types with the Show menu:

◆ From the Show menu inside any pane select the object type you want to show in the pane (Figure 2.29).

The object type selected becomes visible in the view pane.

You can temporarily enlarge a pane to get a better view of its contents.

To focus a pane to full screen:

1. Move the mouse over the pane you would like to make larger (**Figure 2.31**).

2. Tap the ⎧Spacebar⎫ once.

The pane expands to full view (covering any other panes) (**Figure 2.32**).

✔ Tip

■ Tap the ⎧Spacebar⎫ again to reset the pane's size (uncovering any additional panes).

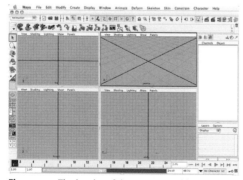

Figure 2.31 The border of the pane turns blue to indicate that it"s selected.

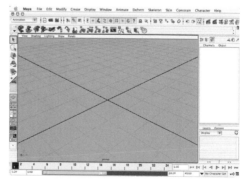

Figure 2.32 Tapping the ⎧Spacebar⎫ zooms the pane; however, *holding down* the ⎧Spacebar⎫ opens the Hotbox. Be careful to use the ⎧Spacebar⎫ correctly.

CHANGING THE LAYOUT

To frame a selected item in a view:

1. Select the item you would like to zoom the camera on by clicking on it.

2. Press ⨍.
   The view zooms to the object (**Figure 2.33**).

✔ Tips

- You can make all of the view panes frame the selected item at the same time by pressing Shift ⨍.

- You can toggle between the previous view and the next view by using the square bracket keys (⟮ and ⟯).

To frame all objects in a view:

◆ Press ⓐ.
   The view frames all of the objects in the scene (**Figure 2.34**).

✔ Tip

- You can make all of the view panes frame all of the objects at the same time by pressing Shift ⓐ.

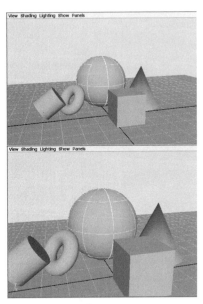

Figure 2.33 Press ⨍ to zoom in closer to a selected object.

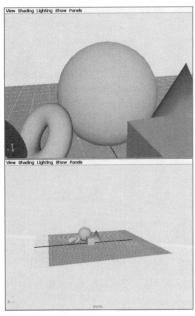

Figure 2.34 When ⓐ is pressed, the camera moves from the view on top to the view on the bottom. Now all of the objects in the scene are framed within the view.

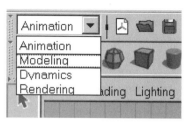

Figure 2.35 Each menu set holds menus specific to the type of process you're working on. If you're in the modeling stage of a project, you can use the Modeling menu set to access modeling-related menus.

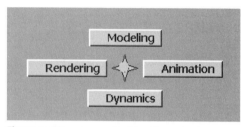

Figure 2.36 You can use Marking Menus to change your menu sets when you've hidden the status line or you just want to speed your workflow.

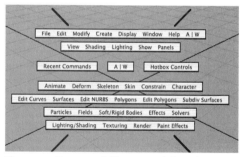

Figure 2.37 You can quickly open and close the Hotbox by holding down the [Spacebar].

Maya has four main menu sets: Animation, Modeling, Dynamics, and Rendering. Each of these sets holds menus specific to its topic as well as the common menus File, Edit, Modify, Create, Display, and Window. The common menus are always accessible from the main menu—regardless of which menu set you're currently using.

To change the menu set:

◆ On the left side of the status bar use the pop-up menu to select the appropriate menu set (**Figure 2.35**).

or

◆ In any view pane hold down the [h] key and the left mouse button to select a menu set from the Marking Menu. (Most objects have a menu specific to their object type called a Marking Menu.) (**Figure 2.36**).

or

◆ Press [F2] for the Animation menu set, [F3] for the Modeling menu set, [F4] for the Dynamic menu set, and [F5] for the Rendering menu set.

To show and hide the Hotbox:

1. Show the Hotbox by holding down the [Spacebar] (**Figure 2.37**).

2. Hide the Hotbox by releasing the [Spacebar].

CHANGING THE LAYOUT

To show and hide specific menu sets in the Hotbox:

1. Show the Hotbox by holding down the Spacebar in any pane.

2. Hold down the left mouse button over the Hotbox Controls to show the Hotbox Controls Marking Menu (**Figure 2.38**).

3. Move the mouse over the menu set name you want to show—Show Animation, in this example.

   This opens an additional Marking Menu.

4. Select Show/Hide (menu set name) (**Figure 2.39**).

   The menu set is shown if it was hidden, and vice versa.

To show all menu sets in the Hotbox:

1. Show the Hotbox by holding down the Spacebar in any pane.

2. Hold down the left mouse button over the Hotbox controls to show the Hotbox Controls Marking Menu.

3. Select Show All to show all the menu sets in the Hotbox (**Figure 2.40**).

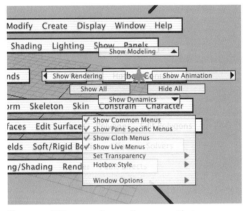

Figure 2.38 You can change the menus that are shown in the Hotbox by using the Marking Menu in the Hotbox Controls.

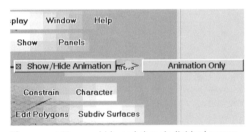

Figure 2.39 You can hide and show individual menus to control the size and accessibility of the Hotbox.

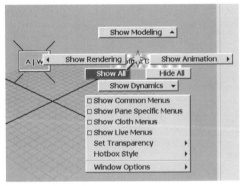

Figure 2.40 One advantage of using the Hotbox is that you can turn on all of the menu sets at once, or you can activate just one or two.

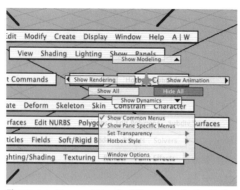

Figure 2.41 You can hide all of the menus in the Hotbox.

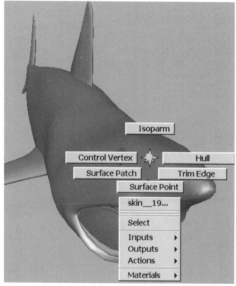

Figure 2.42 Each object has an associated menu set, called a Marking Menu, which you can access by right mouse–clicking the object.

To hide all menu sets in the Hotbox:

1. Show the Hotbox by holding down the (Spacebar) in any pane.

2. Hold down the left mouse button over the Hotbox Controls to show the Hotbox Controls Marking Menu.

3. Select Hide All to hide all the menu sets in the Hotbox (**Figure 2.41**).

   Hiding all of the menus in the Hotbox leaves only the Recent Commands and the Hotbox Controls menus available for selection. Along with these two menus, all of the Hotbox's Marking Menus are still accessible.

Most objects have a menu specific to their object type called a Marking Menu. The Marking Menu holds shortcuts to the selected object's most commonly used commands. If you're in the habit of using Marking Menus, you'll save yourself a lot of time.

To show an object's Marking Menu:

1. Move your pointer directly over an object.

2. Click the object using the right mouse button to show its Marking Menu (**Figure 2.42**).

✔ Tip

■ Once you're familiar with the location of specific commands in the Marking Menus, you can quickly drag in the direction of the command you want to select without waiting for the menu item names to appear.

To show and hide the grid:

◆ From the Display menu select Grid to toggle the grid on and off.

✔ Tip

■ You can adjust the size, closeness, and colors of the grid lines in the Grid options.

The Channel Box provides an easy way to adjust many of a selected object's attributes. Located on the right side of the interface in the default layout (**Figure 2.43**), the Channel Box can also be retrieved after being hidden, or toggled on and off using the steps outlined below.

To show or hide the Channel Box:

◆ Click the "Show or hide the Channel Box/Layer Editor" icon 📊 on the right side of the status line. (The status line sits directly below the main menu bar.)

or

◆ From the Display menu select UI Elements > Channel Box/Layer Editor (**Figure 2.44**).

The Channel Box appears on the right side of the Maya interface.

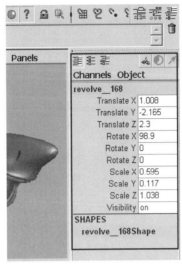

Figure 2.43 The Channel Box can be hidden to save screen space or shown to give the user easy access to keyable object attributes.

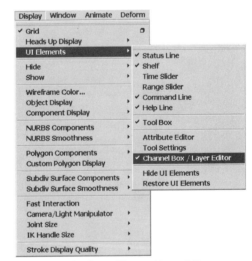

Figure 2.44 The Channel Box and Layer Editor can be shown together to make better use of available screen space.

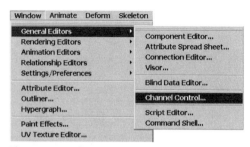

Figure 2.45 Attributes can be removed from or added to the Channel Box via the Channel Control window.

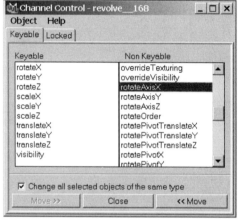

Figure 2.46 The Non Keyable area of the Channel Control window holds attributes that can be added to the Channel Box.

Figure 2.47 You can move additional attributes to the Keyable area to add them to the Channel Box.

By default, the Channel Box holds the keyable attributes of the selected object. You can add attributes to the Channel Box list by following the steps outlined below.

To add preset attributes to the Channel Box:

1. Create or select an object to add an attribute to.

2. From the Window menu select General Editors > Channel Control (**Figure 2.45**). The Channel Control window opens.

3. Under the Keyable tab select the attribute name in the Non Keyable area of the Channel Control window (**Figure 2.46**).

4. Click the Move button << Move.

5. The attribute is added to the Keyable list of attributes (**Figure 2.47**).

6. Click the Close button to close the Channel Control window.

   The new attribute is shown in the Channel Box (**Figure 2.48**).

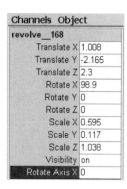

Figure 2.48 The Channel Box displays the newly added attribute, ready for use.

CHANGING THE LAYOUT

49

The Attribute Editor contains additional attributes not available in the Channel Box. The Channel Box is a great shortcut for accessing many of an object's attributes; however, it's too small to hold all of them. The Attribute Editor remains empty until an object is selected.

To show or hide the Attribute Editor:

◆ Click the "Show or hide the Attribute Editor" icon 🎛 on the right side of the status line.

Make a selection to view its attributes.

or

◆ From the Display menu select UI Elements > Attribute Editor (**Figure 2.49**).

The Attribute Editor appears on the right side of the Maya interface.

or

◆ Press [Ctrl]/[Control][a].

The Attribute Editor opens (**Figure 2.50**).

or

◆ From the Window menu select Attribute Editor (**Figure 2.51**).

The Attribute Editor opens in a new window.

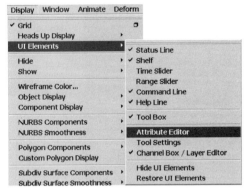

Figure 2.49 The Attribute Editor can be opened from the Display > UI Elements menu.

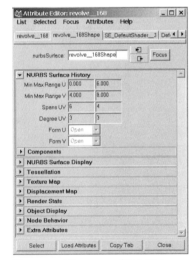

Figure 2.50 When opened in a new window, the Attribute Editor can be moved around and minimized (to get it out of the way).

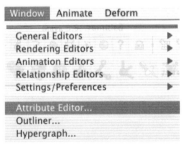

Figure 2.51 The Attribute Editor can be opened in a new window.

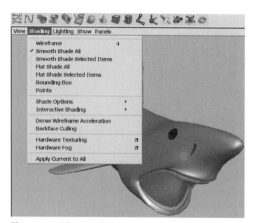

Figure 2.52 The Shading menu controls the display mode for each individual pane.

About Display Options and Smoothness

By using Maya's display options, you can change the way objects are viewed within the pane. You can view your scene in wireframe, smooth-shaded, flat-shaded, bounding-box, or points mode, and you can change your display options to match your current needs. Bounding-box and points mode, for example, can be used to speed interaction when tumbling around a complex scene. Wireframe mode is handy for selecting components (because you can see all of an object's components at once), and smooth and flat shading can provide a more complete surface view (which makes it easier to model a surface). Each of the display options is useful for specific situations, so switching between them can improve workflow.

Included among the display options are hardware texturing and lighting options, which provide quick feedback when adding texture or lighting to a scene. Most of these settings have associated keyboard shortcuts.

You can display objects in one of three smoothness levels: rough, medium, or fine. Objects are displayed rough by default, but you can change the setting using the shortcuts described below. Choosing a setting of rough can ease component selection because fewer surface lines are shown. A fine setting comes closest to matching the final surface—which means this is the setting to use when you need to focus on fine details.

To change the display options from the Shading menu:

◆ From the Shading menu in any pane select one of the following shading options: Wireframe, Smooth Shade, Flat Shade, Bounding Box, or Points (**Figure 2.52**).

Shading and smoothness shortcuts

⌨1 = Rough smoothness (**Figure 2.53**)

⌨2 = Medium smoothness (**Figure 2.53**)

⌨3 = Fine smoothness (**Figure 2.53**)

⌨4 = Wireframe mode (**Figure 2.54**)

⌨5 = Shaded mode (**Figure 2.55**)

⌨6 = Hardware Texturing (**Figure 2.56**)

⌨7 = Hardware Lighting (**Figure 2.57**)

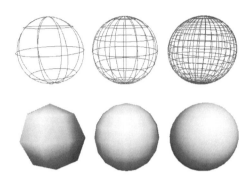

Figure 2.53 Rough smoothness (left) shows the object in low resolution. Medium smoothness (middle) shows the object with some additional resolution but not enough to obstruct the view of the object. Fine smoothness (right) provides the closest representation of the surface's shape.

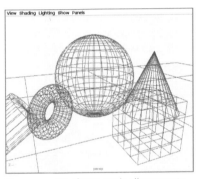

Figure 2.54 Wireframe mode allows you to see through objects and view their geometry on the front and back of the surface.

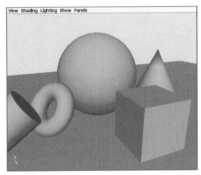

Figure 2.55 Shaded mode presents the surface in gray by default to show its final skin.

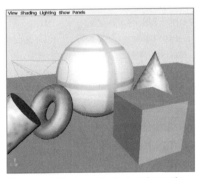

Figure 2.56 Hardware Texturing shows the surface textures within the pane.

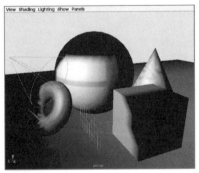

Figure 2.57 Hardware Lighting shows the scene's lighting scenario interactively within the pane by generalizing the effects that the lights would have on the scene—somewhat of a very rough version of the final render. The Hardware Lighting option can save large amounts of rendering time because you can see the results as soon as you change a light's position.

CREATING PRIMITIVES AND TEXT

3

As premade geometry sets that simplify the creation of more complex shapes, primitives are the building blocks of 3D modeling. To understand this, just take a look at the objects around you: Everything in nature, no matter how complex, can be broken down into a few primitive shapes—something you can do right now with the objects in front of you. Is the object you're looking at built around many cylinders like a metal chair, or is it a squashed cube like a door or a wall? Many objects combine a number of different primitives. Take, for example, the bicycle: Its wheels combine a cylinder (for each spoke) and a slim torus (which defines the tires' shape). Likewise, you can use a number of primitives to create a detailed face from a simple sphere, or employ just a few well-placed cubes to construct a building.

Because they can be manipulated in a variety of ways, primitives have become an important part of Maya and other 3D programs. NURBS primitives can speed workflow because the curves have already been drawn and, in many cases, have been replaced with surface geometry. You can stretch, cut, scale, translate, trim, and rebuild them, making them essential to your workflow and great time-savers as well.

Maya includes three primary types of primitives: *NURBS, polygons,* and *subdivisions.* To help you understand which type is appropriate for the task at hand, this chapter takes a close look at NURBS (**Figure 3.1**) and polygons (**Figure 3.2**), explaining the strengths and weaknesses of each. Subdivisions, a more advanced topic, are covered in detail in Chapter 8.

Figure 3.1 The NURBS primitives (top to bottom): sphere, cube, cylinder, cone, plane, torus, circle, and square.

Figure 3.2 The Polygon primitives (top to bottom): sphere, cube, cylinder, cone, plane, and torus.

Weighted control points

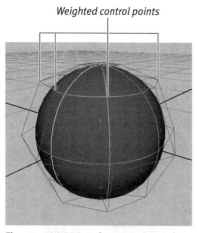

Figure 3.3 NURBS surfaces are changed using weighted control points.

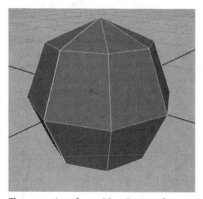

Figure 3.4 A surface with a degree of 1, or setting of linear.

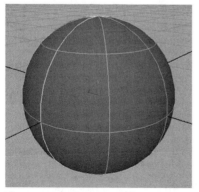

Figure 3.5 A surface with a higher degree will appear smoother.

About NURBS

NURBS curves, surfaces, and primitives are an important part of Maya modeling. You can use NURBS objects to produce long, smooth surfaces (such as car hoods) or sharp, angular surfaces (such as stop signs). NURBS objects make it possible for you to adjust the look of a surface by manipulating just a few weighted control points (**Figure 3.3**).

Each of the NURBS curves and surfaces has an associated degree that controls the smoothness of the NURBS object. A surface degree of 1, or a setting of *linear*, will produce a straight connection between each control point, creating a very angular surface (**Figure 3.4**). As you raise the degree of the NURBS object, you create a smoother curve and surface (**Figure 3.5**). The higher the degree of the curve, the more points are needed to define it. For more about NURBS degrees, see Chapter 7.

continues on next page

NURBS, or *nonuniform rational B-spline*, describes objects whose shapes are defined by mathematical equations. Luckily for us, Maya takes care of most of the math behind the scenes. *B-spline* refers to the underlying curve that defines all NURBS objects. When creating a NURBS object, you use multiple curves to produce a wire representation of the surface's appearance. After using curves to lay down the shape of the surface, you add a skin atop the curves to create the final surface: This process of creating a surface that extends from one curve to the next is called *lofting* (**Figure 3.6**).

You can break down NURBS objects into separate components that work together to define the shape of the NURBS object. Components include (among others) *CVs* (control vertices), *edit points*, and *hulls*— each of which can be manipulated to sculpt the surface or define the curves' shapes. (You can manipulate components together or separately to change the shape of an object.) For more information on NURBS components, see Chapter 7.

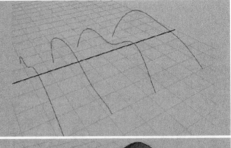

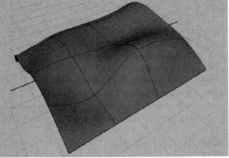

Figure 3.6 The top object has curves only; the bottom object has curves plus a skin.

ABOUT NURBS

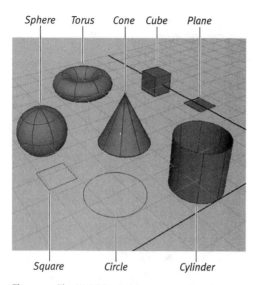

Sphere Torus Cone Cube Plane

Square Circle Cylinder

Figure 3.7 The NURBS primitives are used as starting points for more complex models.

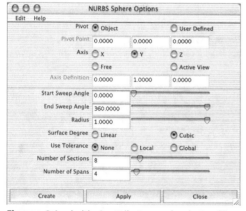

Figure 3.8 A primitive's attributes can be changed in its Options dialog box.

SHAPES	
nurbsSphereShape1	
INPUTS	
makeNurbSphere1	
Radius	1
Start Sweep	0
End Sweep	360
Degree	Cubic
Sections	8
Spans	4
Height Ratio	2

Figure 3.9
The construction history allows you to change an existing surface's attributes.

About NURBS Primitives

NURBS primitives represent a collection of frequently used, predefined curves and surfaces. Maya includes eight NURBS primitives: *sphere, cube, cylinder, cone, plane, torus, circle,* and *square* (**Figure 3.7**).

These predefined primitive surfaces are not only time-savers for creating simple objects; you can also use them as a starting point for more detailed shapes. The circle and square primitives are NURBS curves without surfaces attached to them; the other six NURBS primitives are predefined surfaces ready to be placed in the Maya scene or further manipulated.

Each primitive includes a number of attributes that you can set for an object. You can change each primitive's attributes in its Options dialog box *before* you create an object (**Figure 3.8**). In addition, most primitives include a construction history that's attached to their surfaces: This is where you can adjust and fine-tune the surface's properties *after* it's been created (**Figure 3.9**). The construction-history attributes appear in the Channel Box under each primitive's makeNurb heading. In this chapter, we'll show you how to create NURBS primitives and change some of their attributes (both before and after the object has been created). For more information on construction history, see Chapter 1.

Creating NURBS primitives

NURBS primitives are found in the Create > NURBS Primitives submenu (**Figure 3.10**). You create a primitive by selecting the primitive's name from the submenu. You can also create a NURBS primitive through the Hotbox, as described below. And by simply clicking their icons in the Surfaces Shelf, you can quickly create any of the primitive NURBS surfaces (**Figure 3.11**).

When you create a primitive surface or curve, Maya will place the object's center point at the origin of the scene (at 0, 0, 0 coordinates). This centers most objects over the *y*-axis line (so that half of the object is above the axis, and half is below) (**Figure 3.12**). The exception is the cone, whose center point is at its base. You can create NURBS primitives by following the steps that follow.

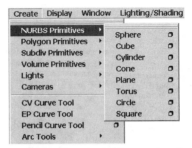

Figure 3.10 NURBS primitives are found in the Create > NURBS Primitives submenu.

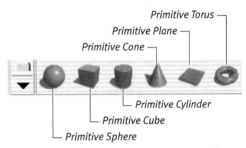

Figure 3.11 You can quickly create NURBS primitives by clicking their icons in the Surfaces Shelf.

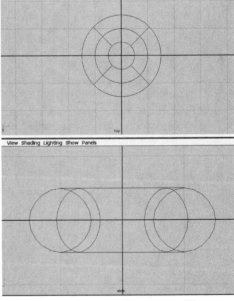

Figure 3.12 Maya places the center point of the primitive at the origin of the scene.

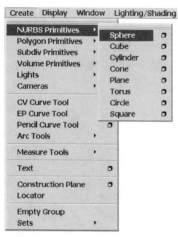

Figure 3.13 Select the name of the primitive you want to create from the NURBS Primitives submenu.

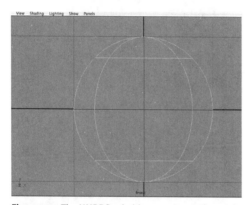

Figure 3.14 The NURBS primitive appears at the origin of the Maya scene (the sphere is shown).

Figure 3.15 You can use the Hotbox to select the NURBS Primitives submenu (the cube is shown).

To create a NURBS primitive using the main menu:

1. From the Create menu select the NURBS Primitives submenu.

2. Select the name of the primitive you want to create—in this case, the sphere (**Figure 3.13**).

   The NURBS primitive appears at the origin of the Maya scene (**Figure 3.14**).

The Hotbox is a great time-saver for creating objects and primitives because you can do so without accessing the main menu. You can display the Hotbox from anywhere within the Maya window, providing even faster access to Maya's menus.

To create a NURBS primitive using the Hotbox:

1. Hold down ⌈Spacebar⌉ anywhere in the scene to show the Hotbox.

2. From the Create menu in the Hotbox select the NURBS Primitives submenu.

3. Select the name of the primitive you want to create—in this case, the cube (**Figure 3.15**).

   The NURBS primitive is created at the origin of the Maya scene (**Figure 3.16**).

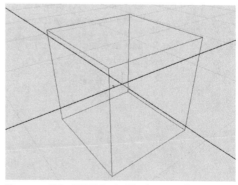

Figure 3.16 The NURBS primitive is created at the origin of the Maya scene (the cube is shown).

ABOUT NURBS PRIMITIVES

Maya's Surfaces Shelf contains shortcut icons for all of the primitive NURBS surfaces (**Figure 3.17**). By selecting these primitives from the Shelf, you can save yourself the two or three steps required to select the same primitive from the Create menu.

Figure 3.17 The default Shelf in Maya holds shortcut icons for the sphere and cone NURBS primitives.

To create a NURBS primitive using the Shelf:

◆ From the Surfaces Shelf, select the NURBS primitive icon for the object you would like to create (for example, a sphere 🔘 or cone 🔺).

The primitive is created at the origin of the Maya scene (**Figure 3.18**).

✔ Tips

■ If the Shelf is not already open, open it by going to the Display menu and selecting UI Elements > Shelf (**Figure 3.19**).

■ To add primitives or other objects to the Shelf, hold down (Shift) and (Ctrl)/(Control) while selecting the menu item in the main menu. This stores the command you selected from the menu in the Shelf with its currently selected options. Thus, if you were to change the object's attributes in the Options dialog box before adding it to the Shelf, you could have one sphere in the Shelf with an end-sweep angle of 20 and another with an end-sweep angle of 360—another way to speed your workflow for commonly used settings.

■ You can remove items from the Shelf by pressing the middle mouse button while dragging the items to the trash.

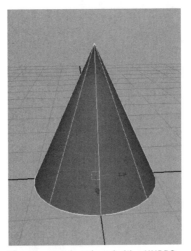

Figure 3.18 Select the primitive NURBS icon in Shelf 1; here the cone has been chosen.

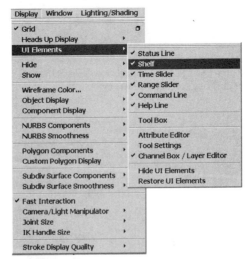

Figure 3.19 To view the Shelf, select UI Elements > Shelf.

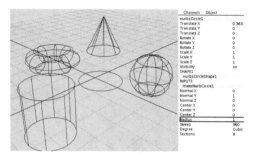

Figure 3.20 The radius attribute, which is common to the objects shown above, makes the object larger.

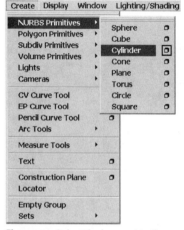

Figure 3.21 Select the box next to the name of the primitive for which you want to set the radius.

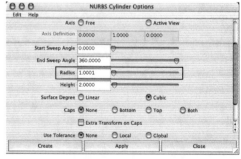

Figure 3.22 Adjust the Radius slider to half the diameter that you desire for the primitive.

Changing Attributes of NURBS Primitives

Each NURBS primitive has an associated set of attributes. Some attributes are common to all NURBS primitives, and others are specific to just one or two. By changing these attributes, you can alter a surface's appearance.

You change all NURBS primitive attributes in the same way. In this section, we'll show you how to change the radius attribute of a NURBS primitive. You can follow the same steps to change other object attributes. The following section defines many of the NURBS primitives' attributes.

The radius attribute is common to the NURBS primitive sphere, cone, cylinder, torus, and circle (**Figure 3.20**).

To set the radius of a NURBS primitive sphere, cone, cylinder, torus, or circle from the Create menu:

1. From the Create menu select the NURBS Primitives submenu.

2. Select the box next to the name of the primitive for which you want to set the radius—in this case, the cylinder (**Figure 3.21**).

3. In the selected primitive's Options dialog box, adjust the Radius slider to half the desired diameter of the primitive (**Figure 3.22**).

✔ Tip

- You can type in a value larger than the slider's highest value.

To change the radius of a NURBS primitive for an existing object:

1. Select a primitive NURBS sphere, cone, cylinder, torus, or circle.

2. Click the makeNurb title under the INPUTS heading in the Channel Box to show the selected primitive's changeable attributes (**Figure 3.23**).

3. Click once in the Radius field to select it (**Figure 3.24**).

4. Change the number to the size you want the radius to be.

5. Press (Enter) to complete the radius change (**Figure 3.25**).

✔ Tips

■ You can also click once on the attribute's name (in our example, Radius) in the Channel Box, and then click and drag the middle mouse button left or right in the View window to interactively change the object's radius.

■ If the construction history is turned off, the makeNurb node will not be available in the Channel Box.

■ The makeNurb history will not be available on a duplicated object unless you go into the Edit > Duplicate options and check Duplicate Upstream Graph.

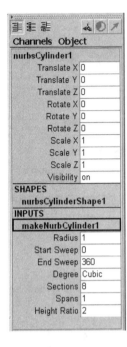

Figure 3.23 Select the makeNurb title under the INPUTS heading in the Channel Box (the cylinder is shown).

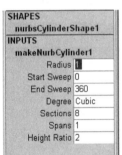

Figure 3.24 Click the Radius field once to select it (cylinder settings are shown).

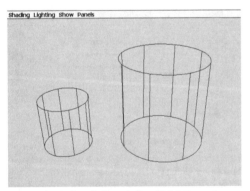

Figure 3.25 Before (left) and after (right) the radius change (the cylinder is shown).

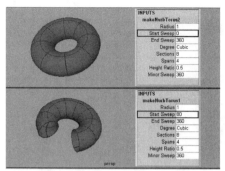

Figure 3.26 Adjusting the start sweep causes the beginning and end of the surface to be separated (the torus is shown). The picture on top shows the torus before the start sweep has been adjusted. The picture on the bottom shows the torus after the start sweep has been adjusted.

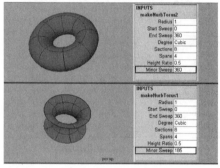

Figure 3.27 Adjusting the Minor Sweep attribute unfolds the surface along the U direction (the torus is shown). The picture on top represents the torus before minor sweep has been adjusted; the picture on the bottom shows the result of the adjustment.

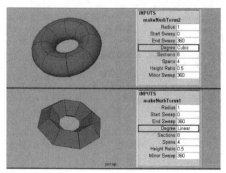

Figure 3.28 If the Degree attribute is set to Cubic (default), the surface will be curved (top). If the Degree attribute is set to Linear, the surface will be planar and faceted (bottom).

NURBS primitive attributes

The following are some important NURBS primitive attributes, with their definitions. You set these in the Channel Box or in the object's Options dialog box.

◆ **Radius**—The radius of an object is half of its diameter. Adjusting the radius scales the object proportionally on all three axes.

◆ **Start Sweep**—Adjusting the start sweep causes the surface to separate from its end in a clockwise direction. The result is a slice of the surface, or a surface of less than 360 degrees (**Figure 3.26**).

◆ **End Sweep**—Adjusting the end sweep has a similar effect to adjusting the start sweep; however, instead of working clockwise from the end point, it works counterclockwise from the starting point to open the surface. The result is a slice of the surface, or a surface of less than 360 degrees.

◆ **Minor Sweep**—Adjusting the Minor Sweep attribute, which is specific to the torus primitive, unfolds the surface along the U direction, creating (for a torus) a slice of the surface similar to a spool (rather than a full doughnut shape) (**Figure 3.27**).

◆ **Degree**—A NURBS primitive can be linear or cubic. If the Degree attribute is set to Linear, the surface is planar and faceted. If the Degree attribute is set to Cubic (default), the surface is more curved and smooth (**Figure 3.28**).

continues on next page

CHANGING ATTRIBUTES OF NURBS PRIMITIVES

◆ **Sections**—Adjusting the Sections attribute adds more detail to the surface in the U direction, which makes it easier to edit its shape (**Figure 3.29**).

◆ **Spans**—Adjusting the Spans attribute adds detail to the surface in the V direction, which makes it easier to edit its shape (**Figure 3.30**).

◆ **Height Ratio**—This is the ratio of the height in relation to the depth. If the height ratio is set to 2, the height will be twice the size of the depth.

◆ **Length Ratio**—This is the ratio of the length in relation to the depth. If the length ratio is set to 2, the length will be twice the size of the depth.

◆ **Patches U and Patches V**—Patches U and V are specific to the plane and cube primitives. Adjusting these attributes will increase the surface geometry in the U or V direction (**Figure 3.31**).

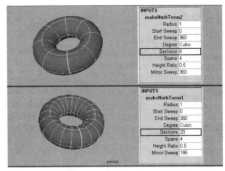

Figure 3.29 Adjusting the Sections attribute adds more detail to the surface in the U direction.

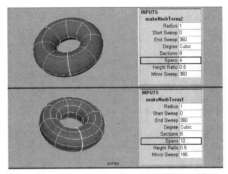

Figure 3.30 Adjusting the Spans attribute adds isoparms in the V direction.

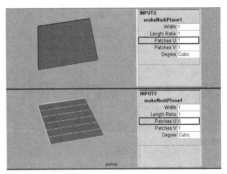

Figure 3.31 Adjusting Patches U and Patches V attributes increases the surface geometry in the U or V direction.

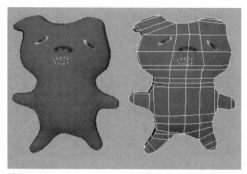

Figure 3.32 A low-polygon model renders fast and can be developed quickly (this one is by Andrew Britt).

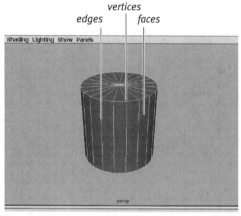

Figure 3.33 Faces, edges, and vertices make up the polygon components.

About Polygons

Polygon meshes facilitate extremely flexible modeling because they can be used to produce high-quality, smooth surfaces as well as low-resolution, fast-rendering surfaces. Games can use only a small amount of polygons per surface (called *low-poly* models) in order for game engines to render them on the fly. Thus, polygons are the surface type of choice for game and Internet developers. A proficient modeler can create a good-looking, fast-loading model by using just a few well-placed polygons (**Figure 3.32**).

Polygons have many components, which you use to manipulate the final look of the surface. The components themselves are made up of *faces, edges,* and *vertices* (**Figure 3.33**)—all of which combine to help define the shape of the polygonal object. Each of these components can be manipulated individually, giving the creator precise control of polygon construction.

continues on next page

You can create polygons, or *polys* for short, one at a time, slowly adding to the surface's resolution. Or you can start with a very simple poly object (for example, a poly primitive; see the next section), and use the Smooth command to add more individual polys, increasing the surface's resolution and smoothness (**Figure 3.34**). To learn more about the Smooth command, see Chapter 8.

Subdivisions are an important part of a polygonal mesh. The number of subdivisions in the poly surface determines how smooth the final surface will render (**Figure 3.35**). Decreasing the number of subdivisions results in fewer faces, making the surface appear much more angular. You can set the number of poly subdivisions before or after you create an object. You can also subdivide individual polygons, giving you precise control over the final number of polygons.

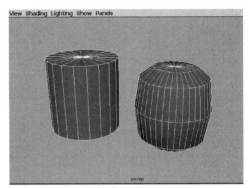

Figure 3.34 You can start with a simple poly object, like a poly primitive (left), and use the Smooth command to add more individual polys (right).

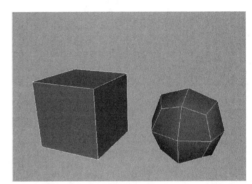

Figure 3.35 The smoothness of the final surface is determined by the number of subdivisions in the poly surface. The default surface is on the left; subdivisions have been added on the right.

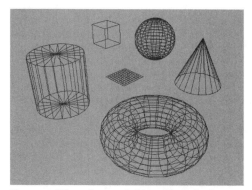

Figure 3.36 The polygon primitives (clockwise from left): cylinder, cube, sphere, cone, torus, and plane (center).

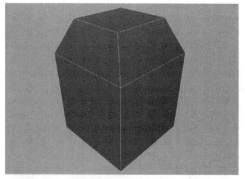

Figure 3.37 Polygon primitives can be extruded, split, subdivided, merged, beveled, and separated (among other things). Here, a beveled primitive cube is shown.

About Polygon Primitives

Polygon primitives, like NURBS primitives, represent a collection of frequently used predefined surfaces. These predefined primitive surfaces can save you time in creating objects and give you a head start on creating more detailed shapes.

Maya includes six polygon primitives: sphere, cube, cylinder, cone, plane, and torus (**Figure 3.36**). You can use polygon primitives to speed workflow because each face that describes the surface has already been drawn for you.

Once you've created polygon primitives, you can (among other things) extrude, split, subdivide, merge, bevel, and separate them. This allows for fast modeling of objects and precise control over the number of faces used for the surface—which means you can control the amount of render time needed to produce the final image (**Figure 3.37**).

Creating polygon primitives

Polygon primitives are found in the Create menu within the Polygon Primitives submenu. You can access polygon primitives via the Hotbox, as described below. By clicking their icons in the Polygons Shelf, you can quickly create any of the poly primitives.

When you create a poly primitive, Maya places the center point of the object at the origin of the scene (just as it does when you create a NURBS primitive).

You can create poly primitives by following the steps outlined below.

To create a polygon primitive using the main menu:

1. From the Create menu select the Polygon Primitives submenu.

2. Select the name of the primitive you want to create (the torus is shown here) (**Figure 3.38**).

   A polygon primitive is created at the origin (0, 0, 0) of the Maya scene (**Figure 3.39**).

The Hotbox is a great time-saver because it allows you to select objects and primitives without returning to the main menu. You can display the Hotbox from anywhere in the Maya window, making access to the Maya menus even faster.

To create a polygon primitive using the Hotbox:

1. Hold down (Spacebar) anywhere in the scene to display the Hotbox.

2. From the Create menu in the Hotbox select the Polygon Primitives submenu (**Figure 3.40**).

3. Select the name of the primitive you want to create (the cone is shown here) (**Figure 3.41**).

   A polygon primitive is created at the origin of the Maya scene (**Figure 3.42**).

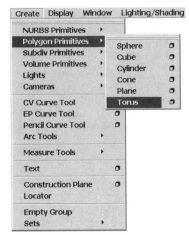

Figure 3.38 You can create a polygon primitive by choosing Create > Polygon Primitives. Here the torus primitive is selected.

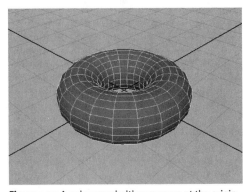

Figure 3.39 A polygon primitive appears at the origin of the Maya scene; the torus is shown.

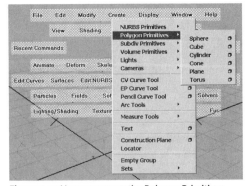

Figure 3.40 You can access the Polygon Primitives submenu via the Hotbox.

Figure 3.41 Select the name of the primitive you want to create.

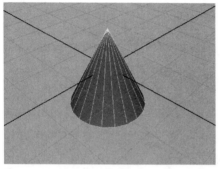

Figure 3.42 A polygon primitive appears at the origin of the Maya scene.

Figure 3.43 Shortcut icons for the polygon primitives in the Polygons Shelf.

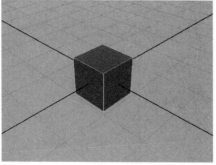

Figure 3.44 The primitive appears at the origin of the Maya scene (the cube is shown).

The default Shelf in Maya holds shortcut icons for the cube and cylinder polygon primitives (**Figure 3.43**). Selecting these primitives from the Shelf can save the two or three steps you would take to select the primitive from the Create menu.

To create a polygon primitive using the Shelf:

◆ From the Polygons Shelf, select the icon of the polygon primitive you would like to create—for example, the cube ▣ or cylinder ▣.

The primitive is created at the origin of the Maya scene (**Figure 3.44**).

✔ Tips

■ If the Shelf is not already open, open it by going to the Display menu and selecting UI Elements > Shelf.

■ To add primitives or other objects to the Shelf, hold down (Shift) and (Ctrl)/(Control) while selecting the primitive in the Create menu.

Changing a Polygon Primitive's Attributes

Like NURBS primitives, each poly primitive has a number of attributes that you can set for the object before or after it's created. You can change each primitive's default attributes in the Options dialog box before you create an object (**Figure 3.45**). Most of these primitives have a construction history attached to their surface, which means you can fine-tune surface properties after the surface has been created (**Figure 3.46**). The construction-history attributes appear under each primitive's poly heading in the Channel Box.

You change all of the polygon primitives' attributes in the same way. In the text that follows we'll show you how to change the Subdivisions Height attribute of a polygon primitive. You can follow the same steps to change other object attributes. The next section defines many of the poly primitives' other attributes.

The Subdivisions Height attribute (common to all of the polygon primitives) determines the number of times the surface's height is divided. By raising the number, you add polygons to describe the surface along the height of the object (**Figure 3.47**). If you lower the number, you will use fewer polygons to describe the surface along the height of the object (**Figure 3.48**).

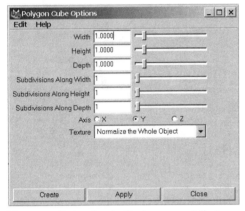

Figure 3.45 Each poly primitive has many attributes that can be set for the object before or after it is created.

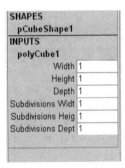

Figure 3.46 You can fine-tune polygon primitives after the surface has been created by adjusting their poly attributes.

Figure 3.47 If you raise the Subdivisions Height attribute, you are adding polygons to describe the surface along the height of the object.

Figure 3.48 Additional polygons are added to the surface along its height.

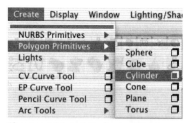

Figure 3.49 Select the box next to the name of the primitive for which you want to set Subdivisions Height.

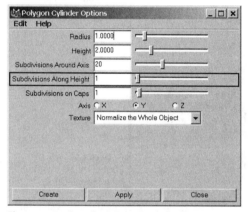

Figure 3.50 Adjust the Subdivisions Along Height slider to the amount of divisions you want along the height of the surface.

To set the Subdivisions Height attribute of a polygon primitive from the Create menu:

1. Go to the Create menu, and select the Polygon Primitives submenu.

2. Select the box next to the name of the primitive for which you want to set Subdivisions Height (the cylinder is shown here) (**Figure 3.49**)

3. In the Options dialog box, adjust the Subdivisions Along Height slider to the number of divisions you want along the height of the surface (**Figure 3.50**).

4. Click Create to create a new primitive with the new Subdivisions Height settings.

✔ Tip

■ You can type in a value that's higher than what the slider will allow.

To change the Subdivisions Height attribute of a polygon primitive after the object has been created:

1. Select a polygon primitive.

2. Select the poly(object) title under the INPUTS heading in the Channel Box (**Figure 3.51**).

3. Click the Subdivisions Height field to select the number there (**Figure 3.52**).

4. Change the number to reflect the number of times you want to divide the height.

5. Press [Enter] to complete the change (**Figure 3.53**).

✔ Tip

■ You can also click the attribute's name (Subdivisions Height in our example) in the Channel Box, and then click and drag the middle mouse button left or right in the view window to interactively change the Subdivisions Height value.

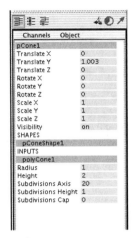

Figure 3.51 Select the poly(object) title under the INPUTS heading in the Channel Box (the title of a cone is shown).

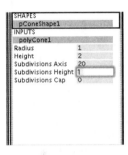

Figure 3.52 Click the Subdivisions Height field to select its contents (the number for the cone is shown).

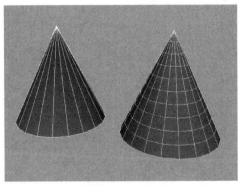

Figure 3.53 Press [Enter] to complete the change. The cone with default settings is on the left; the cone with the altered Subdivisions Height setting is on the right.

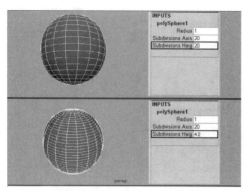

Figure 3.54 Adjusting the Subdivisions Height attribute adds or subtracts polygons to or from the height (a sphere is shown).

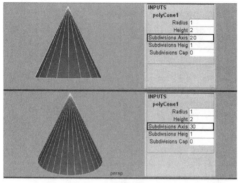

Figure 3.55 Adjusting the Subdivisions Axis attribute adds or subtracts polygons to the object along the center axis.

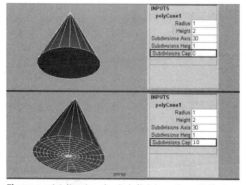

Figure 3.56 Adjusting the Subdivisions Cap attribute adds or subtracts polygons to or from the object's cap, radiating out from the center.

Polygon primitive attributes

The following are some of the most important polygon primitive attributes.

◆ **Subdivisions Height, Width**—These attributes adjust the number of times the height or width of the surface is divided. Adjusting these attributes adds or subtracts faces in the direction of the axis (**Figure 3.54**).

◆ **Subdivisions Depth**—This attribute adjusts the number of times the depth of the surface is divided. Adjusting this attribute adds or subtracts faces along the depth of the object.

◆ **Subdivisions Axis**—This attribute adjusts the number of times the surface is divided along the center axis. Adjusting this attribute adds or subtracts faces to the object in the same way you would add slices to a pizza (**Figure 3.55**).

◆ **Subdivisions Cap**—Two poly primitives have caps, the cone and the cylinder. Caps are pieces of geometry used to cover a surface's round hole(s). The cylinder has a cap on the top and bottom of its surface; the cone only has a cap on the bottom of its surface. The Subdivisions Cap attribute adjusts the number of times the surface's cap is divided. Adjusting this attribute adds or subtracts faces to or from the object's cap—like a water droplet sending concentric circles out from the center (**Figure 3.56**).

continues on next page

◆ **Radius**—An object's radius is half its diameter. Adjusting the Radius attribute scales the object proportionally on multiple axes.

◆ **Section Radius**—This attribute is only used by the torus polygon primitive. Adjusting the section radius fattens or slims the torus' doughnut-like shape (**Figure 3.57**).

◆ **Width, Height, and Depth**—These attributes adjust the object's width, height, or depth.

◆ **Twist**—This attribute is used only by the torus polygon primitive. Adjusting the twist moves the faces around the center axis inside the tube shape from 0 to 360 degrees (**Figure 3.58**).

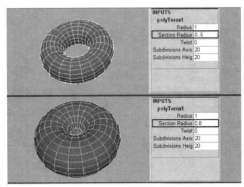

Figure 3.57 Adjusting the section radius fattens or slims the torus' shape.

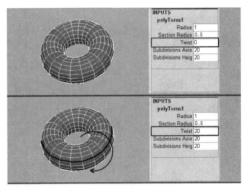

Figure 3.58 Putting a twist on a torus.

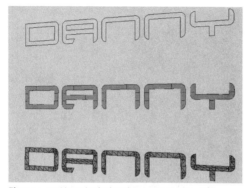

Figure 3.59 Maya includes three types of text (from top): curves, trims, and polys.

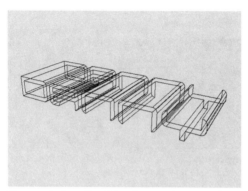

Figure 3.60 Once the 2D text is created, you can do anything to it that you would do to any other curve or surface. This is an example of a loft.

About Text

You can create three types of text in Maya: *curves, trims,* and *polys* (**Figure 3.59**). You can find all of these text types in the Create > Text Options dialog box. Each text type has its place, and the type you use will depend on the application.

All of the text types in Maya create flat text objects made of curves, trimmed surfaces (see Chapter 7), or polygons. Although text starts out flat, there are many ways to make it three-dimensional. Once the two-dimensional text is created, you can do anything to it that you would do to any other curve or surface. For instance, if you create text made of curves, you can loft—a function that creates a surface over two or more curves— between a copy and an original (**Figure 3.60**). You can also take text made of polygons and extrude it to make it three-dimensional. See Chapter 7 for more on lofting.

The Curves text-type option creates versatile text with curves but no attached surfaces. This means you can make the front face of the text planar to create a surface over it, or you can leave it open and loft between two copies of the text to make it three-dimensional while leaving a hole for the front face, as in Figure 3.60.

Notice that the text is created in separate, selectable pieces. For instance, the letter *D* would have a curve for the outside part of the letter and another curve for its center.

To create curve-based text:

1. From the Create menu select the box next to Text (**Figure 3.61**).

2. In the Options dialog box click the Text field, and type in new text.

3. Click the arrow next to the Font field and select the font for the text. Then click Create (**Figure 3.62**).

4. Make sure Curves is selected for the Type option (**Figure 3.63**).

5. Click Create to complete the text.

   Text appears in the Maya scene with the bottom-left corner of the text at the origin (**Figure 3.64**).

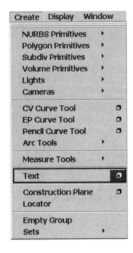

Figure 3.61 Go to the Create menu and select the box next to Text.

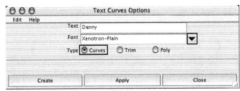

Figure 3.62 Click the arrow next to the Font field, and select the font for the text.

Figure 3.63 Make sure the Curves button is selected for Type.

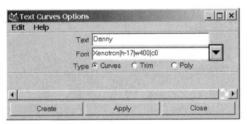

Figure 3.64 Text is placed in the Maya scene with the bottom-left corner of it at the origin.

Figure 3.65 Trim text type can save you some steps if you're looking for text with surface geometry on its front face.

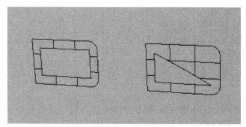

Figure 3.66 You can manipulate the curve's components to change an individual letter's shape.

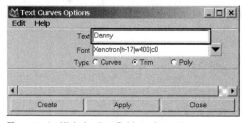

Figure 3.67 Click the Text field, and type in new text.

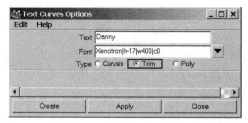

Figure 3.68 Make sure the Trim button is selected for Type.

Another text-type setting is Trim. Using this text type is the same as selecting the curves and making them planar (see Chapter 7). This text type can save you some steps if you're looking for text with surface geometry on its front face (**Figure 3.65**).

With trimmed text, you have surfaces attached to curves through history, allowing you to manipulate the curves to change an individual letter's shape (**Figure 3.66**).

To create trimmed text:

1. From the Create menu select the box next to Text.

2. In the Options dialog box click the Text field, and type in your new text (**Figure 3.67**).

3. Click the arrow next to the Font field, and select the font for the text. Click OK.

4. Make sure Trim is selected for the Type option (**Figure 3.68**).

5. Click Create to complete the text.

   Text appears in the Maya scene with the bottom-left corner of the text at the origin, as in Figure 3.64.

ABOUT TEXT

The third text type setting is Poly. It's best to use this text type if you want to work the text into other polygon surfaces. This text type includes numerous options for controlling the number of polygons used on the text, as well as other helpful text attributes.

The Poly text type also uses surfaces attached to curves through history, allowing you to manipulate the curves to change an individual letter's shape.

To create poly-based text:

1. From the Create menu select the box next to Text.

2. In the Options dialog box click the Text field, and type in new text.

3. Click the arrow next to the Font field, and select the font for the text.

4. Make sure Poly is selected for Type; use the default options for best results (**Figure 3.69**).

5. Click Create to complete the text.

   Text appears in the Maya scene with its bottom-left corner at the origin (**Figure 3.70**).

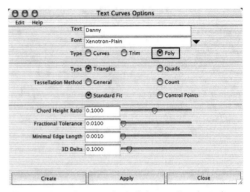

Figure 3.69 Make sure the Poly button is selected for Type.

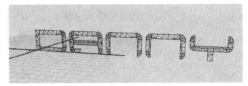

Figure 3.70 Text appears in the Maya scene with its bottom-left corner at the origin.

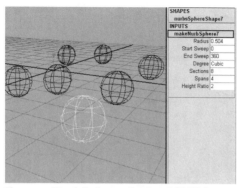

Figure 3.71 The default name for the 7th NURBS sphere created in the scene would be nurbsSphere7.

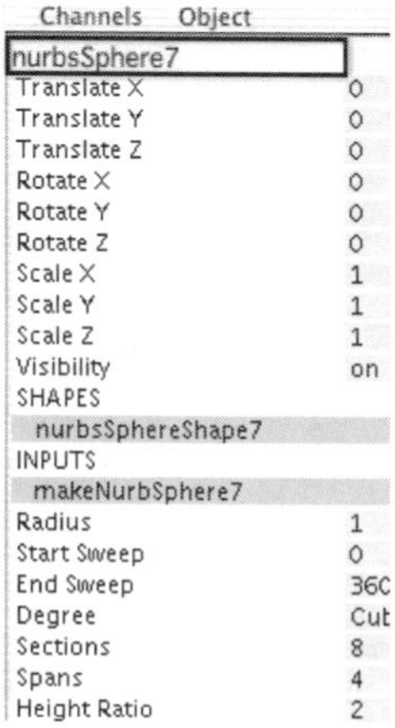

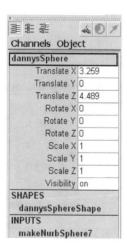

Figure 3.72 Select the object's default name at the top of the Channel Box.

Figure 3.73 Replace the default name with the new name.

Naming Objects

Each time you create an object, Maya gives it a default name. This name is a description of the actual object, followed by the number of times that object type has been used. For example, nurbsSphere7 would be the default name for the seventh NURBS sphere created in the scene (**Figure 3.71**). To make an object easy to find later, you will want to change its default name to something more descriptive. For example, if you created a sphere that you intended to use as a head, you could change its name to *head*. This keeps things organized and clear as you to add objects to your scene.

To change an object's name:

1. Create an object, or select an existing one by clicking it.

2. Select the object's default name at the top of the Channel Box (**Figure 3.72**).

3. Replace the default name by typing in a new name—for example, dannysSphere (**Figure 3.73**).

4. Press (Enter) to complete the name change.

continues on next page

✔ Tip

- You can also change an object's name via the Attribute Editor's Transform panel (the first tab) (**Figure 3.74**). Once the object is selected, you can access the Attribute Editor with Ctrl a/Control a.

Every time you create a primitive or other object in Maya, a node is created to represent the object. You can view this node and any of its connections in the Hypergraph. You can also change the name of the object in the Hypergraph. For more information on the Hypergraph, see Chapter 1.

To change an object's name in the Hypergraph:

1. Create an object, or select an existing one.

2. From any view select Panels > Panel > Hypergraph to change the current view into a Hypergraph (**Figure 3.75**). This menu is at the top of each view's panel.

3. Press f to zoom in on the selected object's node.

4. Hold down Ctrl/Control and double-click the node's object name (**Figure 3.76**).

5. Replace the default name with the new name—for example, dannysSphere.

6. Press Enter to complete the name change.

Figure 3.74 You can also change the object's name in the Attribute Editor's Transform panel (the first tab).

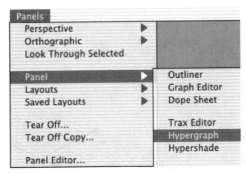

Figure 3.75 From any view select Panels > Panel > Hypergraph to change the current view into a Hypergraph.

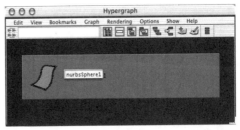

Figure 3.76 Hold down Ctrl/Control, and double-click the node's object name to change it.

NAMING OBJECTS

SELECTION MODES, HIDING AND TEMPLATING

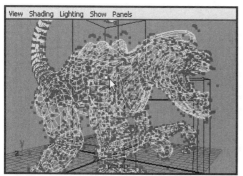

Figure 4.1 A model can have hundreds of selectable points. Luckily, Maya provides helpers for selecting specific ones: Here, the component Pick mask is used to select one of this creature's many points.

A Maya scene can include hundreds of joints, thousands of polygons, and *hundreds of thousands* of points—all of which can amount to a major headache when you're trying to locate just one small point in the middle of huge amounts of geometry (**Figure 4.1**). Not to worry: Maya provides a number of tools that you can use to hide, template, layer, and select objects, eliminating much of the frustration of organizing and selecting objects.

For new users, however, selecting a specific object type or piece of an object (known as a *component)* can be tricky. For instance, a curve may be positioned in front of the surface you are trying to select, making it difficult to select it without using the Pick Mask. The object might be a curve, light, surface, or any of an array of other object types, each of which can be turned off using the Pick mask (**Figure 4.2**). You use the Pick mask controls to mask certain object types (so that only the object types you wish to select are displayed). For example, if you're only interested in selecting curves, you can turn off the ability to select other object types (**Figure 4.3**). Once you do this, when you try to click anything *except* a curve, nothing will happen. When you click a curve, however, it will become selected. We'll devote much of this chapter to this useful tool and the selection process.

Sometimes you'll find that certain objects inhibit your view of other objects. This is where hiding, templating, and layering come in to play. You can use these functions to separate objects so that they no longer hinder your view, making it easier to select the objects that you *are* interested in.

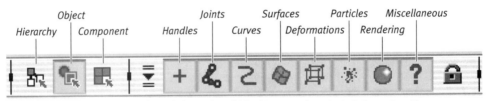

Figure 4.2 The controls in the Pick mask determine which objects can be selected at any given time.

Figure 4.3 Individual object types, such as curves, can be selected in the Pick mask to limit a selection to that type of object.

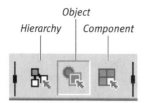

Figure 4.4 Hierarchy, object, and component Pick mask buttons control whether an object or an object component can be selected.

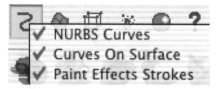

Figure 4.5 Each Pick mask has additional masking selections that you can view by clicking its icon with the right mouse button.

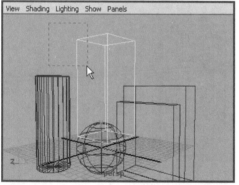

Figure 4.6 Using a marquee can be an easy way to select multiple objects.

Selecting Objects and Using the Pick Mask

Most commands in Maya require that you select an object, or object component, in order for the command to be executed. To do so, you will need to use the Pick mask. Sometimes referred to as the Selection mask, this tool is used to select an object or component by type (not just by where you click on the object).

The Pick mask has three modes: *Hierarchy, Object,* and *Component* (**Figure 4.4**). Each of these modes also has multiple subsets to help you mask off everything but the specific object or component you're interested in. Under each of these subsets you can mask off even more objects to further limit your selection. To view additional subsets, click the mode's icon with the right mouse button (**Figure 4.5**). You can toggle between Object mode (which allows you to select entire objects) and Component mode (which allows you to select pieces of an object) by pressing F8.

This chapter describes the function of each Pick mask mode.

To select an object:

1. Choose the Select by Object Type icon 🔲.

2. Move the mouse over an object.

3. Click the object to select it.

   or

   Drag a marquee that overlaps part of the object you want to select (**Figure 4.6**).

4. Release the mouse button to select the object(s).

To add objects to a selection:

◆ While holding down Shift, click each object you want to add to the current selection.

or

◆ While holding down Shift, draw a marquee that overlaps part of each object you want to add to the selection.

✔ Tip

■ If you drag a marquee around part of an object that's already been selected, you will deselect the object.

To subtract objects from a selection:

◆ While holding Shift, click each object you want to subtract from the current selection. The objects are subtracted.

or

◆ While holding down Shift, draw a marquee that overlaps part of each object you want to subtract from the current selection.

To invert the selection:

1. Select an object (**Figure 4.7**).

2. From the Edit menu select Invert Selection (**Figure 4.8**).

   Deselected objects become selected; selected objects become deselected (**Figure 4.9**).

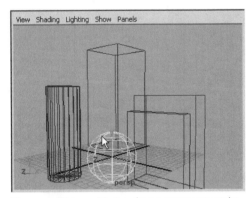

Figure 4.7 Click an object or drag a marquee to make a selection.

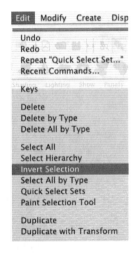

Figure 4.8 From the Edit menu select Invert Selection.

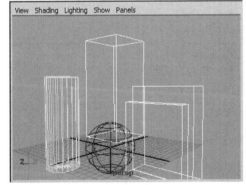

Figure 4.9 When Invert Selection is used, deselected objects become selected, and selected objects become deselected.

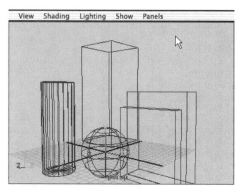

Figure 4.10 Click in the background of a pane to deselect all objects, or (Shift)-click a selected object to deselect it.

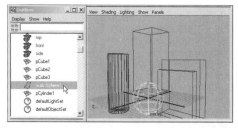

Figure 4.11 Select Outliner from the Window menu, and click the name of the object you want to select.

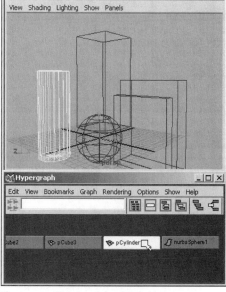

Figure 4.12 Click the node of the object you want to select.

To deselect all objects:

◆ Click once in open space to deselect all objects, or (Shift)-click a selected object to deselect it (**Figure 4.10**).

To select an object using the Outliner:

1. From the Window menu select Outliner.

2. Click the name of the object you want to select (**Figure 4.11**).

   The object becomes selected.

To select an object using the Hypergraph:

1. From the Window menu select Hypergraph.

2. Click the node of the object you want to select (**Figure 4.12**).

   The object becomes selected.

Selecting objects using Hierarchy mode

Hierarchy mode is used to select objects within a hierarchy. You can select the top node in a hierarchy; a descendent, called a *leaf* (**Figure 4.13**); or a templated object. There are three major masks in Hierarchy mode, all of which are defined in **Table 4.1**. In the following examples we will first group two spheres to create a hierarchy, then show how to select objects within that hierarchy. For more information on hierarchies, see Chapter 6.

To select the top object in a hierarchy:

1. Create two spheres.

2. Drag a marquee around the spheres to select both (**Figure 4.14**).

3. From the Edit menu select Group.

   The two objects are grouped together.

4. From the Window menu select Outliner (**Figure 4.15**).

   The Outliner window opens.

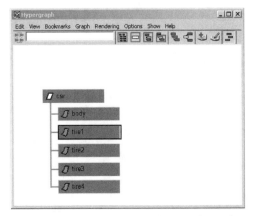

Figure 4.13 A *leaf* is a node lower down in a hierarchy, such as tire4 in this figure.

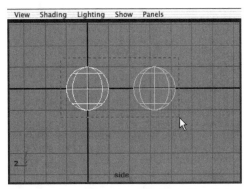

Figure 4.14 A marquee selects all objects it touches; you don't need to box in the entire object.

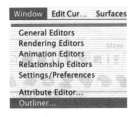

Table 4.1

Hierarchy Mode Selection Masks

ICON	NAME	FUNCTION
🔖	Root	Selects the top node in a hierarchy.
🗏	Leaf	Selects a descendant object.
▦	Template	Selects a templated object. You must select a templated object before untemplating it.

Figure 4.15 The Outliner lists all the nodes in the scene.

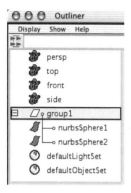

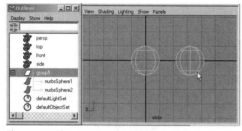

Figure 4.16 Clicking the plus sign expands the view of all of the object names in the hierarchy.

Figure 4.17 The group node at the top of the hierarchy becomes selected no matter which object in the hierarchy you originally selected.

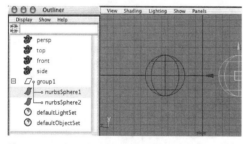

Figure 4.18 The selected node becomes gray, and the top node in the hierarchy becomes green.

5. Click the plus (+) sign to the left of the group name in the Outliner to show the entire hierarchy (**Figure 4.16**).

6. Set the Pick mask to Select by Hierarchy mode by clicking its icon 🔳 in the Status Line.

7. Set the submask to Select by Hierarchy: Root by clicking its icon 🔳 in the Status Line.

8. Click one of the objects.

 The group node at the top of the hierarchy becomes selected, in turn selecting both of the spheres beneath it (**Figure 4.17**).

To select an object within a hierarchy:

1. Follow Steps 1 through 6 of the preceding task.

2. Set the submask to Select by Hierarchy: Leaf by clicking its icon 🔳.

3. Click one of the objects.

 The object clicked, not the group node, becomes selected (**Figure 4.18**). In the outliner, the selected node is shown in gray.

✔ Tip

■ You can move up the hierarchy to the group node by pressing the up arrow.

Selecting objects using Object Type mode

Selecting by Object Type mode (usually just called *Object mode)* selects entire objects. There are eight masks for Object mode, all of which are described in **Table 4.2**.

This mask is extremely useful when you want to select an object of a specific type that has other object types overlapping it—preventing the object from being selected. Take, for example, a character that has already been set up for animation—with joints, Inverse Kinematics, also known as *IK*, handles, selection handles, and geometry sitting directly on top of each other. It can be difficult to select the joints behind the geometry. To get around this problem, you can use the Object Pick mask to turn off all object types *except* for joints (**Figure 4.19**). Now the only selectable objects are the joints themselves, making them much easier to select.

Table 4.2

	Object Mode Selection Masks	
ICON	NAME	FUNCTION
	Handles	Selects selection handles and IK handles.
	Joints	Selects skeleton joints.
	Curves	Selects NURBS curves, curves on surfaces, and paint effects strokes.
	Surfaces	Selects NURBS, polys, and sub-division surfaces as well as planes.
	Deformations	Selects lattices, clusters, non-linears, and sculpt objects.
	Dynamics	Selects particles, emitters, fields, springs, rigid bodies, and constraints.
	Rendering	Selects lights, cameras, and textures.
	Miscellaneous	Selects IK end effectors, locators, and dimensions.

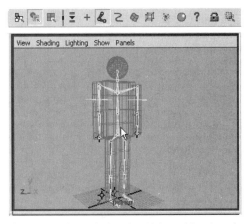

Figure 4.19 When only the Joints Pick mask is selected, joints are the only object type that can be selected.

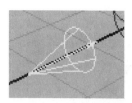

Figure 4.20 Zoom the camera up to an object by pressing [f]; press and hold [Shift][f] to zoom the object in all the views.

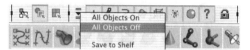

Figure 4.21 Select All Objects Off in the Pick mask to set the mask to select nothing.

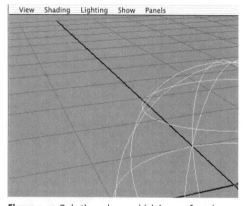

Figure 4.22 Only the sphere, which is a surface, is selected (even though the marquee overlaps the spotlight).

To select surfaces only with the Object Pick mask:

1. From the Create menu select NURBS primitive > Sphere.

2. From the Create menu select Lights > Spotlight.

3. Press [f] to bring the objects closer to the camera view (**Figure 4.20**).

4. Set the Pick mask to Select by Object Type by clicking the icon.

5. Click the arrow to the right of the Object Pick Mask icon, and select All Objects Off from the pop-up menu (**Figure 4.21**). All object types are turned off in the Pick mask.

6. Set the submask to Select by Object Type: Surfaces by clicking its icon.

7. Drag a marquee around the two objects. Because it is a surface, the sphere becomes selected. However, since the spotlight is *not* a surface, it isn't selected (**Figure 4.22**).

✔ Tip

■ You can follow the same steps to mask any object type.

SELECTING OBJECTS AND USING THE PICK MASK

Selecting parts of objects using Component mode

Every Maya object is made up of components, which define the final shape of a curve or surface. A curve, for example, is made up of hulls, CVs, and edit points (**Figure 4.23**). The positions of each of these components determine the look of the curve. Each object's components can be selected and edited individually using Component mode and Maya's manipulation tools. (For more information on curve and surface components, see Chapter 7.)

There are eight major masks in Component mode, all of which are defined in **Table 4.3**.

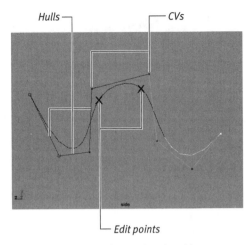

Hulls — CVs

Edit points

Figure 4.23 There are three main selectable components of a curve: hulls, CVs, and edit points.

Figure 4.3

Component Mode Selection Masks

Icon	Name	Function
■	Points	Selects NURBS CVs, poly vertices, subdiv vertices, lattice points, and particles.
●	Parameter Points	Selects NURBS edit points, curve points, surface points, and subdiv UVs.
✎	Lines	Selects NURBS isoparms and trim edges, poly and subdiv edges, and springs.
◈	Faces	Selects NURBS patches, and poly and subdiv faces.
✐	Hulls	Selects NURBS hulls.
◉	Pivots	Selects rotate, scale, and joint pivots.
+	Handles	Selects selection handles.
?	Local Rotation	Selects local rotation axes and image planes.

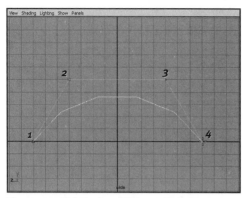

Figure 4.24 Click the four CVs to create the curve.

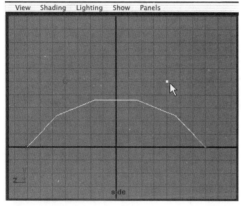

Figure 4.25 Click one or more curve CVs to select them.

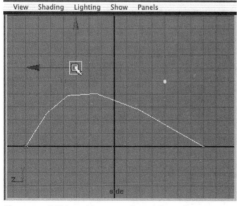

Figure 4.26 CVs can be moved to re-form the curve.

To select and move a curve's CVs:

1. Draw a curve using the CV Curve tool ▧, or open a file that uses curves (**Figure 4.24**). See chapter 7 for more on creating curves.

2. Click the Select by Component icon ▧ in the Pick mask.

3. Click the Set the Component Type icon ▧ arrow and select All Components Off from the menu.

4. Click the Points Submask icon ■.

5. Select the curve to show its points.

6. Click one or more curve CVs to select them (**Figure 4.25**).

7. Click the Move icon ▧ in the toolbar. The Move tool manipulator appears.

8. Click and drag the Move tool manipulator to move the CVs and manipulate the curve (**Figure 4.26**).

The Pick mask has preset shortcuts that when pressed set it to specific settings.

Pick mask shortcuts

F8 —Toggles between Object and Component modes.

F9 —Sets the Pick mask to select vertices (**Figure 4.27**).

F10 —Sets the Pick mask to select edges (**Figure 4.28**).

F11 —Sets the Pick mask to select faces (**Figure 4.29**).

F12 —Sets the Pick mask to select UVs (**Figure 4.30**).

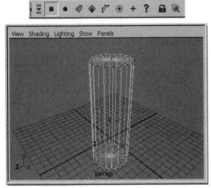

Figure 4.27 Press F9 to have the Pick mask change to select vertices (without selecting other common components).

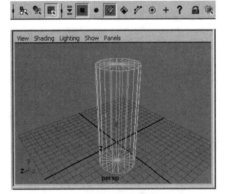

Figure 4.28 Press F10 to have the Pick mask change to select edges (without selecting other common components).

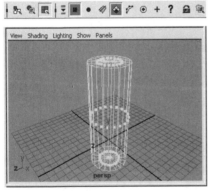

Figure 4.29 Press F11 to have the Pick mask change to select faces (without selecting other common components).

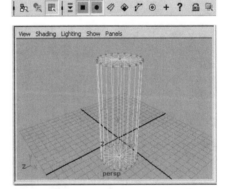

Figure 4.30 Press F12 to have the Pick mask change to select UVs (without selecting other common components).

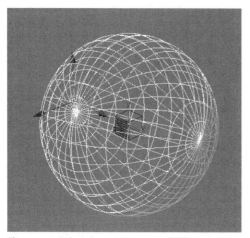

Figure 4.31 Select the points you would like to use for a saved selection.

Often, you will want to select the same group of points or the same objects again and again; however, making the selection more than once can be tedious and unnecessary. You can save time by saving and naming the selection for later use—a function called a Quick Select Set. You can use a Quick Select Set again and again to reselect the same objects and components.

To create a Quick Select Set:

1. In Component mode select multiple points (**Figure 4.31**), or in Object mode select multiple objects.

2. From the Create menu select Sets > Quick Select Set (**Figure 4.32**).

   The Create Quick Select Set dialog box opens.

3. Enter a set name in the "Enter Quick Select Set name" field (**Figure 4.33**).

4. Click OK.

   The named selection is now available from the Edit > Quick Select Sets > [set name] menu (**Figure 4.34**).

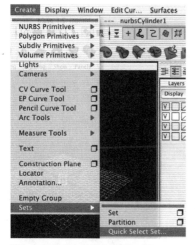

Figure 4.32 Select Quick Select Set to lock in your selection for future use.

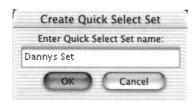

Figure 4.33 Give your selection set a descriptive name to make later use easier.

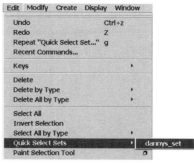

Figure 4.34 After creating a Quick Select Set, you can remake the selection by choosing Edit > Quick Select Sets > [set name].

To hide a selected object:

1. Select an object to hide (**Figure 4.35**).

2. From the Display menu choose Hide > Hide Selection (**Figure 4.36**), or press ⟨Ctrl⟩/⟨Control⟩⟨h⟩.

   The selected object becomes hidden from view (**Figure 4.37**).

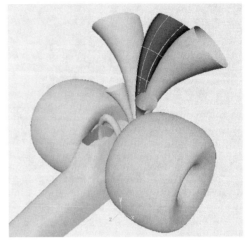

Figure 4.35 Select one or more objects to hide.

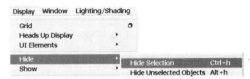

Figure 4.36 Hide the selection by choosing Display > Hide > Hide Selection.

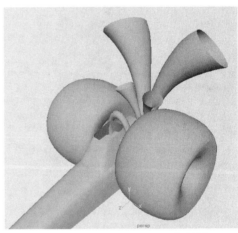

Figure 4.37 The selection becomes totally hidden from view. You can show all objects at once or show the last object hidden.

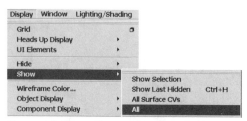

Figure 4.38 Choose Show > All to show all objects that have been hidden.

Figure 4.39 Choose Show > Show Last Hidden to have the last object hidden appear.

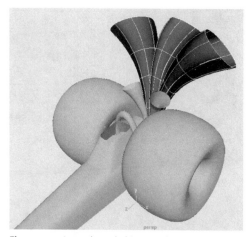

Figure 4.40 Any selected object can be templated. A templated object appears gray until it has been selected.

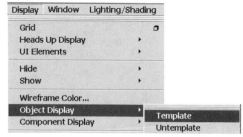

Figure 4.41 From the Display menu select Object Display > Template.

To show all hidden objects:

◆ From the Display menu choose Show > All (**Figure 4.38**).

All hidden objects become visible.

To show the last hidden object:

◆ From the Display menu choose Show > Show Last Hidden (**Figure 4.39**), or press Ctrl / Control Shift h.

The last object hidden becomes visible.

Templating an object allows you to see how it's placed without it getting in the way of other selections. When you template an object, it turns gray and becomes selectable only via the Select Template Pick mask.

To template an object:

1. Select the objects you want to template (**Figure 4.40**).

2. From the Display menu select Object Display > Template (**Figure 4.41**).

3. The object becomes grayed out (**Figure 4.42**) and is only selectable with the Hierarchy: Select Template Selection mask.

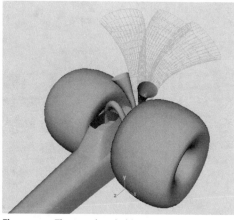

Figure 4.42 The templated objects are gray when not selected and pink when selected with the Template Selection mask.

SELECTING OBJECTS AND USING THE PICK MASK

95

To untemplate an object:

1. Set the Pick mask to Hierarchy mode and click the template icon 🖫 to select templates.

2. Select the templated objects you want to untemplate (**Figure 4.43**).

   The selected templated objects become light pink.

3. From the Display menu select Object Display > Untemplate (**Figure 4.44**).

   The objects become untemplated.

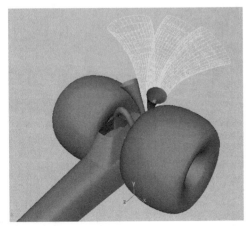

Figure 4.43 To select a templated object you must set the Hierarchy Pick mask to Select Template.

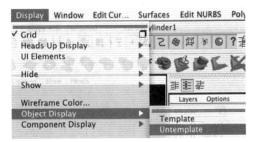

Figure 4.44 To untemplate an object, select Object Display > Untemplate.

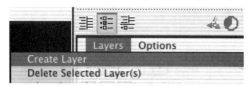

Figure 4.45 You can create additional layers in the Layers menu.

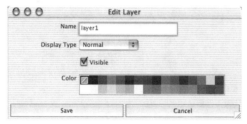

Figure 4.46 The Edit Layer dialog box holds the Name, Display Type, and Color options.

Figure 4.47 Select a descriptive name for the layer.

Figure 4.48 Select a color swatch for the objects on the layer. The wireframes of any objects on the layer will become the color of the selected swatch.

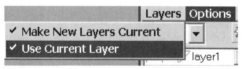

Figure 4.49 To have each new object be placed on the current layer, choose Use Current Layer from the Layer Options menu.

- You can make each new layer the current layer by choosing Make New Layers Current from the Layer Options menu.

- You can delete a layer by clicking on the layer with the right mouse button and selecting Delete from the menu.

About Layers

Layers are used to separate objects so they can be viewed and edited separately. Each layer can have an associated color, which makes objects on that layer easily recognizable. A layer can be hidden, shown, templated, or referenced. Objects can be moved from layer to layer as needed, and new layers can be created at any time.

To create, rename, and color-code a layer:

1. Open the Channel Box, and click the Layer Editor icon ▤ .

2. From the Layers menu in the Layer Editor select Create Layer (**Figure 4.45**), or click the Create Layer icon ▨ .
   A new layer is created, called layer1.

3. Double-click on layer1 to open the Edit Layer dialog box (**Figure 4.46**).

4. Type a descriptive name for the layer in the Name field (**Figure 4.47**).

5. Choose Normal.
   The Display Type pop-up menu lets you choose to have the objects on the layer viewed as normal (or standard), as a template, or as a reference.

6. Select a color swatch (**Figure 4.48**).
   The wireframe of each object on the layer will display in the selected color.

7. Click Save.

✔ Tips

- By default, new objects created reside on the default layer, not the newly created layer. To place each new object on the current layer, choose Use Current Layer from the Layer Options menu (**Figure 4.49**).

To move an object to a different layer:

1. Select the objects you want to move (**Figure 4.50**).

2. With the right mouse button, click on the layer to which you want to move the objects. Then choose Add Selected Objects from the menu (**Figure 4.51**).

To delete a layer:

1. In the Layer Editor select the layer(s) you want to delete.

2. Select Layer > Delete Selected Layer(s). The layer is removed from the Layer Editor.

✔ Tips

■ If a layer containing objects is deleted, those objects are assigned to the default layer.

■ To delete unused layers, select Layer > Select Unused Layers and then select Layer > Delete Selected Layer(s).

To toggle a layer's visibility:

◆ In the Layer Editor, click the square furthest left of the layer name.

If the layer is currently visible, it will become invisible; if the layer is invisible, it will become visible.

To add an annotation to an object:

1. Select the object you would like to annotate.

2. From the Create menu select Annotation... .

The Annotate Node dialog box appears.

3. Type your annotation in the Enter Annotation field, then press OK.

An annotation appears with a line pointing to the annotated object.

Figure 4.50 Select the objects you want to move to a new layer.

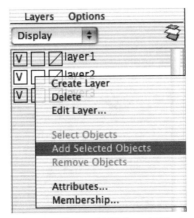

Figure 4.51 Choose Add Selected Objects to move objects to a different layer.

TRANSFORMING OBJECTS AND COMPONENTS

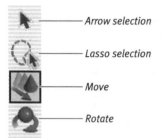

- Arrow selection
- Lasso selection
- Move
- Rotate

Figure 5.1 Maya's manipulation tools.

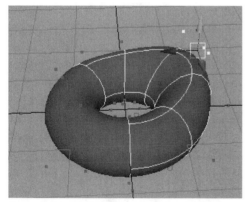

Figure 5.2 The Move tool's translation manipulator is used to move objects and components around the scene.

Maya gives you many ways to move, rotate, and scale objects around a scene, and many shortcuts for completing these common tasks. To move an object (referred to as *translating* an object), you can type in the coordinates in the Channel Box or use one of the many manipulation tools (**Figure 5.1**) to drag the object freely around the scene or constrain it to an axis.

Using the same tools you would employ to manipulate objects in the scene, you can also manipulate *parts* of an object, known as *components*. Each object type has its own components that can be translated (**Figure 5.2**), rotated, and/or scaled to change their look and position, in turn changing the appearance of the object.

Maya's developers have done a great job of making the program easy to learn while still providing plenty of depth: Most tools include advanced features that you can explore as your knowledge base grows. The Duplication options provide a good example of this. Once you get used to using them, you can employ a number of advanced options like duplicating an object multiple times by setting the number of copies, or indicating exactly where you want to place the duplicated object in the scene.

Moving, Rotating, and Scaling Objects

Maya provides multiple tools for moving, rotating, and scaling objects and components. Each of these tools has axes that you can grab and move to transform an object. These axes, called *manipulators* (**Figure 5.3**), are used to translate (move), rotate, or scale the object. Manipulators make it easy to constrain objects along a particular axis: You simply click and drag the colored line for the axis along which you want to constrain the object. The colors remain consistent for each tool. RGB colors coincide with the *x-y-z* axes (**Figure 5.4**): The manipulator's *x* axis is red; the *y* axis is green; and the *z* axis is blue. If you forget an axis' color, simply check the View axis in the lower left-hand corner of each pane (**Figure 5.5**). The axis selected on the manipulator is always yellow.

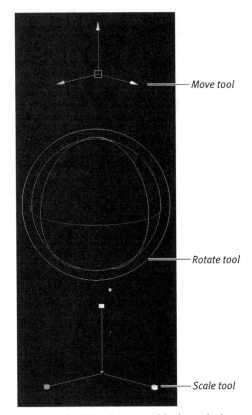

Move tool

Rotate tool

Scale tool

Figure 5.3 The Move, Rotate, and Scale manipulators.

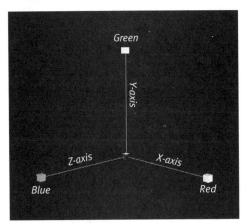

Figure 5.4 RGB colors match the *x-y-z* axes.

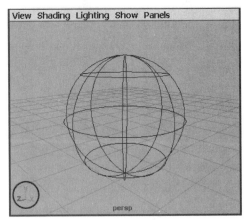

Figure 5.5 Check the View axis in the lower-left corner of each pane to remind yourself which color is associated with each axis.

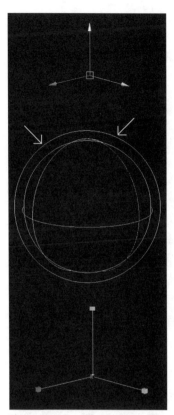

Figure 5.6 You can freely translate an object by selecting the center of the Move tool's manipulators, scaling proportionally with the center of the Scale tool's manipulator, or clicking and dragging anywhere in the sphere of the Rotate tool to rotate freely.

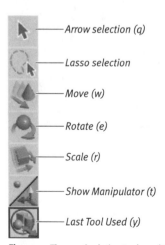

— Arrow selection (q)

— Lasso selection

— Move (w)

— Rotate (e)

— Scale (r)

— Show Manipulator (t)

— Last Tool Used (y)

Figure 5.7 The manipulation tools and their shortcut keys.

In addition to constraining an object along an axis, you can freely manipulate the object by clicking and dragging the square in the middle of the Move and Scale tool manipulators, or by clicking and dragging anywhere on the inside of the Rotate manipulator (**Figure 5.6**).

Each of the tools in the toolbar, with the exception of the Lasso tool, has an associated shortcut—all of which are easy to remember because they coincide with the q w e r t y keys on the keyboard. You can just press a tool's key to turn on its manipulator.

The q w e r t y keys and the manipulators they turn on are as follows (**Figure 5.7**):

q Arrow Selection tool

w Move tool

e Rotate tool

r Scale tool

t Show manipulator

y Last tool used

✔ Tip

- Be aware that these keys will not work if the Caps Lock key is on. In Maya, capitals represent different hotkeys with different functions mapped to them. For example, the Move, Rotate, and Scale tools' associated keyboard shortcuts are w, e, and r, respectively. However, when those same keyboard letters are capitalized, they're used as follows: W keyframes translation; E keyframes rotation; and R keyframes scaling.

101

To translate an object or component using the Move tool:

1. Select an object or component by clicking it.

2. Press ⓦ or click the Move tool icon 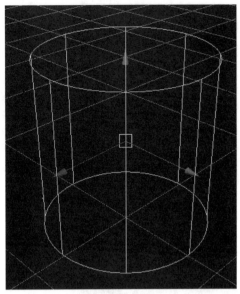 in the toolbar.

   The Move manipulator will now be visible on the object or component (**Figure 5.8**).

3. With the left mouse button, click and drag the manipulator's arrow in the direction you want the object to move (**Figure 5.9**).

   This translates the object along the selected axis.

   or

   Hold down Shift, and then with the middle mouse button click and drag in the direction you want the object to move (**Figure 5.10**).

   This selects the appropriate manipulator axis and translates the object in that direction. This is particularly useful if you've just created an object at the origin but moved the camera away from the grid. You can pull the object into your camera view if you know the direction of the origin.

Figure 5.8 The Move manipulator is used to move the object around the scene.

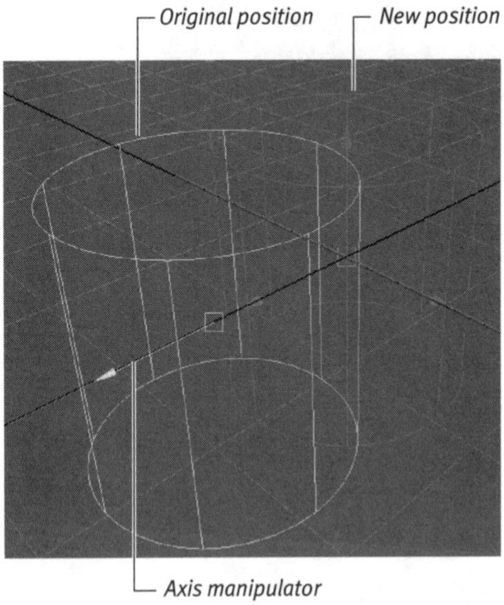

Original position   *New position*

Axis manipulator

Figure 5.9 Click and drag the axis to which you want the object constrained so that you can maintain precise control over the surface's position. This is particularly useful in the perspective view.

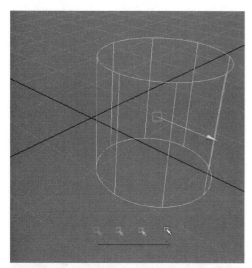

Figure 5.10 By dragging left and right with the middle mouse button, you can change values interactively. Here, a translation value is changed; therefore, the object is moved.

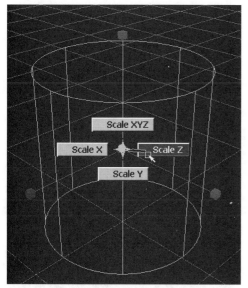

Figure 5.11 The Scale tool's Marking Menu includes shortcuts for scaling proportionally as well as along an axis.

✔ Tips

■ You can also hold down x to activate grid snap. In addition, if you drag with the middle mouse button anywhere on the grid, the object will snap to that location.

■ You can use the + and − keys to enlarge or shrink the manipulators.

■ From anywhere in a view pane you can hold down the keyboard shortcut for the Move (w), Rotate (e), or Scale (r) tool and press the left mouse button to bring up that tool's Marking Menu (**Figure 5.11**). Maya 4.5's Transform Marking Menus now include shortcuts to many of the tools' options.

To scale an object or component:

1. Select an object or component by clicking it.

2. Press ⒭ or click the Scale tool icon in the toolbar.

   The Scale manipulator should now be visible on the object or component (**Figure 5.12**).

3. With the left mouse button, click the small square of the axis on which you want to scale the object or component, and drag in the direction you want the object to scale (**Figure 5.13**).

   or

   While pressing ⒮⒣⒤⒡⒯, Click and drag with the middle mouse button anywhere in the pane in the direction in which you want the object to scale (**Figure 5.14**).

   This selects the appropriate manipulator axis and scales the object in that direction.

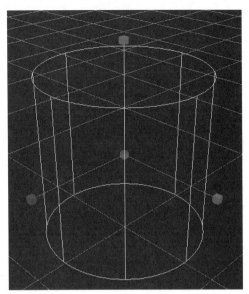

Figure 5.12 You use the Scale tool's manipulator to scale an object proportionally or along a single axis.

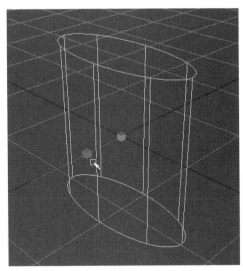

Figure 5.13 Click and drag a Scale tool's axis to scale it along a particular axis.

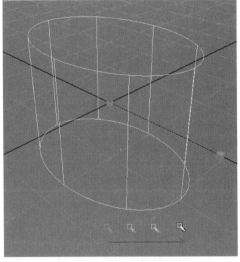

Figure 5.14 This cylinder is being scaled along the x axis by clicking and dragging with the middle mouse button.

Figure 5.15 The Rotate manipulator is used to rotate the surface on one or more axes.

To rotate an object or component:

1. Select an object or component by clicking it.

2. Press e or click the Rotate tool icon  in the toolbar.

   The Rotate manipulator is now visible on the object or component (**Figure 5.15**).

3. Click with the left mouse button on the circle of the axis you want to rotate the object or component around, and drag in the direction you want the object to rotate (**Figure 5.16**).

✔ Tips

- You can click anywhere within the Rotate manipulator sphere, and click and drag to rotate the object without being constrained to any axis.

- Once the axis you want to use is yellow on the manipulator, you can click and drag anywhere in the pane with the middle mouse button to rotate the object around that axis without touching the axis or the object.

- The light-blue outer ring rotates the object or component around an axis that always faces the camera view (**Figure 5.17**).

Figure 5.16 Click and drag the axis circle to which you want the object constrained. A gray pie slice shows you how many degrees you have rotated the object.

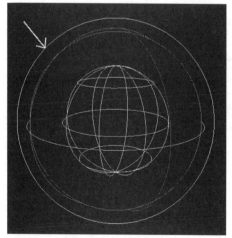

Figure 5.17 The light-blue outer ring rotates the object or component.

MOVING, ROTATING, AND SCALING OBJECTS

To translate, rotate, or scale an object or component using the Channel Box:

1. Select an object or component by clicking it.

2. In the Channel Box, click once in the field next to the attribute you want to change (**Figure 5.18**).

3. Type a new value in the selected field. The object reflects the value change (**Figures 5.19** and **5.20**).

   or

   Click to select the Attribute's name, and then move the mouse over a view pane. Hold down the middle mouse button and drag left or right to interactively change the value of the selected attribute (**Figure 5.21**).

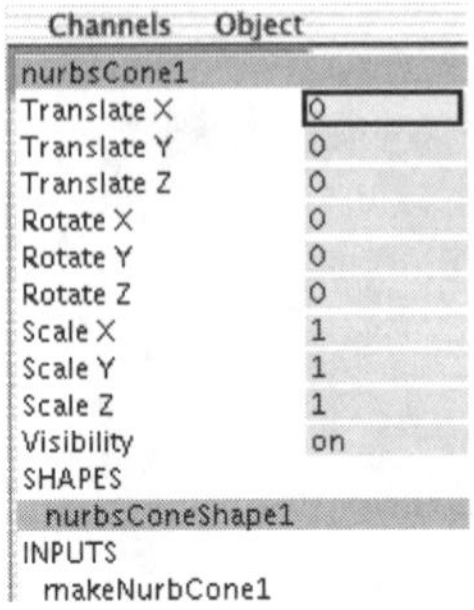

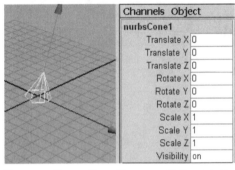

Figure 5.18 Click the field name of the attribute you want to change (in this case, Translate X).

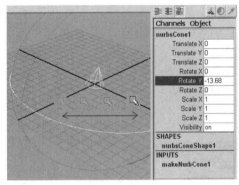

Figure 5.19 The position of the cone with Translate X set to *0*.

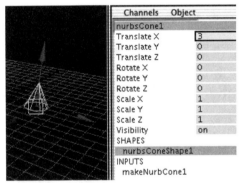

Figure 5.20 Changing the Translate X value to *3* moves the cone three units in the positive *x* direction.

Figure 5.21 You can use the middle mouse button to interactively change values anywhere in a pane.

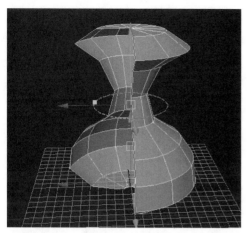

Figure 5.22 The additional manipulator on the Show Manipulator tool controls additional Revolve attributes, saving you from going to the Channel Box. In this example, the revolve was changed to less than 360 degrees by moving the manipulator at the center of the object.

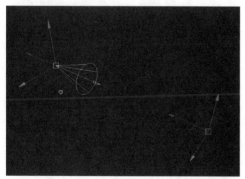

Figure 5.23 Two manipulators appear, giving you more precise control over what objects the spotlight is pinpointing and the direction in which the light is aimed.

Using the Show Manipulator tool:

The Show Manipulator tool ✍ lets you access the Input node of an object (known as its *construction history)* to alter a surface or curve. This tool is most useful for surfaces that originated from curves because the manipulator provides shortcuts to altering the INPUT node attributes (**Figure 5.22**). (For more information, see Chapter 7, "NURBS Curves and surfaces.")

Another great use of the Show Manipulator tool is to direct a spotlight or camera. When used on a spotlight, the light will have two manipulators instead of one—one to move the light, and one for the light to point at, which makes adjusting lighting easier.

The Show Manipulator tool most commonly appears with two manipulators. In the case of a spotlight, one manipulator translates the camera, while the second indicates where the spotlight will be aimed. Follow the steps below to create a spotlight and aim it using the Show Manipulator tool.

To aim a spotlight using the Show Manipulator tool:

1. From the Create menu select Lights > Spotlight.

2. Click the Show Manipulator icon ✍ in the toolbar.

   The spotlight now has one manipulator at its base and another in front of the light (**Figure 5.23**).

continues on next page

MOVING, ROTATING, AND SCALING OBJECTS

3. Select the manipulator at the base of the spotlight (**Figure 5.24**).

4. Move the manipulator up the *y* axis.

   The spotlight moves with the manipulator but continues to point at the second manipulator (**Figure 5.25**).

5. Select the manipulator in front of the spotlight.

6. Move the manipulator along the *z* axis.

   The spotlight remains in place but continues to point at the manipulator (**Figure 5.26**).

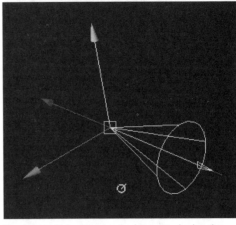

Figure 5.24 Select the manipulator attached to the spotlight to translate the light.

Figure 5.25 You can move the manipulators separately or together (which you would do when you want to maintain the same relationship between the manipulators).

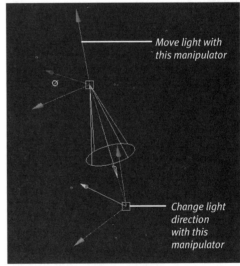

Move light with this manipulator

Change light direction with this manipulator

Figure 5.26 To place a light directly on an object, you can group one of the show manipulators to it: The spotlight will then always shine on that object.

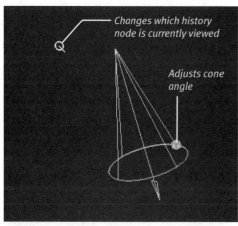

Figure 5.27 Most objects will display a blue ring from which you can access that object's input nodes.

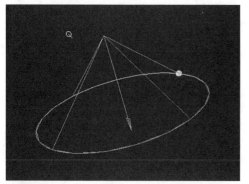

Figure 5.28 The cone angle controls the width of the light beam.

7. Click twice on the light-blue ring.

   The manipulators change into a ring around the cone of light. Each time you click the ring, it takes you through the cone's History nodes (**Figure 5.27**).

8. Click and drag on the square atop the circle that surrounds the cone.

   The cone angle will change interactively as you drag the mouse (**Figure 5.28**).

To use the Lasso Selection tool to select a set of components:

1. Create a primitive NURBS sphere.

2. Press 8.

3. Click the Lasso selection icon in the toolbar.

4. Drag in a circle around the CVs you would like to select (**Figure 5.29**).

5. Release the mouse.

   The CVs within the circle become selected (**Figure 5.30**).

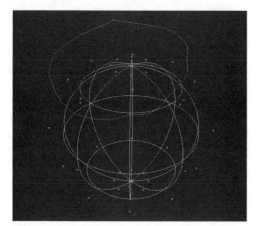

Figure 5.29 The Lasso Selection tool will close itself after the mouse is released.

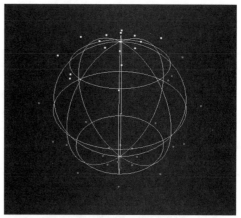

Figure 5.30 The top CVs become selected because they were within the selection circle.

MOVING, ROTATING, AND SCALING OBJECTS

Duplication Options

Maya provides duplication shortcuts for modeling objects with repetitive geometry—for example, a staircase. To model a staircase, you could use one elongated cube and one duplicate action to produce the whole staircase in a minimum number of steps (**Figure 5.31**).

You can use the Duplicate tool for simple object duplications as well as for more complex duplications, including rotations, translations, and scales of an object. What's more, the Duplicate option includes additional valuable tools for mirroring and creating instances of objects.

You can duplicate objects either with or without their INPUTS, History nodes (**Figure 5.32**). (See Chapter 1 for more information on construction history.) It's important to note, however, that history duplication is set to *off* by default.

Mirroring and instancing objects

In addition to translating objects, you can use the Duplication options to create a mirror image of an object (that is, a reversed copy of the original). Body parts make good candidates for mirroring because many (eyes, ears, arms, and legs) include near-identical versions on the other side of the body (**Figure 5.33**). If you mirror one of these objects—say an ear—you can create a second object in the perfect mirrored position with just a click of your mouse.

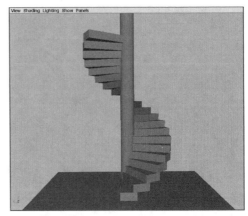

Figure 5.31 This staircase was made with two objects and one duplication.

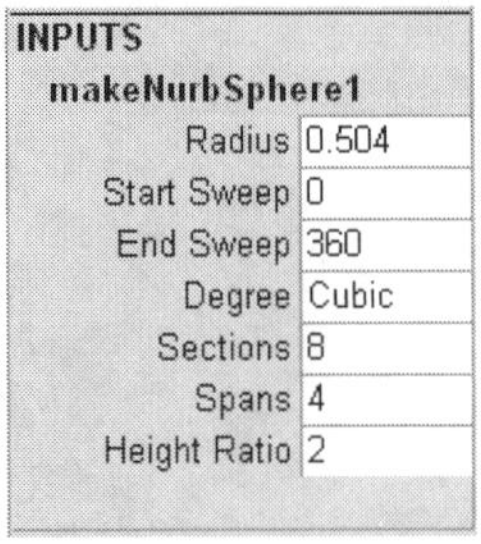

Figure 5.32
The sphere's Inputs node holds its editable history attributes.

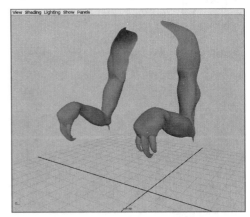

Figure 5.33 By mirroring an arm, you can save time in modeling a second arm.

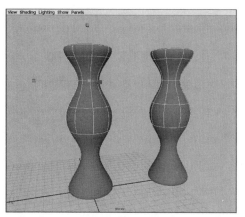

Figure 5.34 Instances of objects will mimic the edits of the first object interactively.

In addition to duplicating and mirroring objects, you can create *instances* of objects—duplicates that retain a connection to the shape of the original (**Figure 5.34**). The beauty of this is that you can then edit the original and have each of the instanced objects follow those edits interactively. For example, if you were creating a building with multiple identical pillars, you could create one pillar and then create a number of *instances* of it to get those additional pillars. If you later decide to change the look of the pillars, all you have to do is edit one, and the rest will be updated automatically.

To duplicate an object:

1. Select an object by clicking it.

2. From the Edit menu select the box next to Duplicate (**Figure 5.35**).

   This opens the Duplicate Options window.

3. Enter the amount of duplicates desired in the Number of Copies field (**Figure 5.36**).

4. Click Duplicate [Duplicate].

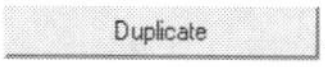

   The specified number of copies are duplicated and placed on top of each other.

Figure 5.35 From the Edit menu select the box next to Duplicate to open the Duplicate Options window.

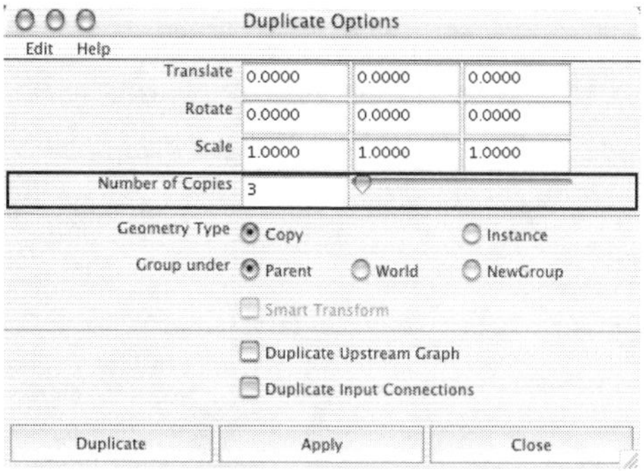

Figure 5.36 Enter the number of duplicates you desire in the Number of Copies field.

To duplicate an object with rotation:

1. Select an object by clicking it.

2. From the Edit menu select the box next to Duplicate.

   This opens the Duplicate Options window.

3. Select a rotation amount for each additional copy, and type that amount in the Rotate field of the axis you want to rotate around (**Figure 5.37**). The fields are, left to right. *x* axis, *y* axis, and *z* axis.

   If you've used a sphere, you'll only notice a rotation in wireframe mode.

4. Click the Duplicate button to duplicate the object.

✔ Tips

- You can use the same technique to translate or scale a copy.

- You can reset the duplication options to their original state by selecting Edit > Reset Settings inside the Options window.

Now that you have a general idea of how to duplicate an object, let's put the options into action and create a simple staircase. We'll use the same technique we employed to create a simple copy with rotation, but now we'll use the Translate, Rotate, and Scale options together.

The key to successfully creating a duplicate with translation is placing the pivot point in the correct position for the objects to rotate around (**Figure 5.38**).

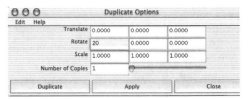

Figure 5.37 Enter the amount of rotation desired in the first field of the Rotate attribute. The first field is the rotate *x* field.

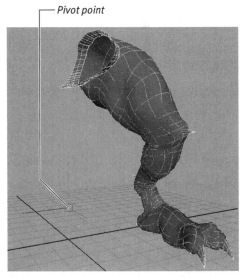

Figure 5.38 The pivot point's placement determines the placement of a duplicated surface.

Channels	Object
CUBE	
Translate X	0
Translate Y	0.5
Translate Z	0
Rotate X	0
Rotate Y	0
Rotate Z	0
Scale X	1
Scale Y	1
Scale Z	1
Visibility	on

Figure 5.39 Type *0.5* in the Translate Y field to move the cube's bottom so that it sits on the grid.

Channels	Object
CUBE	
Translate X	0
Translate Y	0.5
Translate Z	0
Rotate X	0
Rotate Y	0
Rotate Z	0
Scale X	6
Scale Y	1
Scale Z	1
Visibility	on

Figure 5.40 Type *6* in the Scale X field to scale the *x* axis of the object by six units.

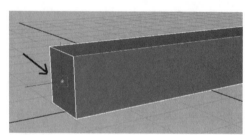

Figure 5.41 The pivot point determines the point in space that the staircase will rotate around.

To create a simple staircase:

1. From the Create menu select Poly Primitive > Cube.

   A cube is created at the origin.

2. Type *0.5* in the Translate Y field in the Channel Box and press ⌅Enter (**Figure 5.39**).

   This moves the cube up so that its base sits on the grid.

3. Type *6* in the Scale X field in the Channel Box and press ⌅Enter (**Figure 5.40**).

   This widens the cube.

4. Press ⓦ or click the Move tool icon in the toolbar.

5. Press ⌊Insert⌋ (⌊Home⌋) on the keyboard to go into pivot-point edit mode.

6. Move the pivot point to the far-left edge of the cube, using the *x*-axis manipulator (**Figure 5.41**).

7. Press ⌊Insert⌋/⌊Home⌋ again to turn off pivot-point edit mode.

8. From the Edit menu select the box next to Duplicate to open the Duplicate Options window.

continues on next page

DUPLICATION OPTIONS

9. Set the Duplicate options as follows (**Figure 5.42**):

   ▼ **Translate: 0, 1, 0**—This moves each new duplicate up the *y* axis one unit. Our cube is one unit high, so each copy will sit on top of the previous one.

   ▼ **Rotate: 0, 15, 0**—This rotates each duplicate 15 degrees more than the previous one around the *y* axis.

   ▼ **Scale: .95, .95, .95**—This scales each duplicate proportionately to 95 percent the size of the last. The staircase will get smaller as it goes higher.

10. Enter 20 in the Number of Copies field. This will create 20 new steps.

11. Select Duplicate.

    The specified number of copies are made and placed on top of each other after being rotated and scaled (**Figure 5.43**).

✔ Tips

- It's a good idea to check your options before duplicating. The previous settings will be retained *unless* you reset them. To return the options to their default settings, with the Duplicate Options window open, select Edit > Reset Settings.

- Move the pivot point farther down the *x* axis before duplicating to make room for a pole in the center (**Figure 5.44**).

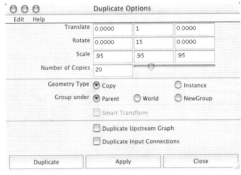

Figure 5.42 Set the Duplicate options as shown to properly duplicate the cube.

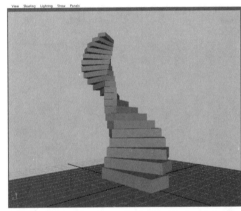

Figure 5.43 A staircase can be built with the click of a button if the proper Duplicate options have been set.

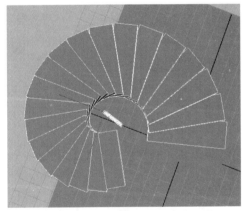

Figure 5.44 Move the pivot point farther from the original object to vary the center of the staircase.

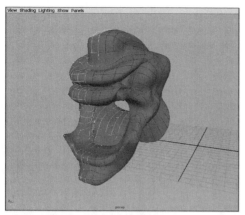

Figure 5.45 You can create half a face and then mirror it to complete the rest of the face.

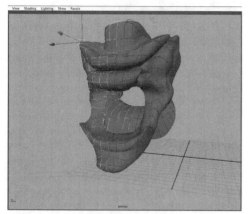

Figure 5.46 By combining instancing and mirroring, you can update both sides of the face with a single movement.

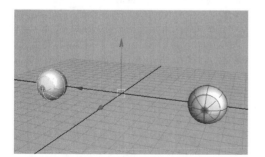

Figure 5.47 Body parts are ideal for mirroring because they have identical counterparts. The pivot point's placement in the scene determines how far apart the mirrored objects end up.

Mirroring an object produces a precise reverse copy of the object. This technique is great for creating one side of a face and then mirroring the face across an axis to complete it (**Figure 5.45**). The pivot point is used as the mirror axis, which means that the farther the pivot point is from the object, the farther the mirrored copy will be from the original. Often, this command is used in conjunction with instancing so that the user can continue to manipulate the original side of the face and have *both* sides of the face reflect those changes. (**Figure 5.46**). (We'll take a closer look at instancing after the following task.)

You can also use instancing to place objects an equal distance away from an axis line, creating a mirrored copy perfectly placed. In the following example, we'll mirror a sphere across an axis, as if to create two eyes (**Figure 5.47**).

To mirror an object:

1. From the Create menu select NURBS Primitives > Sphere, or select an object to mirror.

2. Type *-2* in the Translate X field in the Channel Box (**Figure 5.48**).

   This moves the object two units down the negative *x* axis.

3. Press w or click the Move tool icon ![move icon] in the toolbar.

4. Press Insert/Home on the keyboard to go into pivot-point edit mode.

5. Holding down x, move the pivot point to the origin (**Figure 5.49**).

   x snaps to the grid, which ensures that the pivot point is precisely at the origin.

6. Press Insert/Home to get out of pivot-point edit mode.

7. From the Edit menu select the box beside Duplicate.

   This opens the Duplicate Options window.

8. Select Edit > Reset Settings in the Duplicate Options window to reset the settings, then set the Scale X field to -1.

9. Select Duplicate.

   A mirrored copy is duplicated an equal distance from the pivot point (**Figure 5.50**).

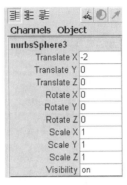

Figure 5.48 Type *-2* in the Translate X field of the Channel Box to move the object two units in the negative *x* direction.

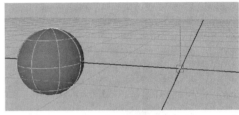

Figure 5.49 Move the pivot point to the origin to send the copy an equal distance away from the origin.

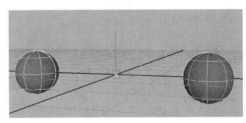

Figure 5.50 A mirrored copy is duplicated an equal distance from the pivot point.

Figure 5.51 Oil drums are instanced to cut down on the amount of edits that need to be made. The objects are rotated to hide their similar attributes.

Figure 5.52 Set the Translate X field (the field on the left) to *2*.

Figure 5.53 Selecting Copy simply duplicates the object; however, selecting Instance results in an additional connection to the original object.

Instancing is a great way to save time, both in modeling and in rendering. An instanced object will follow the edits of the original, making instancing ideal for any object that will have identical copies anywhere else in the scene (**Figure 5.51**). You can still scale, rotate, and move the objects independently once they've been instanced.

To make an instance of an object:

1. Select an object by clicking it.

2. From the Edit menu select the box next to Duplicate.

    This opens the Duplicate Options window.

3. Set the Translate X field to *2* and the rest of the Translate and Rotate fields to *0* (**Figure 5.52**).

    We add a translate here so the copy does not sit directly on top of the original.

4. For Geometry Type, select Instance (**Figure 5.53**).

5. Select Duplicate.

    The duplicate is now an instance, or virtual copy, of the original.

6. With one of the objects selected, press $\boxed{\text{F8}}$ to go into component-selection mode.

continues on next page

DUPLICATION OPTIONS

7. Marquee-select across the top third of the object to select one of its components (**Figure 5.54**).

8. Press ⓦ, and translate the components in any direction.

   Note that the other object follows the translation of the selected surface (**Figure 5.55**).

✔ Tip

■ Once you've created an instance of an object, you can't modify its components independently.

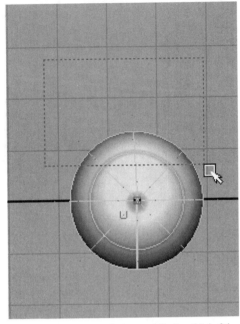

Figure 5.54 Marquee-select across the top third of the object to select CVs to manipulate.

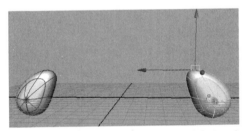

Figure 5.55 The other object follows the translation of the selected surface but in the opposite direction, like an object in a mirror.

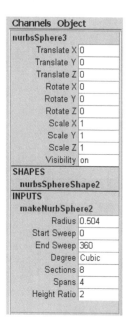

Figure 5.56 A primitive sphere's Inputs node holds the editable history of the sphere.

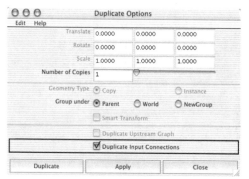

Figure 5.57 Check the Duplicate Input Connections checkbox in the Duplicate Options window to copy the input connections to the new object.

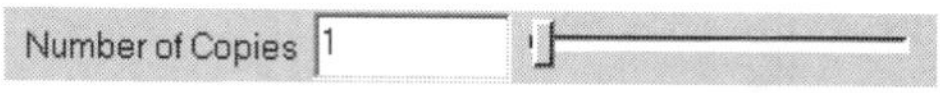

Figure 5.58 The Number of Copies slider determines how many copies of the object will be produced.

Often, you'll want the construction history to remain attached to an object when you create a copy of it. You can do this by selecting the Duplicate Input Connections checkbox in the Duplicate Options window. The objects will then share the same Input node, and both the original and the duplicates will be changed by it.

To duplicate an object with its input connections:

1. Select an object that has input connections attached to it—a primitive sphere, for example (**Figure 5.56**).

2. From the Edit menu select the box next to Duplicate.

   This opens the Duplicate Options window.

3. Check the box next to Duplicate Input Connections (**Figure 5.57**).

   This connects the duplicated object to the Input node of the original. This way, if you alter the Input node of one, the duplicates will be affected as well.

4. Type the number of duplicates you want to produce in the Number of Copies field (**Figure 5.58**).

   continues on next page

5. Click Duplicate.

A copy of the object is made, and its connections are attached to it (**Figure 5.59**). The new object sits directly on top of the original.

6. Select the Move tool, and move the duplicated object away from the original.

7. In the Channel Box select the End Sweep attribute name, and drag the middle mouse button in the View pane to confirm the connections.

The End Sweep is changed on both objects interactively.

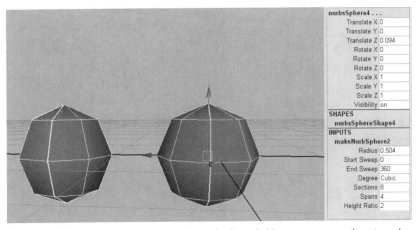

Figure 5.59 When you retain the Inputs node on duplicated objects, you can continue to make individual changes to the surfaces.

Undo	Ctrl+z
Redo	z
Repeat "Duplicate with Transform"	g
Recent Commands...	
Keys	▶
Delete	
Delete by Type	▶
Delete All by Type	▶
Select All	
Select Hierarchy	
Invert Selection	
Select All by Type	▶
Quick Select Sets	▶
Paint Selection Tool	□
Duplicate	Ctrl+d □
Duplicate with Transform	D
Group	Ctrl+g □
Ungroup	□
Level of Detail	▶
Parent	p □
Unparent	P □

Figure 5.60 The Edit > Duplicate with Transform menu.

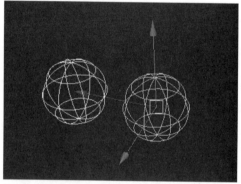

Figure 5.61 Move the sphere the distance you would like your future duplications to copy.

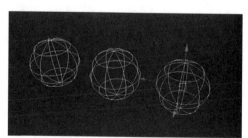

Figure 5.62 Duplicate the object again.

The standard Duplication tool can be cumbersome for simple duplications since there are so many options to adjust, or reset, for even a simple duplication. The Duplicate with Translation tool, on the other hand, comes in handy when all you want to do is make a copy and move it down an axis, or if you only want to produce one or two copies.

To duplicate an object with simple translation:

1. Create a primitive sphere.

2. From the Edit menu select Duplicate with Transform (**Figure 5.60**).

3. Move the duplicated Sphere a few units in the *z* direction (**Figure 5.61**).

4. From the Edit menu select Duplicate with Transform.

   A new Sphere is created the same distance from the second sphere as that one was from the original (**Figure 5.62**).

5. Press (Shift) + (d).

   Another duplicate is made, an equal distance from the last (**Figure 5.63**).

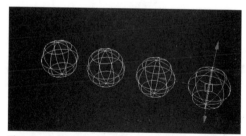

Figure 5.63 Each new copy moves down the axis the same amount as the original copy.

DUPLICATION OPTIONS

GROUPING, PARENTING, AND ALIGNING

6

Grouping, parenting, and aligning provide ways of organizing and controlling an object's relationship to other objects. If you wanted to move a number of objects around a scene simultaneously, you might want to consider grouping those objects so you could move them as a single unit—one selection vs. multiple selections.

You can think of parenting as a distant cousin to grouping. The difference between the two functions boils down to this: Parented surfaces (**Figure 6.1**) have a relationship in which one follows the other (**Figure 6.2**), while objects in a group can act both independently and as a single, grouped entity. We'll be exploring the differences between parenting and grouping throughout this chapter.

Aligning objects, surfaces, and curves can be tricky if you're trying to do it by sight alone. Luckily, Maya offers a few tools to help, including the new Align and Snap Together tools.

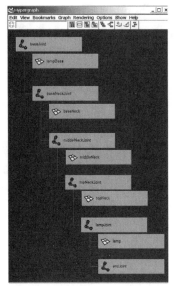

Figure 6.1 Multiple parented surfaces are shown in the Hypergraph.

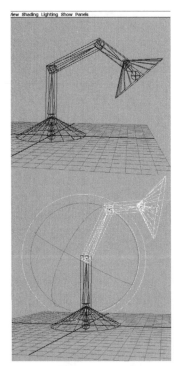

Figure 6.2 When a parent joint is moved, all of the children move along with it.

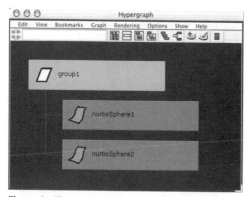

Figure 6.3 The top node is used to change values of the entire group without changing the current values of the individual objects.

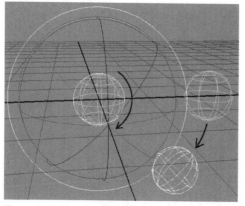

Figure 6.4 Rotating the group node rotates all of the surfaces in the group at the same time around one pivot point.

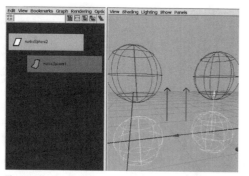

Figure 6.5 The sphere on the left is parented to the sphere on the right. This means that the sphere on the left moves when the sphere on the right is moved.

Grouping vs. Parenting

Grouping two or more objects connects those objects with an additional node, called Group(*n*) (**Figure 6.3**), which you use when you want to perform an action to both, such as moving them at the same time. (The *(n)* in Group(n) represents the number of the group node.) Even though the objects are grouped, you can still select one and move or perform an action on it without affecting the other objects in the group. Alternatively, you can select the Group node and have your actions affect the grouped objects as if they were only one object (**Figure 6.4**).

Parented objects react a bit differently than objects that are grouped. Parented objects have a child-parent relationship. In real life, when a child is holding a parent's hand, the child must follow the parent wherever he or she goes (at least in theory). The same is true in 3D—an object that is parented to another object has to follow the other object around (**Figure 6.5**). When you parent one object to another, no extra node is created. Maya knows which object you want to be the parent and which you want to be the child by the order in which you select them.

GROUPING VS. PARENTING

To group two or more objects together:

1. Select two or more surfaces by dragging a box around them with the Arrow tool (**Figure 6.6**), or Shift-click to select multiple objects.

2. From the Edit menu select Group (**Figure 6.7**).

   The objects are grouped together with an additional node.

3. From the Window menu select Hypergraph.

   The Hypergraph opens in a new window.

4. Press f to zoom the Hypergraph to the selection.

   There is now one more node than the number of objects. This additional node is the group node, named group# (**Figure 6.8**).

✔ Tip

- You can select the Group node and set the Pick mask to hierarchy mode to move the grouped objects together, or you can select a surface's node and set the Pick mask to object mode to move that surface separately from the group.

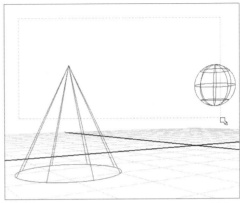

Figure 6.6 You can drag a marquee to select multiple surfaces. The marquee only needs to touch a part of the surface.

Figure 6.7 Select Edit > Group to group objects together.

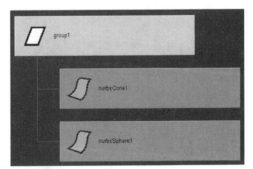

Figure 6.8 The top node is created at the same time the group is created. You use it to control the nodes beneath it.

Figure 6.9 The Group node's default name is group#, with # representing the number of groups created so far.

Figure 6.10 Select Edit > Ungroup to pull objects out of the group.

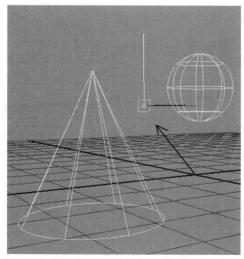

Figure 6.11 The Group node's pivot point is used as the center point for the entire group.

To ungroup an object:

1. Select the Group node in the Hypergraph (**Figure 6.9**).

2. From the Edit menu select Ungroup (**Figure 6.10**).

   The geometry is no longer grouped, and the Group node is deleted.

Once objects are grouped together, they can be translated, rotated, or scaled as if they were a single object. One of the reasons Maya creates an extra group node is to give you an additional pivot point to use as the center point that the objects rotate or scale around. When an object is grouped, the pivot point of the Group node is placed at the origin. The pivot point can then be moved anywhere in the scene to determine its rotation and scale center point.

To translate, rotate, or scale a group:

1. Select the Group node in the Hypergraph, or click one of the grouped objects with the Pick mask set to hierarchy mode to select the Group node.

2. Select the Rotate, Scale, or Move tool in the toolbar, or use their respective hotkeys.

3. Press Insert/Home to go into pivot-point edit mode.

4. Move the pivot point to the position you want the group to rotate around or scale from (**Figure 6.11**).

   You can ignore this step if you're just translating the object.

5. Press Insert/Home to get out of pivot-point edit mode.

continues on next page

6. Translate, rotate, or scale the group by selecting a manipulator's (**Figure 6.12**) axis and dragging left or right in the pane with the middle mouse button to change the axes' value.

✔ Tip

■ You can move the pivot point to the center of a selected Group node by selecting Modify > Center Pivot (**Figure 6.13**).

To move one object within a group:

1. Select the object you want to move with the Pick mask set to object-type mode ![icon].

2. Select the Move tool icon from the toolbox, or press ⓦ.

3. Translate the object by selecting any axis of the Move tool's manipulator, and then dragging left or right in the pane with the middle mouse button to change its value.

The selected object moves, but the rest of the group does not (**Figure 6.14**).

✔ Tips

■ You can follow these same steps to rotate or scale an object within a group without affecting the rest of the group.

■ Once you've selected a member of a group, press ⬆ to move up the hierarchy and select the Group node.

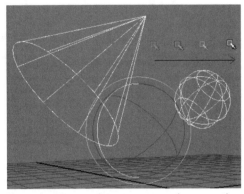

Figure 6.12 You translate, rotate, or scale a group the same way you do an individual object.

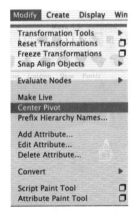

Figure 6.13 The Modify > Center Pivot command is useful for quickly centering the pivot of a group.

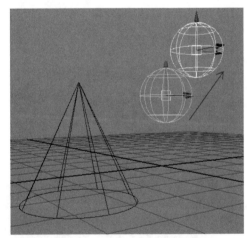

Figure 6.14 Grouped objects can still be edited individually by selecting just that object and not the group node.

GROUPING VS. PARENTING

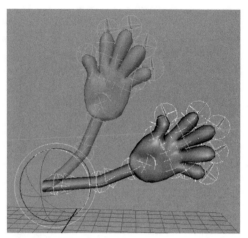

Figure 6.15 The fingers are children of the palm, and the palm is a child of the lower arm. When the lower arm is rotated, all the joints and surfaces below the parent joint follow.

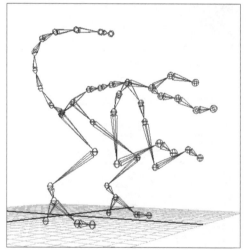

Figure 6.16 An entire hierarchy is formed by parenting one bone to another until they're all connected.

A solid parenting example is a biped skeleton. For our example, we'll use an arm. Your arm starts at your shoulder blade and continues down, connecting your shoulder to your upper arm to your lower arm to your wrist to your palm to your fingers. A relationship is created that forces the fingers to follow the rest of the arm. This relationship is called a parent-child relationship. In this case, the parent is the upper arm and its child is the lower arm. The lower arm is the parent of the wrist, which itself is the parent of the palm. Whenever the upper arm is moved, all the children beneath it move, creating the whole arm movement (**Figure 6.15**).

The overall relationship of the parts of the skeleton is called a *hierarchy* (**Figure 6.16**). A hierarchy determines which objects control other objects. The order of the hierarchy is important to both selecting and translating.

When parenting two objects together, the order in which you select the objects is very important. The second object you select becomes a parent of the first object selected. Once it's parented, the child will follow the parent's translations.

To parent two objects together:

1. Select the object you want to become the child by clicking it.

2. Select the object you want to become the parent by [Shift]-clicking it (**Figure 6.17**).

3. From the Edit menu select Parent, or press [p].

   The second selected object becomes a parent of the first object (**Figure 6.18**).

✔ Tips

■ Because no additional node is added when objects are parented, the pivot point of the parent is used as the center point for controlling the entire hierarchy.

■ If more than two objects are selected, all selected objects become children of the last object selected.

■ You can parent one object to another by using the middle mouse button to drag the child onto the parent in the Hypergraph and Outliner.

To unparent objects:

1. Select each of the children you want to unparent by clicking the first child and then [Shift]-clicking additional children in the Hypergraph or with the Pick mask set to object mode.

2. From the Edit menu select Unparent to unparent the object, or press [Shift]-[p] (**Figure 6.19**).

   This pulls the object out of the hierarchy, so that it now acts separately from the parented hierarchy.

✔ Tip

■ You can also use the middle mouse button to drag the object out of the hierarchy in the Hypergraph and the Outliner, disconnecting the selected object from the rest of the hierarchy.

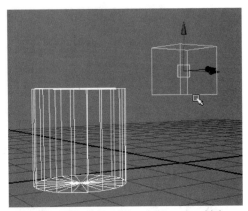

Figure 6.17 [Shift]-click additional objects to add them to the selection.

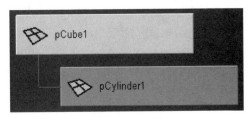

Figure 6.18 The cube is the parent of the cylinder—shown in the Hypergraph by a connecting line.

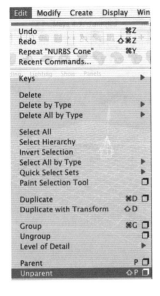

Figure 6.19 Select Edit > Unparent to separate two or more parented surfaces.

GROUPING VS. PARENTING

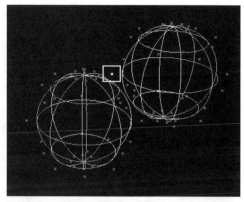

Figure 6.20 You can align one point on one surface to one point on another surface. Here one point on each surface has been selected and the point-to-point command has been run, so that now the two select points are on top of each other (inside the square).

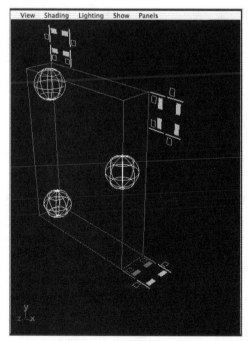

Figure 6.21 Graphical elements are used as quick alignment tools.

About Aligning and Snapping Objects

In the real world, objects touch each other to form other objects. A room, for example, is formed by multiple adjoining walls. You can use Maya's alignment tools to line up objects and components (**Figure 6.20**), saving the additional steps it would take to align objects by eye and eliminating the uncertainty over whether the objects actually touch each other.

In version 4.5, Maya's alignment options are vastly improved with the addition of the Snap Align and Snap Together tools. The Snap Align tool is especially easy to control because it's completely icon-based (**Figure 6.21**)—which means there's no Options window to fuss with. This is a great tool for aligning one object to another, giving you multiple alignment choices (for example, aligning one object to another's center, top, or bottom just by clicking the respective icon). The Snap Together tool takes alignment even further by allowing you to move and rotate an object while aligning it (**Figure 6.22**).

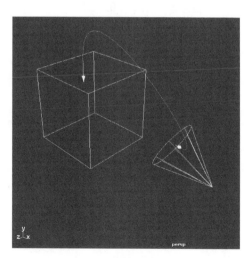

Figure 6.22 Arrows appear when the alignment tool is invoked to show how the alignment command will affect the surfaces when Enter is pressed, completing the command.

Snaps are alignment shortcuts used to quickly align objects or components to gridlines, curves, points, or view planes—for example, moving a selected object to a specific gridline (**Figure 6.23**). You can also use Snaps to make sure curve components and surfaces actually overlap other curves or surfaces. This is important in Maya because many commands require that curves and/or surfaces actually touch in order for the command to work properly. The best way to confirm that a selected point is touching the desired curve is to select the point and use curve snap to move the point to the curve. Snapping can also help bring selected, out-of-view surfaces into view by snapping the selected object to a gridline or curve that is within view.

The four snaps

Let's take a look at the four snaps (**Figure 6.24**) available in Maya 4.5:

♦ **Snap to Grids** ▦ (⟨x⟩⟨)⟩)—Snaps a CV, pivot point, or polygonal vertex to a grid corner. If you turn on this option before you draw a curve, the CVs will snap to the grid corners (Figure 6.23).

♦ **Snap to Curves** ⟨ (⟨c⟩)—Snaps a CV, pivot point, or polygonal vertex to a curve or curve on a surface (**Figure 6.25**).

♦ **Snap to Points** ⟨ (⟨v⟩⟨)⟩)—Snaps a CV, pivot point, or polygonal vertex to another point (**Figure 6.26**).

♦ **Snap to View Planes** ⟨—Snaps a CV, pivot point, or polygonal vertex to a view plane (**Figure 6.27**).

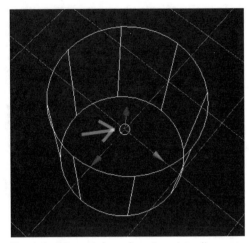

Figure 6.23 Snaps help surfaces jump into alignment with gridlines, curves, and points.

Figure 6.24 The four Snaps, from left to right: Grid, Curve, Points, and View Planes.

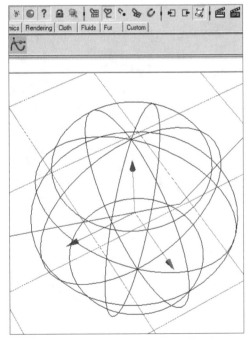

Figure 6.25 Snap to Curves moves the surface into alignment with the curve.

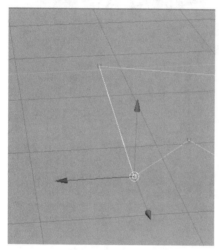

Figure 6.26 The two curve's endpoints are snapped together using Snap to Points.

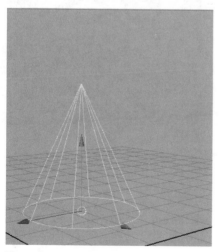

Figure 6.27 Use Snap to View Plane to snap the surface along the plane axis.

To snap an object to the grid:

1. Select an object.

2. Select the Move tool.

3. Hold down ⊠ and drag with the middle mouse button along the grid you would like the object to snap to (**Figure 6.28**).

   or

   Click ⊞ in the status bar and drag with the middle mouse button along the grid you would like the object to snap to.

   The pivot point of the object snaps to the grid corner where you clicked with the middle mouse button.

4. Release the mouse to finalize the snapping position.

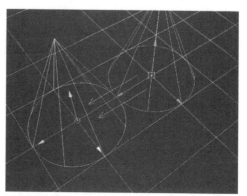

Figure 6.28 The center point of the surface is used to snap from gridline to gridline.

To snap an object to a curve:

1. Select an object.

2. Select the Move tool.

3. Hold down c and drag with the middle mouse button on the curve where you would like the object to snap to (**Figure 6.29**).

   or

   Click ♀ in the status bar and drag with the middle mouse button on the curve where you would like the object to snap to.

   The pivot point of the object jumps to the curve where you clicked with the middle mouse button.

4. Release the mouse to finalize the snapping position.

Figure 6.29 The surface's center point will slide across the curve until you release the mouse button.

To snap an object to a view plane:

1. Select an object.

2. Select the Move tool.

3. Click ✎ in the status bar and drag with the middle mouse button on the view plane where you would like the object to snap to.

   The pivot point of the object snaps to the view plane where you clicked with the middle mouse button (**Figure 6.30**).

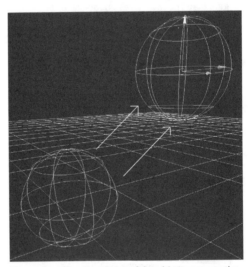

Figure 6.30 The pivot point of the object snaps to the view plane where you clicked with your middle mouse button.

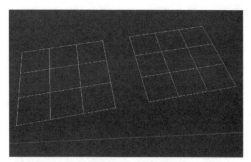

Figure 6.31 Separate two primitive planes so that you can easily view the snapping results.

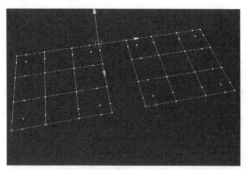

Figure 6.32 Select the point you would like to snap into alignment with another point.

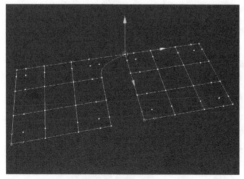

Figure 6.33 Any selected point can be snapped to any edit point or CV.

To snap a point on one surface to a point on another surface:

1. Create two NURBS planes (**Figure 6.31**).

2. Select both planes and press F8.

3. Select a corner CV on one of the planes (**Figure 6.32**).

4. Select the Move tool.

5. Hold down Clear and click and drag with the middle mouse button on a second plane near the CV where you would like the object to snap to.

   The pivot point of the selected CV snaps to the CV on the second plane that's closest to where you clicked with your middle mouse button (**Figure 6.33**).

✔ Tips

■ Although you *can* use the left mouse button when snapping, using the middle mouse button prevents unwanted objects from accidentally being selected.

■ Although we showed snapping points on a curve in this example, the same technique can be used to snap a point on one object to a point on another object. You can snap any point to any other point on a surface or a curve, on the same object or a different object.

ABOUT ALIGNING AND SNAPPING OBJECTS

135

The Snap Align tools

The Snap Align tools are a set of alignment aids for placing multiple objects. Alignment is very important in the world of 3D modeling because an object can appear to be aligned in the Perspective view but be completely off in the Orthographic views (**Figure 6.34**). This happens because the camera angles of Orthographic views are straight on from the side, top, and right; whereas the Perspective view can be viewed at any angle, often giving you an inaccurate perception of the scene.

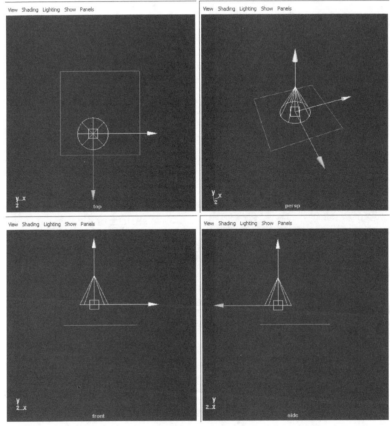

Figure 6.34 The cone seems to be centered on the plane in the Perspective view, but in the Orthographic views, you can see that it's actually very much out of alignment.

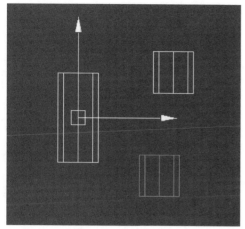

Figure 6.35 The cylinders are different sizes to better illustrate the change after alignment.

Figure 6.36 Min  aligns the surfaces with the minimum *y* value of the two.

The Snap Alignment tools include the Point-to-Point Snaps, Snap Align Objects, Snap Align Tool, and the Snap Together Tool—all of which are essential to a streamlined workflow. Many of the alignment tools are similar; you'll soon determine which one best fits your workflow.

To align two or more objects using the Align Objects tool:

1. Create two primitive cylinders (making one taller along the *y* axis) with some space between them (**Figure 6.35**).

2. Select the cylinders.

3. From the Modify menu select the box beside Snap Align Objects > Align Objects. The Align Objects Options window opens.

4. Select Min  for the Align Mode, and check Align in World Y (unchecking World X and Z) (**Figure 6.36**).

   Setting the World to Y forces the movement to happen along the *y* axis.

continues on next page

ABOUT ALIGNING AND SNAPPING OBJECTS

5. Click Apply.

One cylinder moves up the *y* axis, and one cylinder moves down the *y* axis until the base of each object is aligned (**Figure 6.37**).

6. With the Align Objects Options window still open, select Mid ⊡ for the Align Mode, and check Align in World Y (unchecking World X and Z).

7. Click Align.

One cylinder moves up the *y* axis, and one cylinder moves down the *y* axis until the center of each object is aligned (**Figure 6.38**).

To evenly distribute multiple objects along an axis using the Align Objects tool:

1. Create a primitive cylinder.

2. Duplicate the cylinder four times.

3. Move one of the cylinders up the *y* axis 10 grid units (**Figure 6.39**).

4. Select all of the cylinders.

5. From the Modify menu select the box beside Snap Align Objects > Align Objects. The Align Objects Options window opens.

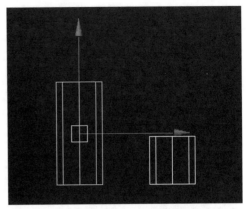

Figure 6.37 The bases of the two surfaces are now placed on the same grid line.

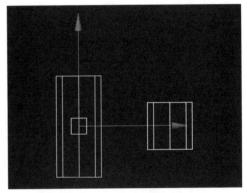

Figure 6.38 The two surfaces are aligned to their centers.

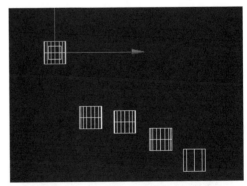

Figure 6.39 Only the placement of the two surfaces farthest away from each other matters now because the rest of the objects will be distributed evenly between them.

Figure 6.40 The Dist option can be used to evenly distribute the selected objects along the selected axes.

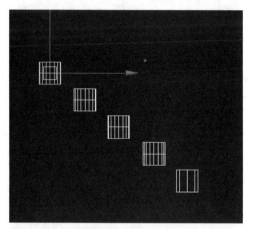

Figure 6.41 The cylinders are perfectly spaced along the *y* axis.

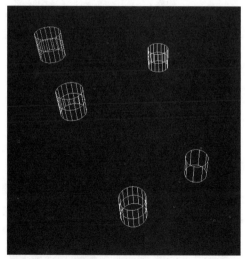

Figure 6.42 The order of selection becomes important because the objects are aligned to the last selected object.

6. Select Dist ![icon] as the Align Mode, and check Align in World Y (unchecking World X and Z) (**Figure 6.40**).

Setting the World to Y forces the objects to be distributed along the *y* axis.

7. Click Apply.

Each of the cylinders moves up the *y* axis until they're all evenly spaced between the two cylinders farthest from the others (**Figure 6.41**).

To align two or more objects using the Align tool:

1. Create five primitive cylinders and randomly space them away from each other (**Figure 6.42**).

2. Select one cylinder by clicking it, then Shift-select each of the others one at a time until all are selected.

continues on next page

ABOUT ALIGNING AND SNAPPING OBJECTS

3. From the Modify menu select the box beside Snap Align Objects > Align Tool.

A gray box appears around the selected cylinders. On the edges of the box are icon manipulators used to align the objects (**Figure 6.43**).

4. Click 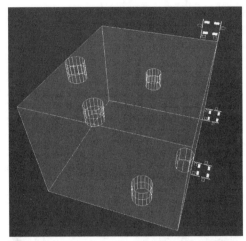 on the surrounding box (**Figure 6.44**).

The cylinders fall into alignment with the selected icon.

5. Press 〔z〕 to undo the alignment, then click on another icon to see its alignment type.

6. Repeat the last step until you feel comfortable with each of the alignment icons functions.

✔ Tip

■ Objects are aligned to the last selected object (blue).

Figure 6.43 A gray bounding box is for visualization purposes only: You need to click the icons for the Align function to work.

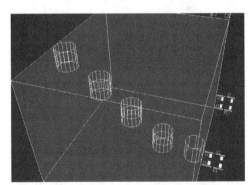

Figure 6.44 Note that each icon actually illustrates which side, or center, on which the alignment will occur.

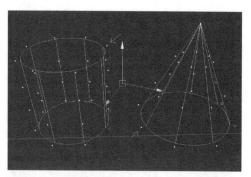

Figure 6.45 You can select any edit point or CV to be aligned with any edit point or CV on another surface.

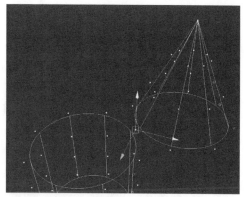

Figure 6.46 The two selected points now appear as one but are actually sitting on top of each other.

To align one point to another point using the Point-to-Point Snap Align tool:

1. Create one primitive cylinder and one primitive cone.

2. Select the objects and press F8.

3. Select one CV from the cylinder, then Shift-select a CV from the cone (**Figure 6.45**).

4. From the Modify menu select the box beside Snap Align Objects > Point to Point.

   The entire object associated with the first selected point moves into alignment with the second object. The two selected points are now stacked on top of one another (**Figure 6.46**).

✔ Tip

■ If you only want the points to move into alignment, not the entire object, use Point Snap (explained earlier in this chapter) instead of the Point-to-Point Snap Align Tool.

ABOUT ALIGNING AND SNAPPING OBJECTS

To align two or three points to two or three points using the 2 and 3 Point-to-Point Snap Align tools:

1. Create one primitive cylinder and one primitive cone.

2. Select the objects and press F8.

3. Select two CVs from the cylinder, then Shift-select two CVs from the cone (**Figure 6.47**).

   or

   Select three CVs from the cylinder, then Shift-select three CVs from the cone.

4. If you selected two CVs on each object, from the Modify menu select the box beside Snap Align Objects > 2 Points to 2 Points. If you selected three points on each object, select the box beside Snap Align Objects > 3 Points to 3 Points (**Figure 6.48**).

   The entire object with the first selected points moves into alignment with the second object's selected points. The points may not stack on top of one another if the spacing between points is different on each of the objects (**Figure 6.49**).

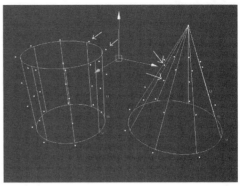

Figure 6.47 The selected set of points will be aligned to the other selected points as closely as possible without changing the shape of the surface.

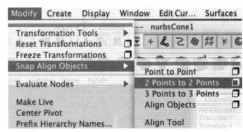

Figure 6.48 The Snap Align Objects drop-down menu holds many of the alignment commands.

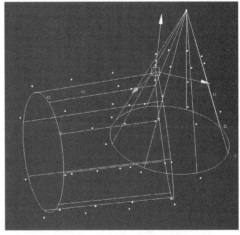

Figure 6.49 The cylinder's placement shifts into alignment with the selected points on the cone's surface.

NURBS Curves
and Surfaces

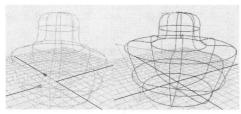

Figure 7.1 You can edit a revolved surface using the original NURBS curve you used to create it.

You can use NURBS curves to create nearly any object—a medieval knight, a detailed car, an alien, or just about any other object you can imagine. Because they can be highly organic, characterized by sinuous, rounded shapes, NURBS surfaces are great for creating trees, faces, and streamlined vehicles.

For anyone who has used other software programs with Bézier curves (for example, Adobe Illustrator), NURBS curve creation should come quite naturally. Although NURBS curves are different than Bézier curves, you create and edit them similarly. Bézier and NURBS curves represent curved lines whose shape you can edit by translating points along the curve (the placement of the original points was specified at the curve's creation). You can use NURBS curves to create a framework for a final surface, outline the profile of surfaces that you plan to later *revolve* to create the final surface, and fine-tune a surface (**Figure 7.1**).

About NURBS Objects

NURBS object creation is a Maya strongpoint because of the precise control it affords the user over the final surface. There are two types of NURBS objects: *curves* and *surfaces*.

NURBS curves have three main components: *CVs (control vertices)*, *edit points*, and *hulls* (**Figure 7.2**). You use these components to create and edit curves in different ways. As you grow familiar with creating NURBS curves, you'll likely come to prefer one component to the others, making it your primary editing method.

In addition to CVs, edit points, and hulls, NURBS surfaces have the following more advanced components: *surface normals*, *patch centers*, and *surface origins* (**Figure 7.3**). You can edit any NURBS surface that was created from a curve (for example, a revolved surface) by editing components of the original curve or by editing the surface's components directly. When a surface is created from one or more curves, it remains linked to that curve through a history connection. Thus, when you modify a curve, you're also editing the surface.

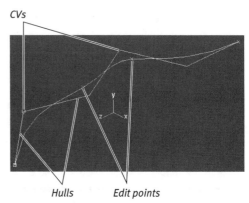

Figure 7.2 NURBS components are used to easily and quickly change the look of the curve or surface.

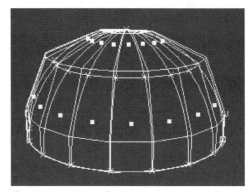

Figure 7.3 NURBS surface components are used to manipulate the look and feel of the surface.

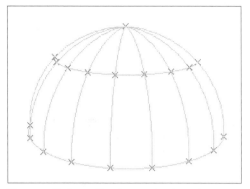

Figure 7.4 Surface edit points can be shown by themselves to make selection and editing easier. You can select each component by clicking its icon, in this case a small *x*.

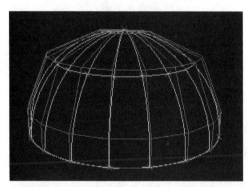

Figure 7.5 Maya allows you to show or hide as many components as you want to view at any given time. This helps you narrow down your selection while still getting a good idea of what the object's other components look like.

Each NURBS component (edit points, CVs, and so on) can be displayed and edited both individually (**Figure 7.4**; edit points are shown) and with other components (**Figure 7.5**; edit points and hulls are shown). NURBS curves are an important part of NURBS modeling because they help you create and edit surfaces. This chapter will provide the foundation you need to control the look of NURBS curves and surfaces.

Creating NURBS Curves

By learning how to create and edit curves, you'll gain a better understanding of how to take full advantage of Maya's modeling tools. Multiple edit points give you precise control over the shape and placement of NURBS curves.

Curves are often used to create a wire representation of a surface. Once you've done this, you can place a skin over the curves to create the final surface (**Figure 7.6**). You can create this final surface using a number of Maya commands, including *lofting*, *extruding*, and *revolving*—all of which we'll examine in depth in this chapter.

Anatomy of a curve

Each NURBS curve has an associated direction, derived from the order in which the CVs were created. A curve's direction is important in determining the look of the final surface. If you don't pay attention to the direction in which a curve is created, you will often get undesirable results when you go to create the final surface. Curves that are oriented in opposite directions can twist and fold the final surface.

The direction of a curve is determined by the first and second CVs created for the curve. The first CV, or *start point,* is represented by a small square. The second CV is represented by the letter *U.* The start point followed by the *U* shows the user the direction in which the curve is headed; this determines the *U* direction of any surface created from the curve (**Figure 7.7**).

Because NURBS curves are used mainly as modeling aids, they don't appear when the scene is rendered.

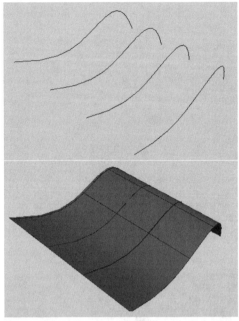

Figure 7.6 Curves used to create a framework for the surface (top), and the same curves with a surface laid over them (bottom).

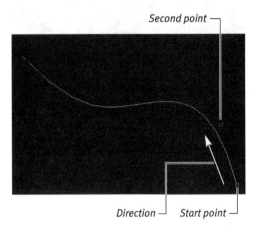

Figure 7.7 The *U* direction of a curve is determined by the first and second CVs created.

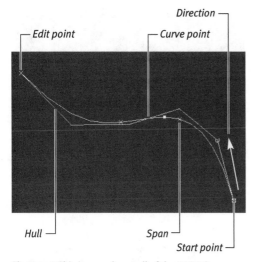

Figure 7.8 This image shows all of the NURBS curve components.

Each curve has the following components (**Figure 7.8**):

Control vertices—CVs are points placed slightly away from the curve and are the components most often used to edit a curve's shape.

Edit points (knots)—Edit points, placed directly on the curve and indicated by a small x, represent another way of editing a curve's shape.

Hulls—Hulls are straight lines connecting each CV. Showing the hulls can help clarify which row of CVs each CV is connected to. By clicking a hull, you select the entire row of CVs along the hull.

Spans—A span is the area between two edit points. Each time an edit point is added, a span is added as well. You can't edit spans directly (like edit points); instead, they represent the results of your edits. You use spans to create and rebuild curves and surfaces. The more spans you add when rebuilding a surface, the more edit points you're adding—which means the more spans you have, the more detailed, and heavy, your surface becomes.

Curve point—A curve point is an arbitrary point on a curve—often used as a point to detach a curve from or to align it with. A curve point can be located anywhere along a curve.

Start point—The start of a curve is the first CV created for the curve, represented by a small square.

Curve direction—The direction of a curve is determined by the first and second CVs created for the curve.

Creating curves of various degrees

Every curve has a certain degree; the higher the degree, the smoother the curve. A curve can have a degree of 1, 2, 3, 5, or 7. A curve with a degree of 1 is a linear curve and only requires two points to define it (**Figure 7.9**). Linear curves and surfaces are characterized by straight lines and sharp corners. A curve degree of 3 will produce a smooth curve without using an excessive number of CVs to describe it (**Figure 7.10**). A curve with a degree of 3 is the most common and versatile curve because it only requires four points and is smooth enough to create a high-quality surface. Because of the accuracy needed for manufacturing, car designers often use degrees higher than 5. For animation, however, a degree of 3 is usually high enough.

Each curve requires CVs that total one more than its degree to create it. For example, a curve with a degree of 3 requires four CVs (Figure 7.10), and a 7-degree curve requires eight CVs, thereby creating a heavier surface (**Figure 7.11**). It is for this reason that a degree of 3 or 5 is usually most ideal.

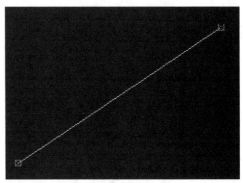

Figure 7.9 A curve degree of 1 creates a linear curve and a linear surface (if a surface is created from the curve).

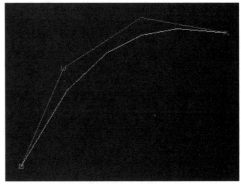

Figure 7.10 A curve degree of 3 produces a smooth curve without using an excessive number of CVs.

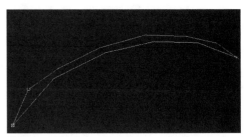

Figure 7.11 This is a 7-degree curve, which means it requires eight CVs.

Figure 7.12 This surface was created with one revolved curve.

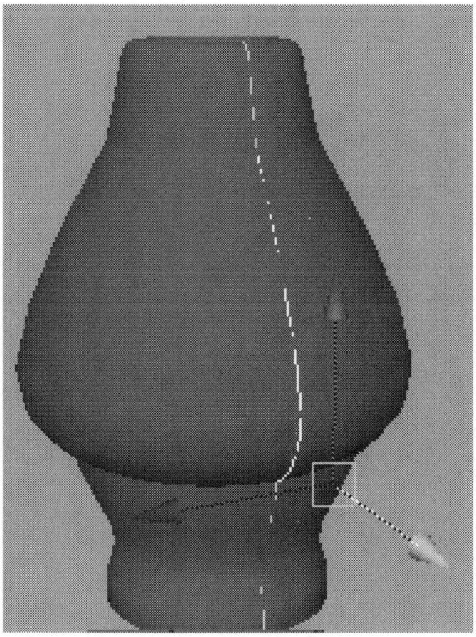

Creating profile curves

You can create many objects by drawing an outline curve in the shape of the object's profile. This profile curve can then be revolved to complete the final surface (**Figure 7.12**). In addition, you can alter the profile curve to tweak the object's shape after the final surface has been created. You can do this because the profile curve and final surface are connected through the object's construction history (**Figure 7.13**).

If you're drawing a profile curve for a vase, glass, pot, or any other object that has thickness to it, you should draw the profile of the inside as well as of the outside (**Figure 7.14**). If you don't draw both profiles, your object will be paper-thin: Since most real objects have some depth or dimension, you need to re-create that thickness in Maya to keep your objects looking realistic. The thickness of the glass is defined by the way you draw the profile curve.

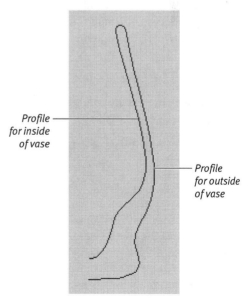

Profile for inside of vase

Profile for outside of vase

Figure 7.13 By tweaking a point of the curve—which is how this revolved surface was created—you can interactively sculpt the object.

Figure 7.14 When drawing a profile curve, make sure you add the inside of the surface to add thickness to the final object.

Typically, you create a curve in one of three ways: with the CV Curve tool, the EP Curve tool, or the Pencil Curve tool.

To create a curve with the CV Curve tool:

1. From the Create menu select CV Curve Tool.

2. In the top view, click in several places.

   A CV will appear with each mouse click, and a curve will appear on the fourth click (**Figure 7.15**).

3. Press (Enter) to complete the creation of the curve.

   The curve becomes highlighted to indicate that it's selected.

To create a curve with the EP Curve tool:

1. From the Create menu select EP Curve Tool.

2. In the top view, click in several places.

   A curve is created once the second edit point is placed, and it continues to take shape with each subsequent point (**Figure 7.16**).

3. Press (Enter) to finish creating the curve.

To create a curve with the Pencil Curve tool:

1. From the Create menu select Pencil Curve Tool.

2. Click and drag in the top view to draw a line.

   The curve is completed once you release the mouse. The Pencil Curve tool tends to be a less efficient way of creating a curve because you end up with more points than you need to describe the shape (**Figure 7.17**).

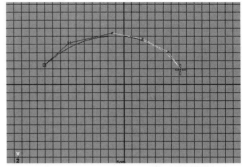

Figure 7.15 This curve was created by placing points using the CV Curve tool.

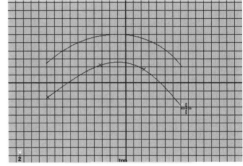

Figure 7.16 This curve was created using the EP Curve tool.

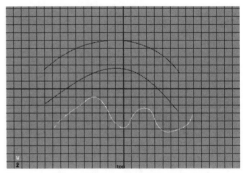

Figure 7.17 The bottom curve was created using the Pencil Curve tool.

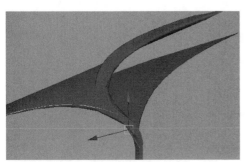

Figure 7.18 Curve direction can cause unwanted surface problems. It is best to keep all curves of the same surface facing in the same direction.

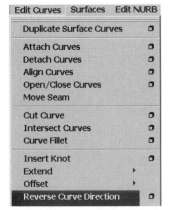

Figure 7.19 Select Edit Curves > Reverse Curve Direction to change the direction of a curve.

As stated earlier, each curve has a direction, called the *U* direction. Sometimes you'll want to reverse a curve's direction because you are getting undesirable surfaces from the curves (**Figure 7.18**).

To reverse a curve's direction:

1. Select a curve in object mode.

2. From the Edit Curves menu select Reverse Curve Direction (**Figure 7.19**).

3. Press F8 to view the new curve direction in component mode (**Figure 7.20**).

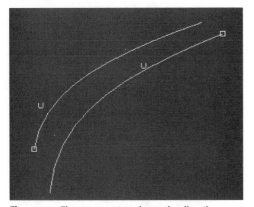

Figure 7.20 The curve on top shows the direction before it was reversed; the curve beneath it shows the direction after the curve has been reversed.

Circular 2D fillets

A *fillet* is a concave junction where two curves or surfaces meet. You can create 2D fillets to combine multiple curves with an arc between them. Sometimes it's easier to create two curves and fillet them together in order to create a corner than it is to draw out one curve with the corner in it. An example might be when you need to create a corner out of two perpendicular curves (**Figure 7.21**).

To create a circular 2D fillet:

1. Create two curves to fillet between (**Figure 7.22**).

2. Click the first curve with the right mouse button, and select Curve Point from the Marking Menu (**Figure 7.23**).

3. Click the first curve, and drag the point to where you want the fillet to arc (**Figure 7.24**).

4. Click the second curve with your right mouse button, and select Curve Point from the Marking Menu.

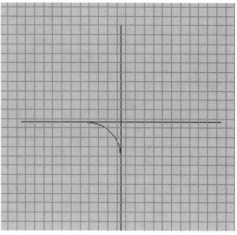

Figure 7.21 A 2D fillet serves as a good tool for adding smooth corners to a set of curves.

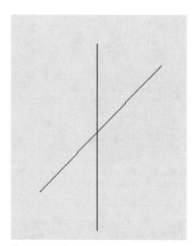

Figure 7.22 Two curves are intersecting.

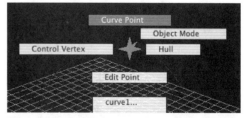

Figure 7.23 A Marking Menu appears when you click the curve with your right mouse button. This is a convenient way to choose which component type you'd like to be able to select.

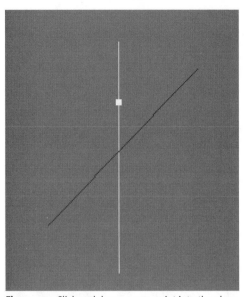

Figure 7.24 Click and drag a curve point into the place where you would like the arc to begin.

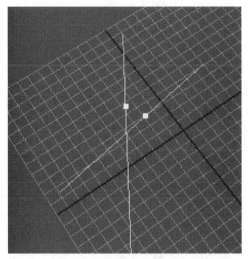

Figure 7.25 The two curve points determine the start and end points of the arc.

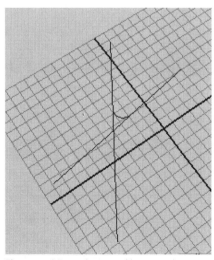

Figure 7.26 An arc is created between the two curve points selected on each curve.

5. (Shift)-click the second curve, and drag the point to where you want the fillet to arc (**Figure 7.25**).

6. From the Edit Curves menu select Curve Fillet.

   An arc is created between the two curve points (**Figure 7.26**).

Opening and closing curves

A curve that does not start and end on the same point is called an open curve (**Figure 7.27**). Many Maya commands will not function correctly on open curves, so the curves must be closed. A closed curve has the same start and end point, making it continuous (**Figure 7.28**).

To open or close a curve:

◆ From the Edit Curves menu select Open/Close Curves (**Figure 7.29**).

An open curve will become closed, and a closed curve will become open.

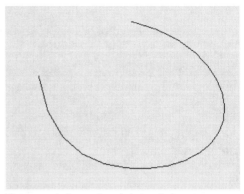

Figure 7.27 An incomplete circle is called an open curve.

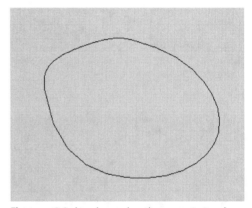

Figure 7.28 A closed curve has the same start and end point.

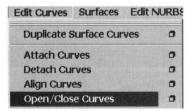

Figure 7.29 The Open/Close Curves command opens a closed curve and closes an open curve.

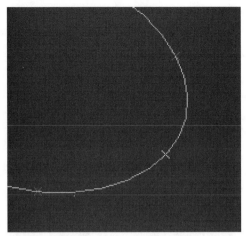

Figure 7.30 An edit point is represented by an x; when selected, it can be used as a curve's breaking point.

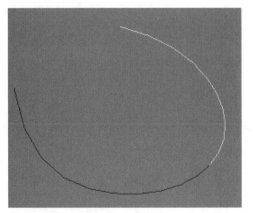

Figure 7.31 Two curves are created out of the detachment at the edit point.

To detach a curve:

1. Select a curve with the Pick mask set to Component: Parm Points mode ⬚.

2. Select the edit point x where you would like to detach the curve (**Figure 7.30**).

3. From the Edit Curves menu select Detach Curves.

   The curve is now broken into two curves (**Figure 7.31**).

✔ Tip

- If Keep Originals is selected in the Detach Curves Options dialog box, you will have three curves after detaching—the original curve and two detached curves. Deselect Keep Originals before you detach to automatically delete the original curve (see the "Keep Originals" sidebar).

Keep Originals

Many of the curve and surface manipulation and rebuild commands have a Keep Originals option. When you rebuild a curve using a command such as Detach, the Keep Originals option lets you retain the original curve in addition to creating the new curve(s) as a result of the specific rebuild command.

Be aware that you may not notice that the original curve or surface is still present because the new curves or surfaces will sit directly on top of the original.

Creating Surfaces from Curves

There are several commands in Maya that you can use to turn curves into surfaces. They include Revolve, Loft, Planar, Extrude, Birail, and Boundary.

To revolve a curve to make a vase:

1. In the front view draw a curve for the shape of the vase's profile, as in the **Figure 7.32**.

2. Select the curve in object mode.

3. In the Surfaces menu select the box next to Revolve (**Figure 7.33**)

   The Revolve Options window opens.

4. Select the axis you want the object to revolve around (**Figure 7.34**). We'll use the *y* axis for our illustration.

5. Click Revolve to create the surface of the vase.

   If you get unexpected results, you may have the object revolving around the wrong axis.

6. Press ③ to increase the smoothness to see the full surface (**Figure 7.35**).

✔ Tips

- You can adjust Start Sweep Angle and End Sweep Angle in Revolve Options to create a revolved surface that is not a complete 360 degrees.

- To interactively change the shape of a revolved surface by changing the angle of the axis revolution, you can use the Show Manipulator tool.

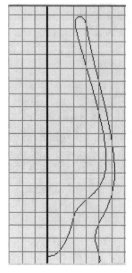

Figure 7.32 A profile curve illustrates the outline of the object used for revolving.

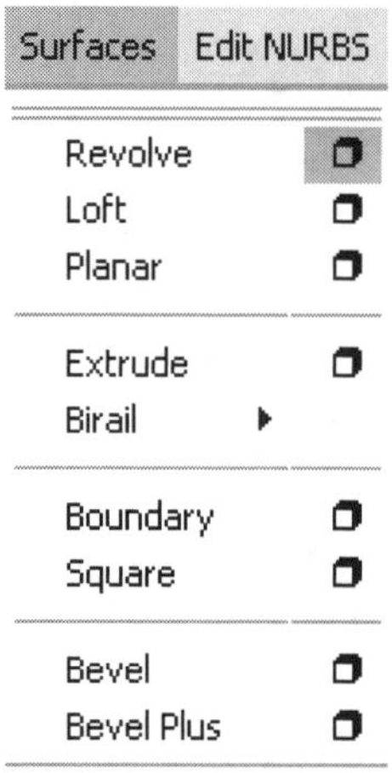

Figure 7.33 From the Surfaces menu select the box next to Revolve to open the Revolve Options window.

Figure 7.34 The revolve axis is very important to the look of the final surface. You want to choose the axis that goes through the middle of the final surface.

Figure 7.35 Increasing surface smoothness helps clarify where the actual revolved surface lies.

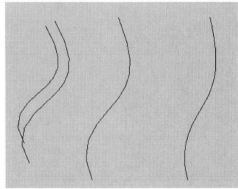

Figure 7.36 When creating curves to loft across, you must consider each curve describing the contour of the final surface.

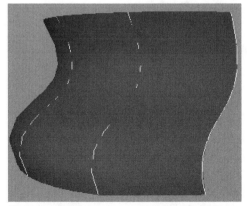

Figure 7.37 A lofted surface maintains a connection to the original curves, so that you can edit them in the future using the original curves.

One of the best ways to create a surface from multiple curves is by using the Loft command. The Loft command creates a surface that extends from one selected curve to the next until each curve is covered with a surface. Each of the isoparms on the final surface is derived from the edit point placement on each curve. As a general rule, you want to have the same amount of edit points on each curve.

To loft across multiple curves:

1. Create two or more curves with which to create a surface (**Figure 7.36**).

2. [Shift]-select each curve in the order in which you would like the surface to loft across them.

    The order in which you select curves is important. The surface will start at the first selected curve and cover each additional curve in the order you select them.

3. With all the curves selected, choose Surfaces > Loft to create a surface over the curves (**Figure 7.37**).

✔ Tip

■ A new surface displays in rough mode and will look as if it is not fully touching the curves that were used to create it. Select the surface and press ③ to view the surface in smooth display mode.

The Extrude command creates a surface by sweeping one curve (the profile) along another curve (the path). The Extrude command is often used to add depth to text and create long, tubelike objects such as power cords.

To extrude a curve:

1. Create a profile curve that is the shape you'd like the final extruded surface to be. For example, if you want to extrude a tube, you could create a circle (**Figure 7.38**).

2. Starting from the already created curve, create a CV curve the length of the final surface you want to create (**Figure 7.39**). This is referred to as the *path curve*.

3. Select the circle, then Shift-select the path curve.

4. From the Surfaces menu select Extrude to sweep the profile curve along the path curve.

   A new extruded surface is created (**Figure 7.40**).

✔ Tip

■ By default, the new surface starts at the angle of the profile curve and mimics its angles. With this default setting, the extruded surface only follows the path curve if the profile curve is perpendicular to the path curve. To ignore the angle of the profile curve and have the curve follow the path curve, select At Path in the Extrude Options window.

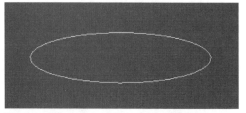

Figure 7.38 Any curve shape can be used for an extrude—for example, if you're looking for a tubelike shape, you could use a closed curve.

Figure 7.39 The second curve you create for an extrude is used for the path and length of the extruded surface.

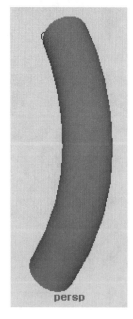

persp

Figure 7.40 A surface is created from the extrude that follows the angle of the profile curve.

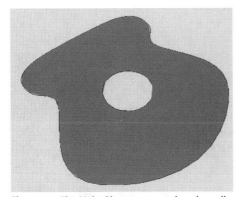

Figure 7.41 The Make Planar command works well for any closed, flat curve out of which you would like to make a flat surface.

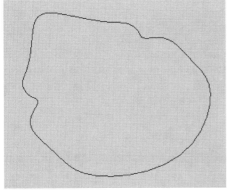

Figure 7.42 This closed curve will determine the outline of the surface. Use grid snap to be sure that all of the points of the curve lie on the same plane.

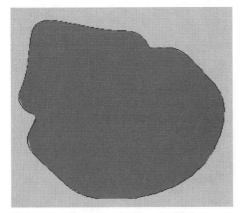

Figure 7.43 A flat surface is created, with the curve used as the border of the surface.

The Make Planar command is used to make a flat surface out of a curve. An example of its use would be to create the flat top of a guitar (that is, the part with the hole in it) (**Figure 7.41**). You could create the outline of the guitar's body with a curve, and then use the Make Planar command to complete the flat surface.

To make a curve planar:

1. Create a closed curve with all the CVs on the same axis (**Figure 7.42**).

2. From the Surfaces menu select Planar. A planar surface is created from the curve (**Figure 7.43**).

✔ Tips

- The curve must be closed or self-intersecting for the Planar command to work.

- All CVs must lie on the same axis for the command to work. To ensure that this is the case, you can grid-snap each CV to a grid plane.

CREATING SURFACES FROM CURVES

The Birail tool is similar to Extrude, except that instead of having one path curve and one profile curve, it has two path curves (rails) and any number of profile curves. The hull of a boat provides a good example: Two path curves can determine the hull's outline, and profile curves can determine its depth and shape (**Figure 7.44**).

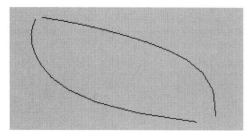

Figure 7.44 The hull of a boat can be created from a few profile curves and two rail curves.

To create a birail surface:

1. Draw two curves to use for the rails of the surface (**Figure 7.45**).

2. Draw a new curve that extends from the first curve to the second curve using curve snap (hold down [c] and click and drag on the rail curve) for the first and last points (**Figure 7.46**).

    The curves must touch each other for the operation to work. Curve snap helps ensure that the profile curve touches both rails.

3. From the Surfaces menu select Birail > Birail 1 Tool (**Figure 7.47**).

    Use Birail 2 Tool if you have two profile curves. Use Birail 3+ if you are using three or more profile curves.

4. Click the profile curves, and then click the rail curves (**Figure 7.48**).

    The birail surface is created.

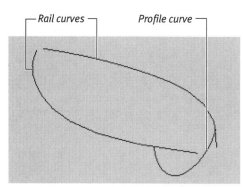

Figure 7.45 You always use two curves for the rails.

Rail curves *Profile curve*

Figure 7.46 For the command to function correctly, your must curve-snap the ends of each profile curve to the rails.

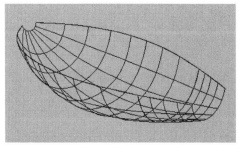

Figure 7.48 A surface is created from the three curves using the Birail tool.

Figure 7.47 From the Surfaces menu select Birail > Birail 1 Tool.

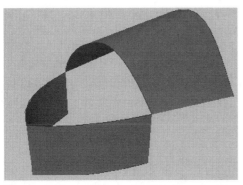

Figure 7.49 The gap between these surfaces would be a good candidate for filling via the Boundary command.

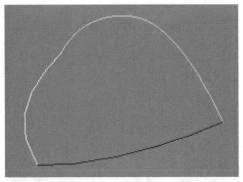

Figure 7.50 With boundary surfaces, as with birail surfaces, it is essential to curve-snap each end point.

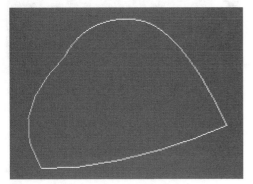

Figure 7.51 You can select curves or isoparms on which to use the Boundary command.

The Boundary command requires three or four curves that intersect or meet at each other's ends. One use for a boundary surface would be when you have three surfaces connecting at a corner and you want to use three of the edges to complete a rounded corner between the surfaces (**Figure 7.49**).

To create a boundary surface:

1. Draw three or four curves with intersecting ends (**Figure 7.50**).

   You can make sure the ends intersect by curve-snapping the first and last CVs to the other curves.

2. Select all the curves that complete the boundary (**Figure 7.51**).

3. From the Surfaces menu select Boundary. The boundary surface is created (**Figure 7.52**).

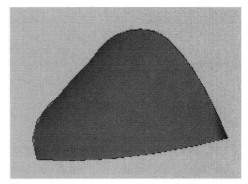

Figure 7.52 A surface is created across the three curves.

To create beveled text:

1. In the Create menu select the box next to Text.

   The Text Curves Options dialog box opens.

2. In the Text field type the text you want.

3. Select a font for the text.

4. Select Curves for Type.

5. Click Create (**Figure 7.53**).

6. From the Surfaces menu select Bevel (**Figure 7.54**).

   The text bevel can be edited with the Inputs node afterward or in the Text Curves Options dialog box before creation.

   The text now appears with a bevel (**Figure 7.55**).

✔ Tip

- You can adjust the width and depth of the extrude in the bevel's Inputs node (accessible from the Channel Box).

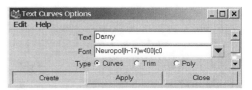

Figure 7.53 In the Text Curves Options window set the Text, Font, and Type options, and then click Create.

Figure 7.54 From the Surfaces menu select Bevel.

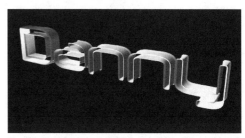

Figure 7.55 The curves that outlined the letters have been turned into beveled surfaces.

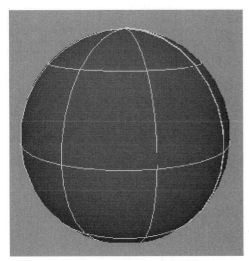

Figure 7.56 The sphere has been selected to make it live so that a curve can be drawn on it. Any surface can be made live.

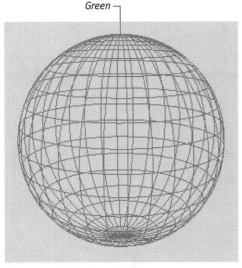

Green ⌐

Figure 7.57 The surface wireframe turns green to indicate it is a live surface.

To draw a curve directly on a surface, you must make the surface live. Once a surface is live, a curve can be created and edited directly on the surface itself.

To make a surface live:

1. Select a surface to make it live (**Figure 7.56**).

2. From the Modify menu select Make Live, or click 🗇 to make the surface live.

   The surface wireframe turns green to indicate that it is a live surface (**Figure 7.57**).

✔ Tip

■ To deactivate a surface that's live, select Make Not Live from the Modify menu.

To draw a curve on a live surface:

1. Make the surface live.

2. From the Create menu select CV Curve Tool (**Figure 7.58**).

3. Click points on the surface where you want to create the curve (**Figure 7.59**).

4. Press Enter to complete the curve.
   A curve is created on the surface.

5. From the Modify menu select Make Not Live to bring the surface back into normal mode (**Figure 7.60**).

✔ Tip

■ You can move the curve along the surface in the *U* or *V* direction using the Move tool.

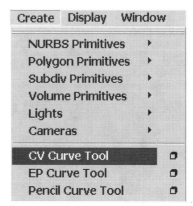

Figure 7.58 From the Create menu select CV Curve Tool.

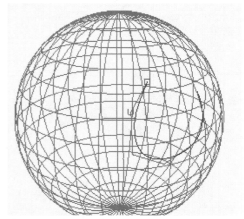

Figure 7.59 It's helpful to tumble your view around the surface to get a straight look at where you want to place each CV.

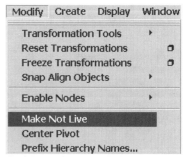

Figure 7.60 From the Modify menu select Make Not Live to return to normal mode.

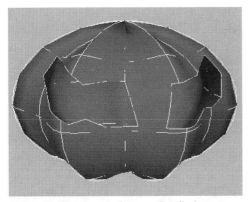

Figure 7.61 Curves on surfaces work well when you want to later trim out part of a surface, as with this pumpkin.

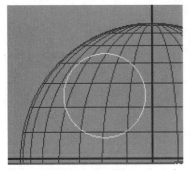

Figure 7.62 This circle will be projected onto the surface of the sphere.

When you project a curve, it creates a new curve on the selected surface. Imagine projecting the image of a curve at an object from a slide projector. The shape of the object may warp the image of the curve. Likewise, when you project a curve in Maya, the resulting curve projected on an object's surface is warped to some degree.

A pumpkin's eyes provide a good example of this: You can draw the shape of the eyes you want to cut out of a pumpkin in the front view, and project these curves onto the pumpkin shape so that you can later trim them out of the surface (**Figure 7.61**). The trim function is often used after projecting a curve onto a surface to cut out the curve shape.

To project a curve onto a surface:

1. Create a surface for the curve to be projected onto—a primitive sphere, for example.

2. In the front view create a curve to project onto the surface; in this example, we'll use a primitive circle (**Figure 7.62**).

3. Select the curve to be projected, and the surface (**Figure 7.63**).

continues on next page

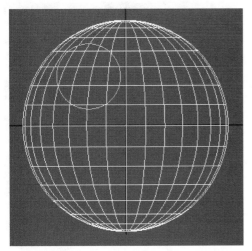

Figure 7.63 Both the curve and the surface must be selected for the projection to work.

4. With the front view active, select Edit NURBS > Project Curve on Surface (**Figure 7.64**).

The curve becomes projected on both sides of the sphere's surface (**Figure 7.65**).

To trim out a hole in a surface:

1. Follow the steps outlined in the previous task.

2. From the Edit NURBS menu select Trim Tool.

3. Click on the sphere.

The object becomes transparent and the lines turn white to indicate that you're in the Trim tool (**Figure 7.66**).

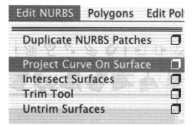

Figure 7.64 The active view becomes the angle from which the curve is projected.

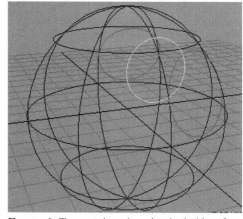

Figure 7.65 The curve is projected on both sides of the object.

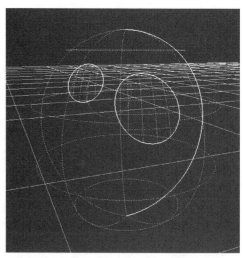

Figure 7.66 The object becomes transparent and each area that has an option to trim is filled with a grid.

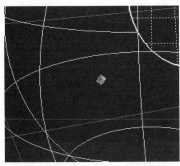

Figure 7.67 The small, yellow diamond indicates that the region will be kept intact.

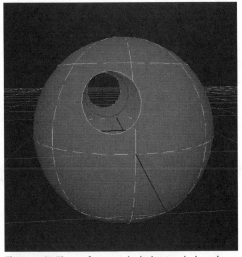

Figure 7.68 The surface now includes two holes where the original curve originally appeared on the surface.

4. Click on the sphere in an area you want to keep—*not* the area in which you want a hole.

A yellow diamond indicates the area you want to retain (**Figure 7.67**).

5. Click 〔Enter〕 to trim the surface.

Because the curve was projected on both sides of the sphere, there are now two holes in the surface (**Figure 7.68**).

✔ Tip

■ You can click on each area you want to retain. In our sphere example, you can click on the main surface of the sphere and inside the area of one of the circles to create only one hole in the surface.

POLYGONS AND SUBDIVIDED SURFACES

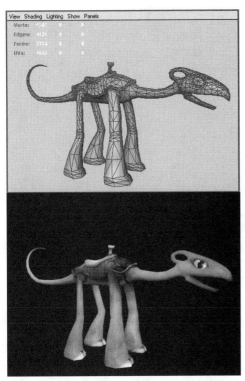

Figure 8.1 This polygon model was designed to have the lowest number of faces possible. The textures make up for the lack of detail. Modeled and textured by Toby Marvin.

Polygons provide a fun, easy way of modeling a surface. A polygon is a surface made up of smaller, flat surfaces with three or more sides. These smaller surfaces are called *faces*. Working with polygons has more of a rigid construction feeling, and working with NURBS has a more pliable, sculptural feeling.

Games make extensive use of polygons because their complexity is limited if they are to offer fast interaction with real-time rendering. If your character has a low *poly* (short for *polygon)* count—that is, a low number of faces—it will render and interact quickly. A character in a game is usually limited to a certain number of polygons in order for the game to run in real time (**Figure 8.1**).

You can, however, use polygons to make smooth, highly detailed, even organic, surfaces (**Figure 8.2**). Some surfaces may be easier to build in polygons than in NURBS surfaces. For example, you can create a character's body from a seamless polygon surface—something you can't achieve using a NURBS surface, which can only be four-sided.

Subdivision surfaces are a recent addition to Maya. They combine some of the best of NURBS and polygons, plus a few tricks of their own. Subdivision surfaces can speed the modeling process because you can choose between viewing the surface in high-res with many points, or low-res with just a few points. If you know how to model polygons, you can model a subdivision surface as well—they use many of the same tools.

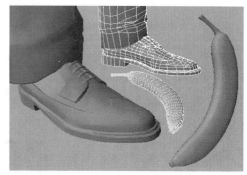

Figure 8.2 Polygons can be used to make both smooth shapes, such as a banana, and hard edges like the ones on this shoe. Shoe and trouser leg modeled by Adrian Niu.

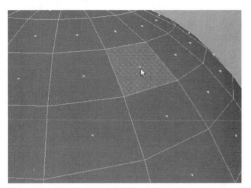

Figure 8.3 The faces are displayed on this sphere. The highlighted face was selected by clicking the dot in the center of the face.

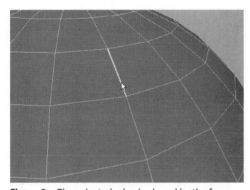

Figure 8.4 The selected edge is shared by the faces on either side of it. Any change to the position or size of this edge will affect all of the faces it touches.

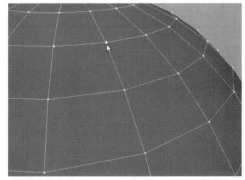

Figure 8.5 The selected vertex is at the corner of four faces.

About Modeling Polygons

The most common way to create a complex polygon model is to start with a primitive poly cube. By transforming this simple object and manipulating its existing components, you can get the basic shape for your model. From there, you can build onto the object by adding more complexity to the surface.

Polygons include four types of components, which are important for both modeling and texturing: *faces, edges, vertices,* and *UV*.

Two of the most commonly used polygon tools are the Extrude Face tool and the Split Polygon tool. Many other tools are used to manipulate a poly surface, including Extrude Edge and Subdivide.

Polygon components

◆ A *face* is one of the many smaller surfaces that make up the polygon object as a whole. You can choose it by selecting the point in the center of each face (**Figure 8.3**).

◆ An *edge* is one border of a polygonal face (**Figure 8.4**).

◆ A *vertex* is at the corner of a face. Vertices become yellow when selected (**Figure 8.5**). If a vertex is moved, it will change the shape of the four faces that include it.

◆ *UVs* are used for creating texture, not for modeling; they become green when selected (see Chapter 14).

✔ Tip

■ Once a face, vertex, or edge is selected, you can move, rotate, or scale the component. For the fastest workflow, use the Marking Menu.

To select and transform polygon components:

1. Create any polygon primitive (see Chapter 3).

2. With the right mouse button, click a polygon surface.

3. Select Vertex from the Marking Menu (**Figure 8.6**).

4. Select some vertices. You can marquee-select by clicking and dragging with the left mouse button (**Figure 8.7**).

5. Press w or click the Move tool icon 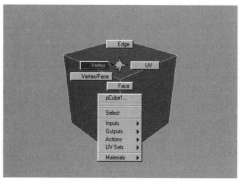 in the toolbar.

6. Move the vertices (**Figure 8.8**).

✔ Tips

■ If you are in wireframe mode, you must click a component of the surface, such as an edge, for the Marking Menu to show up. If you are in shaded mode, you can click anywhere on the surface.

■ Any of the polygon components can be selected and transformed using the method described above.

Figure 8.6 Generally, only one kind of component is displayed at a time. This Marking Menu, accessible from the right mouse button, is a convenient way to switch between the different component displays.

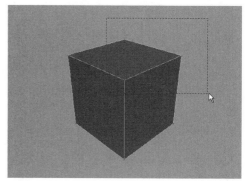

Figure 8.7 Three vertices are selected simultaneously using marquee select.

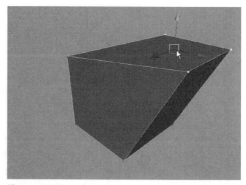

Figure 8.8 The selected vertices are moved using the Move tool. The shape of every face that shares these vertices is changed.

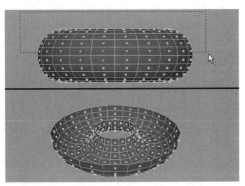

Figure 8.9 In the top picture, the faces of a torus have been selected in the side view. (It's often helpful to switch views to get a better angle on your selection.) In the bottom shot, you see the torus after the selected faces have been deleted.

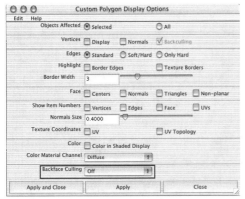

Figure 8.10 In the Custom Polygon Display Options window, you can choose whether to have the display options affect all polygon objects or just the selected one(s)—for Objects Affected, choose Selected or All.

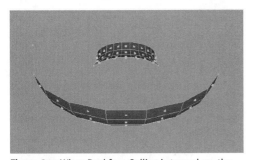

Figure 8.11 When Backface Culling is turned on, the components on the far side of the object disappear so you can't select them. This works for all kinds of polygon components.

When using polygons, you often deal with a large number of components. Maya has several tools to help you select components and to prevent you from selecting some by mistake. These include *Backface Culling*, which prevents you from picking points on the far side of the object, as well as tools that allow you to grow, shrink, and convert your existing selections.

To use Backface Culling:

1. From the Create menu select Polygon Primitives > Torus.

2. Use your right mouse button to click a polygon surface, and select Face from the Marking Menu.

3. In the side view, marquee-select the top half of the torus, and then delete the faces (**Figure 8.9**).

4. From the Display menu select the box next to Custom Polygon Display.

   This opens the Custom Polygon Display Options window (**Figure 8.10**).

5. From the Backface Culling menu select On. Click Apply.

   The portions of the torus on the far side of the camera view disappear. They cannot be selected (**Figure 8.11**).

continues on next page

6. From the Backface Culling menu select Keep Wire. Click Apply.

You can see the wireframe of the back side, but you cannot select components from that part of the surface (**Figure 8.12**).

7. From the Backface Culling menu select Keep Hard Edges. Click Apply.

You can see the hard edges of the back side only—that is, the edges along the sides of holes in the surface (**Figure 8.13**).

8. From the Backface Culling menu select Off. Click Apply.

This resets the Custom Polygon Display Options to their default settings. Now you are able to select the back sides of polygon surfaces again.

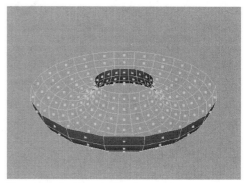

Figure 8.12 Backface Culling is set to Keep Wire. This allows you to see the shape of the object while preventing you from selecting unwanted components on its back side.

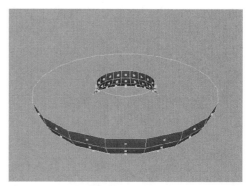

Figure 8.13 Keep Hard Edges lets you see the object's basic shape, but only the edges that border a hole in the object.

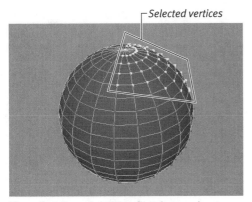

Selected vertices

Figure 8.14 Several vertices of a polygon sphere are selected. With Backface Culling off, points on the back of the sphere were selected as well.

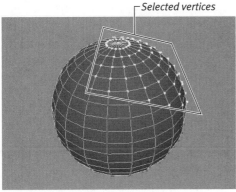

Selected vertices

Figure 8.15 Surgically picking poly vertices one by one can be difficult. One way to save time is to use Edit Polygons > Selection > Grow Selection Region. This selects the points surrounding the ones that are currently selected, making the selected area larger.

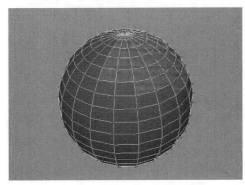

Figure 8.16 The faces that were surrounded by selected vertices are now selected, and the points are deselected.

To grow, shrink, and convert a selection:

1. From the Create menu select Polygon Primitives > Sphere.

2. Use your right mouse button to click a polygon surface, and select Vertex from the Marking Menu.

3. Select several vertices (**Figure 8.14**).

4. From the Edit Polygons menu choose Selection > Grow Selection Region.

   The vertices surrounding the existing selection are also selected. Repeat this step to increase the size of the selected area (**Figure 8.15**).

5. From the Edit Polygons menu select Selection > Shrink Selection Region.

   The region of selected vertices becomes smaller. Repeat this step to further shrink it.

6. From the Edit Polygons menu select Selection > Convert Selection to Faces.

   The vertices are deselected, and the faces they surrounded are selected (**Figure 8.16**).

✔ Tips

- A selection of any kind of polygon component can similarly be converted to edges, vertices, or UVs.

- Some polygon-modeling tools only work on faces, such as Extrude Face. If you've already selected the region as vertices, Convert Selection saves you the time of meticulously selecting the faces one by one in order to run this tool on the faces.

ABOUT MODELING POLYGONS

Extrude Face is a great way to begin constructing your surface. It allows you to pull additional geometry from the surface. You simply select a face or several faces, extrude them, and then manipulate the new faces.

To extrude faces of a cube:

1. From the Create menu select Polygon Primitives > Cube.

2. With the right mouse button click the cube, and select Face from the Marking Menu.

3. Marquee-select all of the faces (**Figure 8.17**).

4. From the Edit Polygons menu select Extrude Face.

   A manipulator appears that you can use to move, rotate, and scale the new faces (**Figure 8.18**). Even though the manipulator only shows up on one face, it affects all the faces that were just extruded. It transforms them locally, which means that they move relative to their *surface normal,* which is a line perpendicular to the center of each individual face.

5. Move one face out from the center of the cube with the Translate manipulator.

   All newly extruded faces will move out from the center as well (**Figure 8.19**). This is very helpful for making symmetrical objects.

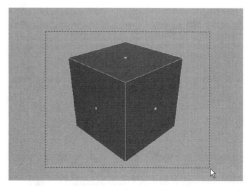

Figure 8.17 When marquee-select is used around the entire object, even the faces on the far side of the object are selected.

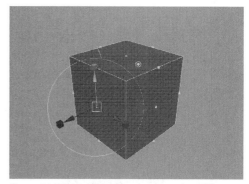

Figure 8.18 This manipulator appears when Edit Polygons > Extrude Face is selected.

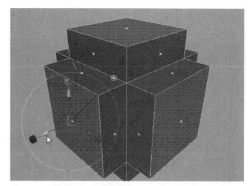

Figure 8.19 When one face is moved outward, all of the faces move outward. By scaling with the Extrude Face tool, all of the selected faces will scale simultaneously, relative to their centers.

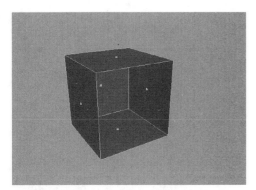

Figure 8.20 One face of the cube is deleted, creating an opening.

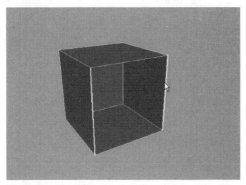

Figure 8.21 The edges on the left and right side of the opening are selected.

✔ Tips

■ When you first extrude a face, points appear on the center of each edge of the face you chose to extrude (Figure 8.18). These points are the new faces that resulted from the extrusion; however, they remain flat until you move or scale the selected face. Beware any time you see these points along an edge: They can cause problems later on in the final rendering because you actually have two surfaces sitting directly on top of each other. To avoid this, make sure you scale or move a face after every extrusion.

■ After extruding a face, you will often want to scale it proportionally. Simply click any of the scale manipulators, and a proportional scale manipulator will appear in the center. To rotate along a single axis, click the outside rotate manipulator, and three rotate manipulators (one for each axis) will appear.

To extrude edges:

1. From the Create menu select Polygon Primitives > Cube.

2. With the right mouse button, click the cube, and select Face from the Marking Menu.

3. Select a face on the side of the cube and press `Delete`.

   The face disappears, and you see the inside of the cube (**Figure 8.20**). (An edge or vertex can also be deleted, but it does not make an opening, just a larger face defined by the edges left behind. To try this, pick some vertices and select Delete Vertex from the Edit Polygons Menu.)

4. With your right mouse button click the cube, and select Edge from the Marking Menu.

5. Select the left edge, and `Shift`-select the right edge of the hole you created (**Figure 8.21**).

continues on next page

6. From the Edit Polygons menu select Extrude Edge.

7. Move the edge out and away from the cube. Two new faces have been created, and the cube should now look like an open box (**Figure 8.22**).

✔ Tip

■ An edge should not be shared by more than two faces. This means that you should only extrude edges that are adjacent to an opening in the polygon. Although you can do otherwise, we don't recommend it (**Figure 8.23**).

The Split Polygon tool is used extensively in polygon modeling. It allows you to split one face into two faces along an edge that you create. You can split multiple faces simultaneously to save time.

Because of the way perspective distorts the view of an object, it can be difficult to select the center of an edge. To help you split a face in the right place, the Split Polygon tool snaps to the center of an edge. This means that if the spot where you want to split is close to the center of an edge, the tool jumps to the precise center.

In general, it's best to limit yourself to three- and four-sided faces, known as triangles and quads, respectively. Quads and triangles respond more predictably to other polygon modeling tools. If a face has five or more sides, you should split it into smaller faces.

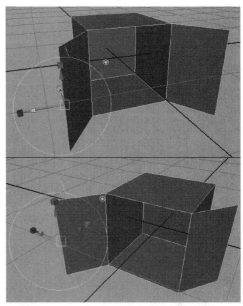

Figure 8.22 The edges have been extruded, which creates new faces. When one edge is moved, the other edge moves in the same direction for one axis but in the opposite direction for the other axis (depending on which side of the cube is removed). Here are two possible results.

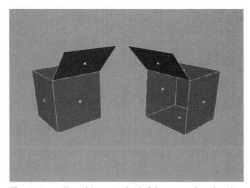

Figure 8.23 The object on the left has an edge that is shared by three faces; the object on the right does not because it has an opening in the front. It's not good construction to have an edge shared by more than two faces. One problem is that the polygon object cannot be converted into Subdivision Surfaces.

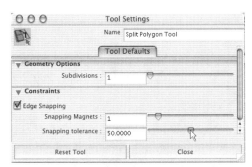

Figure 8.24 The options for the Split Polygon tool make it easy to split a polygon in half, thirds, quarters, and so on.

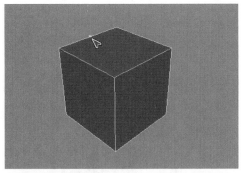

Figure 8.25 A point is placed at the center of an edge with the Split Polygon tool.

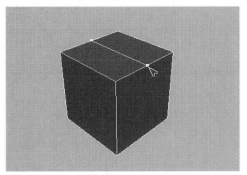

Figure 8.26 The new edge is defined by the two points placed by the Split Polygon tool. If you press (Enter) now, it completes the command. However, you could continue splitting (and go all the way around the cube) by clicking a point on one edge at a time.

To split a face:

1. From the Create menu select Polygon Primitives > Cube.

2. From the Edit Polygons menu select the box next to Split Polygon Tool.

   This opens the Tool Settings window with Split Polygon Tool options.

3. Adjust the slider next to "Snapping tolerance" to about the middle of the range. Close the window (**Figure 8.24**).

4. Click and drag along a top edge to the center. The point should snap to the center of the edge. Release the mouse button (**Figure 8.25**).

5. Click and drag along the edge on the opposite side of the top of the cube to the center of that edge (**Figure 8.26**).

6. Press (Enter). The face is now split in half.

7. With the right mouse button click the cube, and select Edge from the Marking Menu.

continues on next page

8. Select the new edge you created, and move it up. The object should look like a simple house (**Figure 8.27**).

9. From the Edit Polygons menu select Split Polygon Tool.

10. Click and drag up the left side of the cube until the point snaps to the corner. Repeat for the right side (**Figure 8.28**).

11. Press Enter.

Now the five-sided face, which formed the front of the house, is split into a three-sided face and a four-sided face.

✔ **Tips**

■ Make sure that your split always creates an edge. If you click one edge and press Enter without successfully clicking another edge of the same face, it will only put a vertex on that edge—another example of bad construction. To avoid this problem, just make sure to undo if the Split Polygon tool does not make a new edge.

■ Sometimes snapping can make it difficult to split where you want to. To turn off snapping, under the Split Polygon Tool options in the Tool Settings dialog box uncheck the box next to Edge Snapping.

■ You are not limited to snapping to the middle of an edge—you can snap to more than one point of an edge. If you want to snap to a point one-third of the way along an edge, you can select 2 from Snapping Magnets in the Split Polygon Tool options in the Tool Settings dialog box. This creates two points, evenly spaced along the edge, that the tool will snap to.

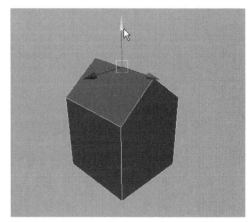

Figure 8.27 The new edge is moved up, creating a simple house shape. Note that the front of the house has five edges. More than four edges is generally considered bad construction.

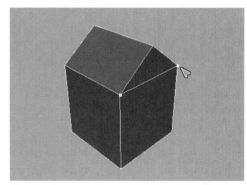

Figure 8.28 A new edge is created, splitting the front face into two separate faces.

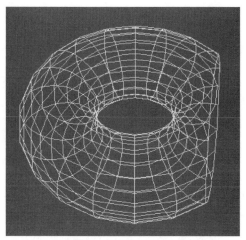

Figure 8.29 The Cut Face tool is an interactive surface-cutting tool that will either delete one side of the cut surface (shown here), or just slice the surface, leaving you with both sides of the cut line.

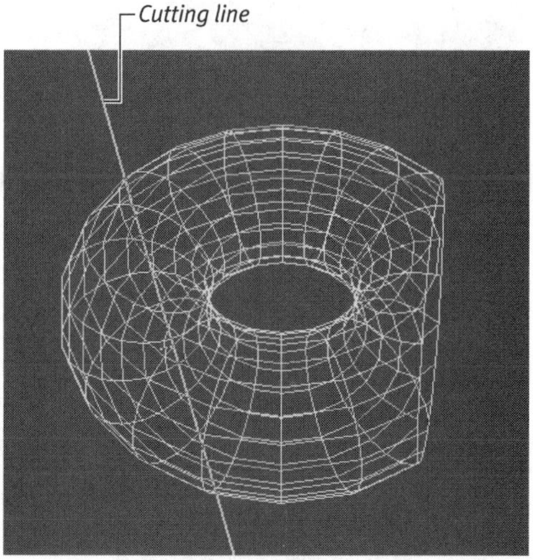

Cutting line

Figure 8.30 The Cut Face tool can be used to slice a piece of a surface by directing the cutting line into the exact position on the surface where you would like the cut to happen.

Splitting multiple polygons using the Split Polygon tool can be a tedious process. Now when you want to cut through an entire surface, you can use the new Cut Face tool (**Figure 8.29**). The surface is cut in the same fashion that a knife would cut through a block of cheese. To be more specific, the Cut Face tool adds edges to a poly (or an entire poly object) through a projected line that you position to your liking (**Figure 8.30**). The chosen line is projected from the view angle of the camera, slicing through all of the selected intersecting polygons.

With the Cut Face Delete option selected, one side of the cut object will be deleted. This option is useful if you later want to create an instance of the object or mirror the object to complete it (as you would the head of a character).

To slice a surface using the Cut Face tool:

1. Create a primitive polygon cube and select it.

2. From the Edit Polygons menu select the box beside Cut Faces.

   The Cut Face Tool Options window opens (**Figure 8.31**).

3. Click Enter Cut Tool.

4. Click and interactively drag the line across a surface to choose a cutting plane.

   A line appears that is used as the cutting plane (**Figure 8.32**).

5. Release the mouse to cut the surface (**Figure 8.33**).

   The line is projected across the object, and cuts are made where it crosses a surface. Notice that no surfaces were deleted, just added.

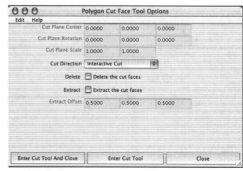

Figure 8.31 The Polygon Cut Face Tool Options provide many commands for cutting the surface in an exact, numeric position, or for interactively placing a cutting line. You can adjust the direction (or the plane) in which the cut will take place.

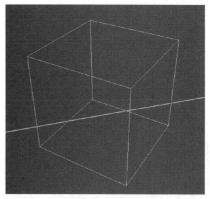

Figure 8.32 The cut line can be moved and rotated until it is perfectly aligned with your cut.

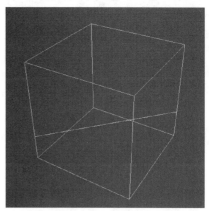

Figure 8.33 The cut line is projected from the selected camera angle to make a cut straight through the surface.

Delete ☑ Delete the cut faces

Figure 8.34 Deleting cut faces removes part of the original surface.

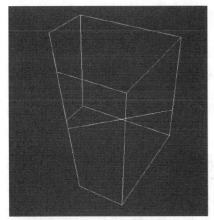

Figure 8.35 The surface on one side of the cutting line is deleted, leaving only a portion of the original surface.

6. In the Cut Face options check the box beside "Delete the cut faces" (**Figure 8.34**).

The Delete option deletes the surface on one side of the cutting line.

7. Click Enter Cut Tool and Close.

The mouse icon becomes an arrow.

8. Click and Interactively drag the line across a surface to choose a cutting plane.

9. Release the mouse to cut the surface.

The surface on one side of the cutting line is deleted (**Figure 8.35**).

✔ Tips

■ A small line, perpendicular to the cutting line appears to show you which side of the line will be deleted.

■ Holding (Shift) will snap the cutting line horizontally, vertically, or at a 45-degree angle, to make a more precise cut.

The Poke Faces tool is another new Maya tool for speeding your polygon-modeling workflow. You can use it to subdivide a selected face, adding more detail to your model and additional selection points.

The Poke Faces tool is similar to Subdivide in that it cuts the selected face into perfect triangles. However, the Poke Faces tool offers several workflow advantages, one of which is that once the surfaces have been divided, you're left with a manipulator to move the new polygons.

To poke the face of a polygon using the Poke Faces tool:

1. Create a primitive polygon cube.

2. With the right mouse button click on the cube's surface and select Face from the Marking Menu.

3. Select one or more faces to poke (**Figure 8.36**).

4. From the Edit Polygons menu select Poke faces.

   Each selected face is split into four faces (**Figure 8.37**).

5. Select the manipulator and move it away from the surface.

   A pyramid-like shape appears as the manipulator is pulled away from the surface (**Figure 8.38**).

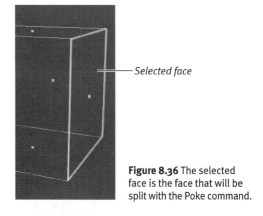

Selected face

Figure 8.36 The selected face is the face that will be split with the Poke command.

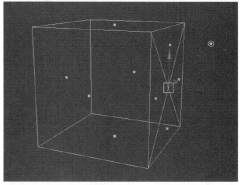

Figure 8.37 Each selected face is split into four faces, each one a perfect triangle.

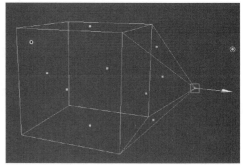

Figure 8.38 The Poke tool creates a manipulator at the center point of the poked face, which is used to pull the new geometry into, or away from, the surface.

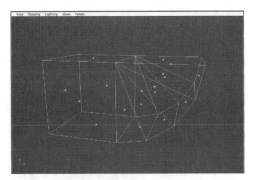

Figure 8.39 A wedged primitive cube.

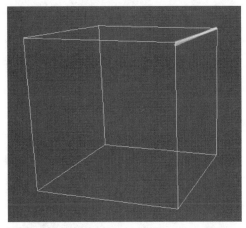

Figure 8.40 The selected edge defines the wedge's axis rotation point.

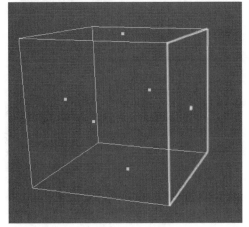

Figure 8.41 The selected edge will determine the direction of the extrusion.

New to Maya 4.5, the Wedge Face tool is a variation of the Extrude Face tool. It creates angled wedges by extruding selected polygonal faces in an arc (**Figure 8.39**). This tool is a great time saver when you're creating poly surfaces that will need to be moved and rotated.

To create a wedge without using the new Wedge Face tool, you would have to extrude the faces of a surface one at a time and then rotate each into position to create the arc shape. Now you can perform the same task in just a few easy steps using the Wedge Face tool.

To wedge the face of a poly:

1. Create a primitive polygon cube.

2. With the right mouse button, click on the surface and select Edge from the Marking Menu.

3. Select a surface edge you would like the extruded surfaces to curve, or arc, around (**Figure 8.40**).

4. With the right mouse button click on the surface and select Face from the Marking Menu.

5. [Shift]-select a face of the same edge (**Figure 8.41**).

continues on next page

6. From the Edit Polygons menu select the box beside Wedge Faces.

The Polygon Wedge Face Options dialog box opens (**Figure 8.42**).

7. Click Apply.

New geometry is created in an arc around the selected edge, ending 90 degrees from the original selected face (**Figure 8.43**).

8. With the right mouse button, click on the surface and select Edge from the Marking Menu.

9. Select a surface edge of the face on the opposite side of the cube that you would like the extruded surfaces to curve, or arc, around (**Figure 8.44**).

10. With the right mouse button click on the surface and select Face from the Marking Menu.

11. (Shift)-select a face of the same edge (**Figure 8.45**).

12. Change Wedge Angle to *120* and Wedge Divisions to *8*, then click Apply.

New geometry is created in an arc around the selected edge, ending 120 degrees from the original selected face and with eight divisions defining the arc (**Figure 8.46**).

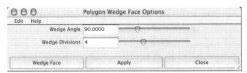

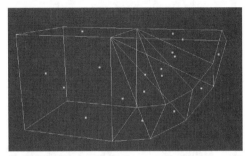

Figure 8.42 In the Polygon Wedge Face Options dialog box, you can set the wedge angle and the desired number of wedge divisions for the new surface.

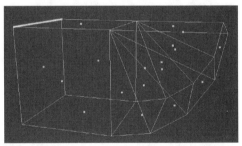

Figure 8.43 New geometry is created in an arc around the selected edge, and additional polygons are created to make the wedge a smoother curve.

Figure 8.44 Surface edges become important to the Wedge command's rotation and extrusion. Select the edge you would like the extrusion to wedge around.

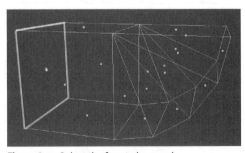

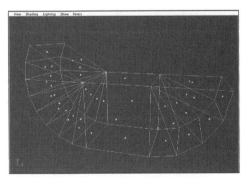

Figure 8.46 You can control the arc amount by changing the Degree attribute.

Figure 8.45 Select the face to be arced.

ABOUT MODELING POLYGONS

Low-res

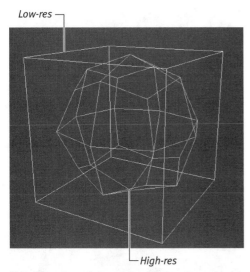

High-res

Figure 8.47 Smooth Proxy allows you to view a smooth version of your model while allowing you to work on a lower-res version. In this screenshot the low-res version of the model looks just like a primitive square; the high-res version looks similar to a sphere.

Low-res

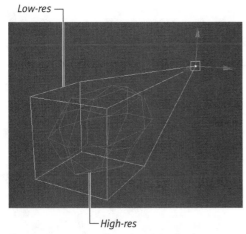

High-res

Figure 8.48 You can adjust the minimal points on the low-res surface to adjust many points on the high res surface.

The new Smooth Proxy tool is ideal for situations when you want to work on a low-res model but still want to see how the model will look when it's smoothed. Using the Smooth Proxy tool, you can view a smooth version of your low-res model (just as if you had applied the Smooth command to it). The original low-res surface remains visible, allowing you to manipulate fewer points while still viewing the final smoothed shape.

When you run the Smooth Proxy command on a polygonal model, Maya creates a new layer that holds the higher-resolution proxy version—convenient for modeling because you can choose between viewing the low-res and smooth version simultaneously or individually (by hiding one of the layers).

To aid surface modeling using the Smooth Proxy tool:

1. Select a polygonal object in object mode.

2. From the Polygons menu choose Smooth Proxy.

   Maya creates a new smooth version of the model while also retaining the original. Both shapes are added to their own layers; you can make one or the other layer invisible to simplify modeling (**Figure 8.47**).

3. With the right mouse button click on the original cube and select Vertex from the Marking Menu.

4. Select and move one of the vertices.

   The high-res version of the model mirrors the manipulations of the low-res model (**Figure 8.48**).

✔ Tip

■ In the Smooth Proxy options you can set how smooth the hi-res version of the model will be by changing the number of subdivisions.

ABOUT MODELING POLYGONS

The Subdivide tool splits a face into quads (four-sided faces) or triangles (three-sided faces). It provides a quick way of adding detail to your surface in the form of additional faces. This should not, however, be confused with subdivision surface. In this example, we'll combine the Subdivide and Extrude Face tools to make a door.

To subdivide a polygon face:

1. From the Create menu select Polygon Primitives > Cube.

   It's common to start out with a cube roughly scaled to the size of an object and then use the Edit Polygon tools to model the surface.

2. Scale the cube to the shape of a door (**Figure 8.49**).

3. With the right mouse button click the cube, and select Face from the Marking Menu.

4. Select the face on the front of the cube.

5. From the Edit Polygons menu select Subdivide. The face should be split into four faces (**Figure 8.50**).

6. From the Edit Polygons menu select Extrude Face.

   The manipulator and the new faces show up.

7. Scale the faces down a little using the Manipulator tool (**Figure 8.51**).

Figure 8.49 The cube is scaled to the shape of a door.

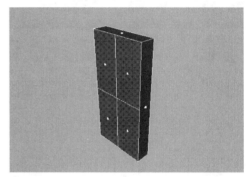

Figure 8.50 The face is subdivided into four smaller faces. A face can be subdivided into more faces by adjusting Subdivision Levels in Edit Polygons > Subdivide > Options.

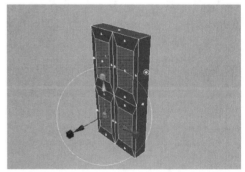

Figure 8.51 The extruded faces are scaled down relative to their centers.

Figure 8.52 A completed four-panel door. Had the face on the opposite side of the door been selected before the Subdivide function, the exact same steps would have modeled the back side of the door simultaneously.

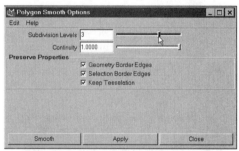

Figure 8.53 Higher subdivision levels in the Polygon Smooth Options dialog box create smoother objects with more faces. The Continuity setting determines how closely the new shape resembles the original (vs. how rounded it is). A low Continuity setting will make the object appear more similar to the original shape; a high Continuity setting will produce a very rounded shape.

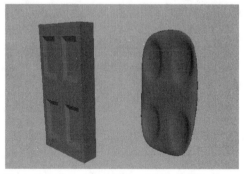

Figure 8.54 The original door and the smoother door, side by side. The basic structure of a polygon object should be complete before you apply the Smooth function. Smoothing produces a dense object with many faces, making it more difficult to work with.

8. From the Edit Polygons menu select Extrude Face again.

The manipulator and new faces appear.

9. Scale the new faces down a little and move them in toward the middle of the object, which should now like a door with four panels (**Figure 8.52**).

Polygons start out with sharp edges and corners. You can round them by using the Polygons > Smooth function, which subdivides surfaces into many smaller polygons to round out their corners and edges.

To smooth a polygon:

1. Select a polygon object, such as the door from the previous section.

2. From the Polygons menu, select the box next to Smooth.

The Polygon Smooth Options dialog box opens.

3. Adjust the slider next to Subdivision Levels to set it to 3 (**Figure 8.53**).

4. Click Smooth.

The object becomes smooth (**Figure 8.54**).

✔ Tips

- You can set Subdivision Levels in the Polygon Smooth Options dialog box as high as *4*; however, *3* is generally high enough (and any higher could give you a cumbersome surface).

- You can change the level of smoothing after the function is complete by clicking polySmoothFace1, which should be at the top of the list of inputs in your Channel Box. You will then see a field labeled Divisions, which you can change from *0* (no smoothing) to *4* (very smooth) (**Figure 8.55**).

- A portion of a polygon surface can be smoothed by selecting the faces of the part of the surface you want smoothed and then applying the Smooth operation (**Figure 8.56**).

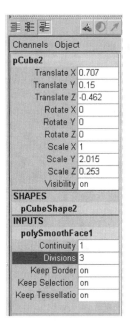

Figure 8.55 The inputs in the Channel Box allow you to change the Smooth options after the function has been run. However, once additional tweaks are made to the surface, going back and changing the options on the polySmoothFace input will produce undesirable results.

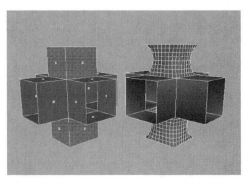

Figure 8.56 On the left, faces on the top and bottom of the object have been selected. On the right, you see the result of that smoothing. The Smooth function works by selecting whole polygon objects or faces of the object; you cannot smooth by selecting vertices or edges.

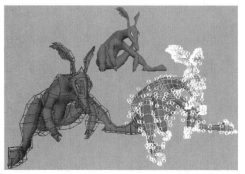

Figure 8.57 This odd creature is called a Huffer. It was designed by Roy Miles and modeled by Andrew Britt using subdivision surfaces. Left, polygon mode; right, standard mode with vertices visible; top, standard mode with no components visible.

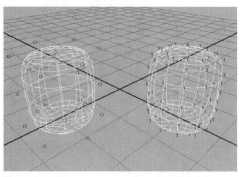

Figure 8.58 These are two copies of a subdivision cylinder. The one on the left is at Display Level 0, while the one on the right is at Display Level 1.

About Subdivision Surface Modeling

Subdivision surface modeling, which combines NURBS and polygons, has two modeling modes, *standard* and *polygon*. In polygon mode, you can use all of the polygon tools on the surface. In standard mode, you work primarily with vertices, which act similarly to NURBS control vertices (CVs). But standard mode also has edges and faces, similar to a polygon. Standard mode has the unique capability of moving between *display levels—* that is, different levels of detail. This allows you to move back and forth between low and high levels of detail on an object (**Figure 8.57**).

In polygon mode, you see the edges of a polygon shape surrounding a smooth surface, which is the subdivision surface. In this mode, all of the components are the same as with any other polygon.

Standard mode includes a different set of components, which can be manipulated at different display levels. Note that subdivision surfaces, like NURBS surfaces, have smoothness levels of rough, medium, and fine that can be activated by the 1, 2, and 3 keys, respectively. However, these should not be confused with display levels, which actually make the surface more complex, as shown in **Figure 8.58**.

Subdivision surface components

Subdivision surfaces have four types of components in standard mode: face, vertex, UV, and edge.

◆ A **face** generally appears offset from the subdivision surface. It can have three or more sides; however, the most efficient subdivision surfaces have four sides. The number in the center indicates which display level it is in (**Figure 8.59**).

◆ A **vertex** generally appears offset from the surface. It is represented by the number of the display level it occupies. When moved, the vertex controls the area of surface nearest to it (**Figure 8.60**).

◆ **UVs** are points that turn green when selected. They are used for texturing, not modeling. See Chapter 14 (**Figure 8.61**).

◆ An **edge** is one border of a face (**Figure 8.62**).

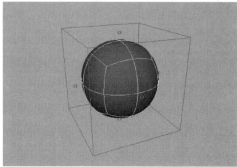

Figure 8.59 This subdivision surface sphere is in Display Level 0 and has its faces displayed.

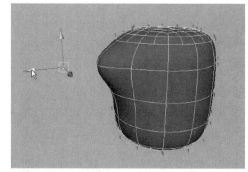

Figure 8.60 A subdivision vertex, at Display Level 1, has been moved. The surface responds much as a NURBS surface responds to moving a control vertex.

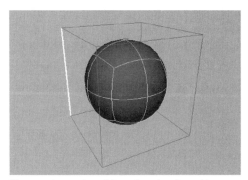

Figure 8.62 An edge of the sphere is selected in standard mode.

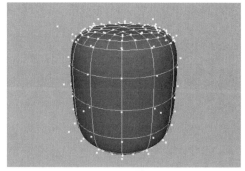

Figure 8.61 UVs don't have associated display levels. Thus, they show up as points, not numbers.

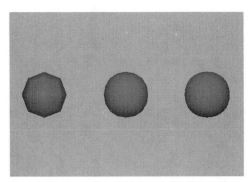

Figure 8.63 From left to right, Rough, Medium and Fine Subdiv Smoothness.

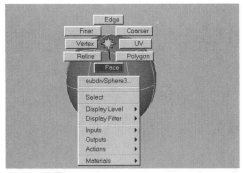

Figure 8.64 The Marking Menu for subdivision surfaces is accessible by clicking the sphere's surface with the right mouse button. Much of what is needed to work with subdivision surfaces is right here.

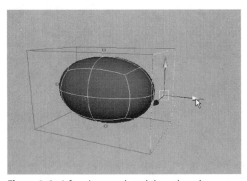

Figure 8.65 A face is moved, and the sphere is elongated.

To select a subdivision surface component:

1. From the Create menu, select Subdiv Primitives > Sphere.

2. Press ③ to go into the fine level of subdivision surface display smoothness (**Figure 8.63**).

    The surface should appear smoother in the view. Changing these settings does not affect the construction of the model, just how it's displayed.

3. With the right mouse button, click the sphere, and select Face from the Marking Menu (**Figure 8.64**).

    The faces should now appear surrounding the sphere.

4. Select and move the face (**Figure 8.65**).

Sculpting subdivision surfaces

Subdivision surfaces allow you the freedom to move back and forth between different levels of detail. The following are a few terms you'll need to understand to manipulate this functionality.

Display level—Subdivision surface objects have different display levels—that is, different levels of refinement. This means that you can work with many points close together on the surface that affect only a small area, or with fewer points farther apart on a surface that affect a large area. You can move back and forth between these levels (**Figure 8.66**).

Refine—This function gives the selected area of the surface a higher level of detail. If it is at Level 1, Refine will make the area of selected points have Level 2 points.

Finer and Coarser—These functions allow you to move quickly to a higher level of detail (Finer) or a lower level of detail (Coarser).

To change display levels on a subdivision surface:

1. From the Create menu, select Subdiv Primitives > Cylinder.

2. Press ③ on the keyboard to go into the fine level of subdivision surface smoothness.

3. With the right mouse button click the cylinder, and select Vertex from the Marking Menu.

4. With the right mouse button click the cylinder, and select Display Level > 2 from the Marking Menu (**Figure 8.67**).

   Many more points appear labeled as 2 (**Figure 8.68**).

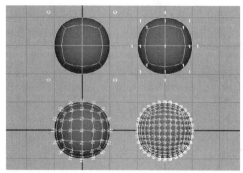

Figure 8.66 A subdivision surface sphere is shown at Display Levels 0 (from top left), 1, 2, and 3. By default, the sphere only has levels 0 and 1. It needs to be refined to access higher levels.

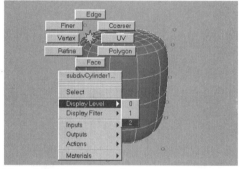

Figure 8.67 Display Level allows you to choose from any of the existing levels.

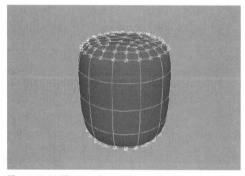

Figure 8.68 The Level 2 vertices only show up on the default cylinder where detail is needed. If you need the 2's to be evenly distributed, go to Display Level 1 and refine.

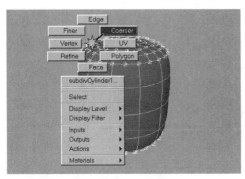

Figure 8.69 Coarser and Finer are another way to change the display level.

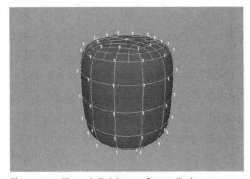

Figure 8.70 The subdivision surface cylinder at Display Level 1.

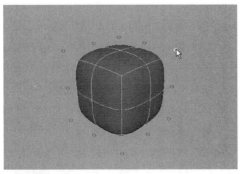

Figure 8.71 A vertex is selected to determine the area that will be refined.

5. With the right mouse button click the cylinder, and select Coarser from the Marking Menu (**Figure 8.69**).

The display level goes down to 1 (**Figure 8.70**).

6. With the right mouse button click the cylinder, and select Finer from the Marking Menu.

The display level goes back up to 2.

To add detail to a subdivision surface:

1. From the Create menu, select Subdiv Primitives > Cube.

2. Press ③ to go into the Fine level of sub-division surface smoothness.

3. With the right mouse button click the cube, and select Vertex from the Marking Menu.

4. Select a vertex (**Figure 8.71**).

continues on next page

5. With the right mouse button click the cube, and select Refine from the Marking Menu.

The zeros are replaced by ones in the area around the original point, and there are now more of them (**Figure 8.72**).

6. With the right mouse button click the cube, and select Refine from the Marking Menu again.

The ones are replaced by even more twos.

7. Select and move a point (**Figure 8.73**).

8. With the right mouse button click the cube, and select Display Level > 0 from the Marking Menu.

9. Select and move a point (**Figure 8.74**).

The changes to the Level 2 points remain while you work with Level 0 points. You can move back and forth between the display levels.

✔ Tips

■ The Refine function also works with edges and faces.

■ You can refine up to a display level of 13. However, we don't recommend that you go above 3 because the speed of interactivity decreases dramatically as the levels increase.

■ You cannot delete a subdivision surface component. However, if you transform any component at a display level of 1 or higher and then try to delete it, the component will return to its original position.

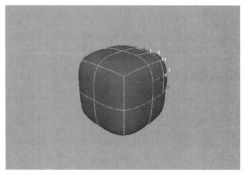

Figure 8.72 With the Refine function, detail is added only around the selected component.

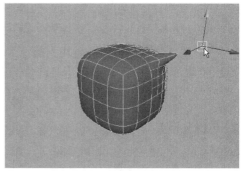

Figure 8.73 A point is selected and moved. This refined area allows for tweaks to small portions of the surface.

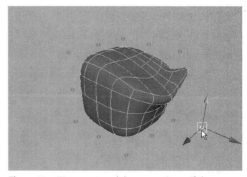

Figure 8.74 You can tweak large portions of the surface by returning the display level to 0.

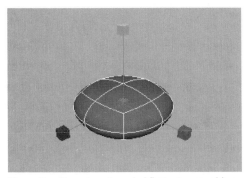

Figure 8.75 The sphere is scaled flatter to resemble a turtle shell.

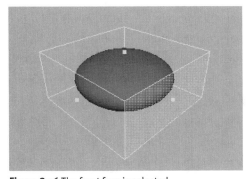

Figure 8.76 The front face is selected.

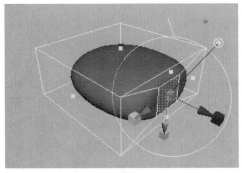

Figure 8.77 The face is scaled down. To get the Proportional scale manipulator in the center, click any of the other scale manipulators.

Subdivision surfaces polygon mode

While standard mode is good for adding fine details, polygon mode is essential for creating the basic structure of the surface. One common tactic is to model a polygon to get the rough form and then convert it to subdivision surfaces. This is helpful because you can work quickly, and the polygon primitive cube has a simpler construction than the subdivision primitive cube.

It's good practice to finish all the manipulation you plan to do in polygon mode before you begin refining the surface in standard mode. This is because you can lose changes made to the surface if you frequently switch between modes.

To model a turtle out of subdivision surfaces using polygon mode:

1. From the Create menu select Subdiv Primitives > Sphere.

2. Press ③ to go into the Fine level of subdivision surface smoothness.

3. Scale the sphere down the *y* axis to make it flatter (**Figure 8.75**).

4. With the right mouse button click the sphere, and select Polygon from the Marking Menu.

   A rectangular polygon shell should appear around the sphere.

5. With the right mouse button click the sphere, and select Face from the Marking Menu. Select the face on the front side of the polygon (**Figure 8.76**).

6. From the Edit Polygons menu select Extrude Face. Scale down the face (**Figure 8.77**).

continues on next page

7. From the Edit Polygons menu select Extrude Face again. Move the face forward and up (**Figure 8.78**).

This will be the neck of the turtle.

8. From the Edit Polygons menu select Extrude Face again. Proportionally scale the face up (**Figure 8.79**).

9. From the Edit Polygons menu select Extrude Face again. Move the face forward (**Figure 8.80**).

This will be the head of the turtle.

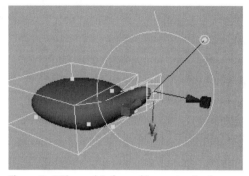

Figure 8.78 The neck is formed by moving the face out and up.

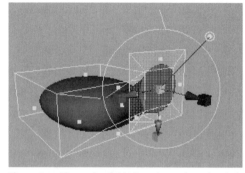

Figure 8.79 The scale of this face determines the size of the back of the turtle's head.

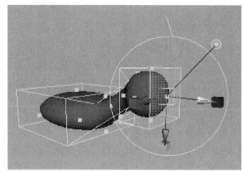

Figure 8.80 Move this face forward to give the head some length.

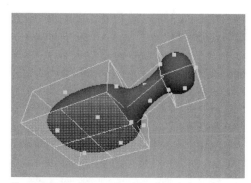

Figure 8.81 Looking at the object from below, the bottom has been subdivided.

10. Select the face on the bottom of the sphere.

11. From the Edit Polygons menu select Subdivide (**Figure 8.81**).

12. From the Edit Polygons menu select Extrude Face. Proportionally scale the faces to be smaller (**Figure 8.82**).

13. From the Edit Polygons menu select Extrude Face again. Move the faces down (**Figure 8.83**).

You've made a turtle!

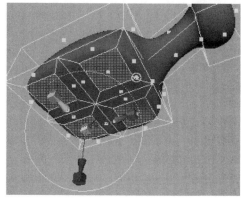

Figure 8.82 The bases of the legs are scaled down simultaneously.

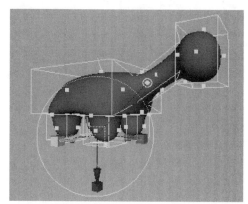

Figure 8.83 Move these faces down to determine the length of the legs. A simple turtle shape is completed.

To model a SubD telephone receiver, starting with a polygon:

1. From the Create menu select Polygon Primitives > Cube.

2. Scale the cube down in the *z* direction so that it is flatter. Scale it down in the *x* direction so that it is narrower (**Figure 8.84**).

3. With the right mouse button click the cube, and select Face from the Marking Menu.

4. Select the top face of the cube.

5. From the Edit Polygons menu select Extrude Face. Move the face up to double the height (**Figure 8.85**).

6. From the Edit Polygons menu select Extrude Face again. Move the top face up so that you have three equal faces on the front of the object (**Figure 8.86**).

7. Select the top and bottom faces of the front of the object.

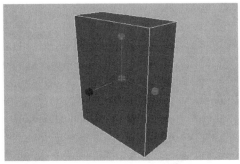

Figure 8.84 The polygon cube is scaled flatter and narrower.

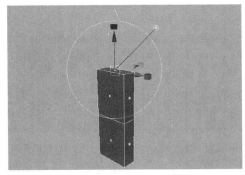

Figure 8.85 The height of the object is doubled by extruding the top face.

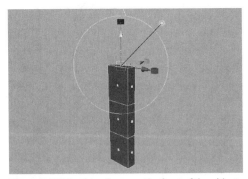

Figure 8.86 The three faces on the front of the object should be about equal.

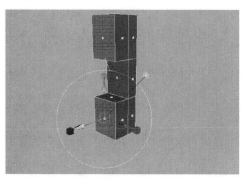

Figure 8.87 Move out the extruded faces to form the receiver and mouthpiece of the telephone.

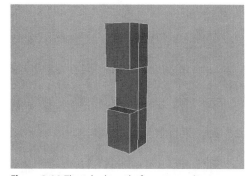

Figure 8.88 The telephone before conversion to subdivision surfaces. The mode has been switched from Pick mask to object.

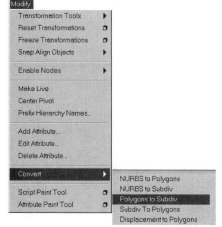

Figure 8.89 Select Modify > Convert > Polygons to Subdiv.

8. From the Edit Polygons menu select Extrude Face. Move the faces along the *z* axis (**Figure 8.87**).

9. Switch the Pick mask mode to object mode by pressing ⌐F8⌐ (**Figure 8.88**). The object should be selected.

10. From the Modify menu select Convert > Polygons to Subdiv (**Figure 8.89**). You've made a simple telephone receiver (**Figure 8.90**).

✔ Tips

- Subdivision surfaces can be turned back into polygons by using Modify > Convert > Subdiv to Polygon.

- You can also convert a NURBS surface to a subdivision surface by selecting NURBS to Subdiv from the Modify > Convert menu. Whether you're converting from NURBS or polygons, you should always start out with a simple surface. An already-dense surface converted to subdivisions will prove very difficult to work with, simply because of the sheer number of points created by the conversion.

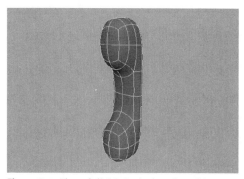

Figure 8.90 The subdivision telephone's surfaces are smooth and rounded.

Subdivision surfaces tend to be smooth all around. To get flatter areas and sharp edges, Maya has provided the Crease tools.

To add a partial crease:

1. Create the telephone receiver according to the instructions from the previous exercise.

   Be sure you are in standard mode. From the Subdiv Surfaces menu select Standard Mode. The remaining steps will not work in polygon mode.

2. With the right mouse button click the surface, and select Edge from the Marking Menu.

3. Select the eight edges that form a cube around the top part of the telephone (**Figure 8.91**).

4. From the Subdiv Surfaces menu select Partial Crease Edge/Vertex (**Figure 8.92**).

5. Repeat Steps 3 and 4 for the mouthpiece of the telephone.

   The mouthpiece and receiver now have a flatter, more squared look (**Figure 8.93**).

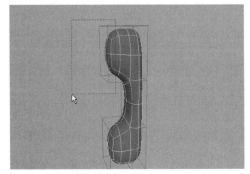

Figure 8.91 With the camera lined up correctly, marquee-selecting makes it easy to select several edges at once.

Figure 8.92 Note that in addition to creasing edges from this menu, you can uncrease them by selecting Uncrease Edge/Vertex.

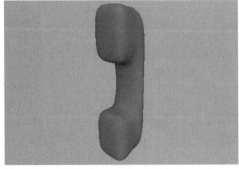

Figure 8.93 This is the resulting telephone receiver after using partial crease on the top and mouthpiece.

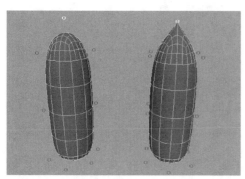

Figure 8.94 Left, the point has been moved up. Right, the surface has a point on top from the Full Crease function.

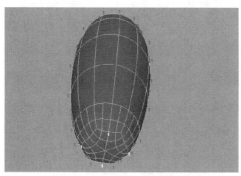

Figure 8.95 Carefully select four evenly spaced points from the bottom of the surface. It helps to tumble around the camera to be sure the right ones are selected.

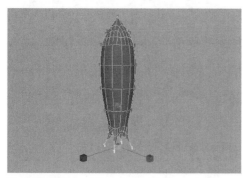

Figure 8.96 The points are moved down, and proportionally scaling them moves them out from the center. They now form the legs of a simple rocket ship.

To add a full crease to vertices:

1. From the Create menu select Subdiv Primitives > Cylinder.

2. Scale the surface along the *y* axis so that it's about three times the original length.

3. With the right mouse button click the surface of the cylinder, and select Vertex from the Marking Menu.

4. Select the point in the middle of the top and move it up.

5. From the Subdiv Surfaces menu select Full Crease Edge/Vertex.

   The top point becomes sharp (**Figure 8.94**).

6. Marquee-select the bottom row of points, and scale them in.

7. With those points still selected, click the surface with the right mouse button, and select Refine from the Marking Menu.

8. Select four evenly spaced points on the bottom of the surface (**Figure 8.95**).

9. From the Subdiv Surfaces menu select Full Crease Edge/Vertex.

10. Move the points down, and scale them out.

    You have created a simple rocket ship (**Figure 8.96**).

To add a full crease to edges:

1. Create the rocket from the previous section (**Figure 8.97**).

2. With the right mouse button click the surface, and select Edge from the Marking Menu.

3. With the right mouse button click the surface, and select Display Level > 0.

4. With the right mouse button click the surface, and select Edge from the marking menu that appears.

5. Select all of the vertical edges.

   To avoid selecting horizontal edges, marquee-select the vertical edges at the bottom, then (Shift)-select those at the middle, and finally (Shift)-select those at the top (**Figure 8.98**).

6. From the Subdiv Surfaces menu select Full Crease Edge/Vertex.

7. Your rocket now has sharp edges (**Figure 8.99**).

✔ Tip

■ You can remove a crease by selecting the edge that the crease is on and choosing Uncrease Edge/Vertex from the Subdiv Surfaces menu.

Figure 8.97 This is the completed rocket ship from the previous section.

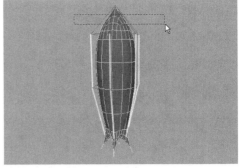

Figure 8.98 By (Shift)-selecting the vertical edges one bunch at a time, you can avoid selecting the horizontal edges.

Figure 8.99 The edges of the rocket ship are sharp, giving it a more interesting shape.

SKELETONS AND INVERSE KINEMATICS

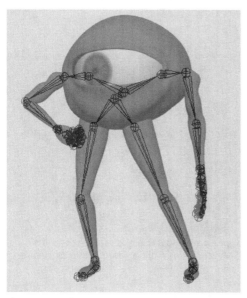

Figure 9.1 Inside this eyeball character you can see the skeleton, which is used to pose and animate the character.

Once you model a character, you need to place a skeleton inside it in order to animate it. The skeleton is built as a hierarchy of individual joints connected by bones.

In general, nature serves as the best template for placing joints: Use pictures of skeletons, human or animal (**Figure 9.1**). A shoulder joint should go at the shoulder; an elbow joint should go at the elbow; and so on. However, you don't need to be too literal. For example, although the human foot has 26 bones, you can animate a shoe with three bones. Wherever you want something to bend, that's where you need a joint.

Joints are hierarchical—that is, the joints at the top of the hierarchy will move those beneath them. The first joint you place will be at the top of the hierarchy and is often referred to as the *root joint*. This is the joint that moves the whole skeleton. Because the knee, ankle, and foot joints are below the hip joint, the rest of the leg moves when the hip joint is rotated. Animating in this fashion is called *forward kinematics* (FK) (**Figure 9.2**).

Inverse kinematics, or IK, refers to animating from the bottom of the hierarchy up. In this type of animation, if you moved the foot around, the knee and hip would rotate accordingly (**Figure 9.3**).

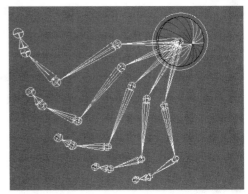

Figure 9.2 Illustrating the principle of forward kinematics, when the hip joint is rotated, all of the joints below rotate with it.

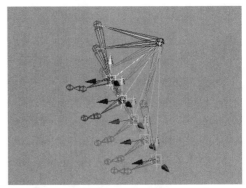

Figure 9.3 The foot is moved using an IK handle. Some animators avoid IK because it tends to move limbs in straight lines rather than natural arcs.

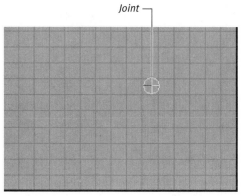

Joint

Figure 9.4 A joint is created in an orthographic view by selecting Skeleton > Joint Tool.

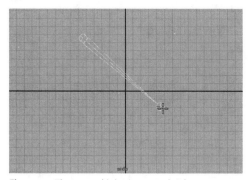

Figure 9.5 The second joint is created. A bone appears between the two joints, demonstrating that they are parented together. The bone is thicker at the parent joint than at the child joint.

About Joints

When you create joints, the bones appear automatically between the joints. The order in which you create joints is important: The first joint that's created resides at the top of the hierarchy; the second joint is parented to the first (making it a child of that joint and forcing it to follow the parent's movement); the third is parented to the second; and so on down the line.

A joint is like a pivot point in a hierarchy. You can't take a joint's pivot point away; the joint always remains with its pivot point. A joint's position in the hierarchy determines which joints will rotate with it: The joints below it rotate with that joint; the joints above it are not affected by that joint's movements. Don't confuse this hierarchy with joints that are above or below each other *physically:* One joint can be above another in the *y* direction but below it within the hierarchy.

To create joints:

1. From the Skeleton menu select Joint Tool.

2. In the side view, click where you want the joint to be placed.

   A joint appears. You should generally use an orthographic view when you create joints (**Figure 9.4**).

3. Click where you want the next joint to be placed.

   A bone appears between the two joints (**Figure 9.5**).

4. Click and drag to place the third joint. When you release the mouse button, the joint will be placed.

   continues on next page

5. Press Enter.

The skeleton is complete, and you're no longer in the Joint tool. The top joint of the hierarchy is selected, which causes the whole skeleton to be highlighted.

✔ Tips

■ It's often a good idea to build a skeleton with grid snap turned on so that all your joints are securely aligned. A convenient way to do this is by holding down x when you place joints.

■ You can make the joints appear bigger or smaller by selecting Display > Joint Size and choosing a size from the list.

■ To delete a joint, select the joint and then press Delete. That joint will be deleted, along with any joints below it in the hierarchy.

Often you'll want to branch off from a joint in the hierarchy. For example, both arms branch off from the chest joint.

To branch off from an existing skeleton:

1. Create the skeleton from the previous page.

2. Click the Joint tool icon 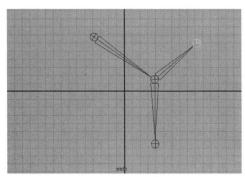.

3. Click the joint from which you want to branch off.

This will *select* the joint, not create a new one.

4. Click where you want the new joint to be placed.

A new joint appears with the bone branched off from the original skeleton (**Figure 9.6**).

5. From the Window menu select Hypergraph to view the resulting hierarchy.

Note that two joints are at the same level in the hierarchy, both parented under the same joint (**Figure 9.7**).

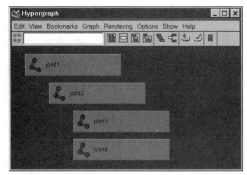

Figure 9.6 A new joint branches off from the existing joints.

Figure 9.7 Joint3 and joint4 are both children of joint2. That means that if joint2 is rotated, joint3 and joint4 will rotate with it.

ABOUT JOINTS

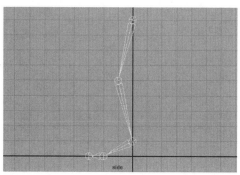

Figure 9.8 This is a typical leg skeleton. Starting from the top, the joints are named hip, knee, ankle, ball, and toe. If the character is wearing shoes, you don't need bones for each toe; one bone is sufficient to rotate the front of the shoe.

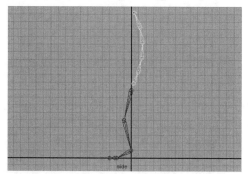

Figure 9.9 A spine joint is created from the bottom up. This makes the bottom joint the parent of the rest of the spine. The rest of the joints are beneath it in the hierarchy even though they are above it in space.

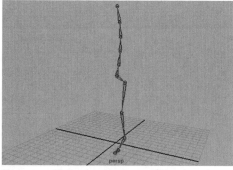

Figure 9.10 The leg has been parented to the spine. Now the bottom joint of the skeleton is the root joint for the whole character. When this joint is moved, the whole character moves.

You can think of bones as a visual representation of your skeleton's joint hierarchy. When you parent one joint to another, a bone appears. If you unparent a joint, the bone disappears. Sometimes it's easier to create separate hierarchies and then place them inside a single skeleton by parenting them.

To parent joints:

1. Create the skeleton of a leg and foot out of five joints in the side view (**Figure 9.8**).

   Press Enter to complete the creation.

2. As a separate hierarchy, create spine joints in the side view, starting from the bottom and working your way up (**Figure 9.9**).

3. In the Front view, move the leg to the side.

4. Select the top joint of the leg and then Shift-select the bottom joint of the spine. Now press p.

   A bone appears between the leg and the spine. It is now one hierarchy (**Figure 9.10**).

✔ Tip

- You can similarly unparent joints. Select the joint you want to unparent and press Shift p. The joint becomes unparented, and the bone disappears.

To save time, once you create a leg or arm, you can mirror the joint, which makes a duplicate leg or arm appear on the other side of the body.

To mirror joints:

1. Create the leg from the previous sections.

2. Select the hip joint (**Figure 9.11**).

3. From the Skeleton menu, select the box next to Mirror Joint.

   This opens the Mirror Joint Options dialog box.

4. For Mirror Across, select YZ (**Figure 9.12**).

5. Click Mirror.

   A new leg appears on the other side (**Figure 9.13**).

✔ Tips

- If the leg was built in the side view, you should mirror it across the YZ plane. To figure out which plane you should use, look at the view axis in the corner of the panel and imagine two of the axes forming a plane that you want to mirror across. If the new leg does not appear in the correct location, undo the mirror joint and try choosing a different plane to mirror across in the Mirror Joint Options dialog box.

- Don't mirror a joint that falls on the center line of the body: If you do, you'll end up with two joints on top of each other.

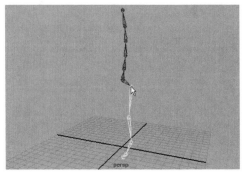

Figure 9.11 The hip joint is selected so that the leg can be mirrored over to the other side.

Figure 9.12 The YZ option is chosen so that the leg will mirror across the YZ plane.

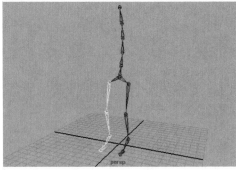

Figure 9.13 The opposite leg is created using the Mirror Joint Options dialog box from the Skeleton menu.

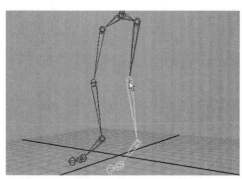

Figure 9.14 The knee joint of the leg has been selected so that it can be moved.

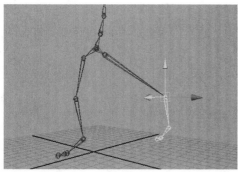

Figure 9.15 As the knee is moved back, the foot bones move with it. Note that the bone between the hip and the knee becomes longer.

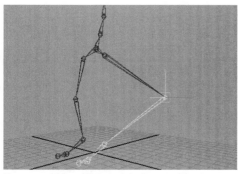

Figure 9.16 When the knee joint is moved in pivot move mode, the foot, which is below it in the hierarchy, stays put.

When you move a joint to position it, all of the joints beneath it in the hierarchy move along with it. You can move a joint *independently* of its position in the hierarchy by using pivot move mode.

To move a joint:

1. Create a skeleton like the one from the previous sections.

2. Select the knee joint (**Figure 9.14**).

3. Press ⓦ.

4. Move the knee backward.
   The rest of the leg moves with it (**Figure 9.15**).

5. Press ⓩ to undo the last move.

6. Press ⟨Insert⟩/⟨Home⟩ on the keyboard.
   You are now in pivot move mode.

7. Move the knee forward.
   The rest of the leg does not move with it (**Figure 9.16**).

8. Press ⓩ to undo the last move. Press ⟨Insert⟩/⟨Home⟩ again to get out of pivot move mode.

ABOUT JOINTS

To insert a joint:

1. Create a skeleton of several joints (**Figure 9.17**).

2. From the Skeleton menu select Insert Joint Tool.

3. Click on a joint and drag out the new joint.

   The new joint will be inserted between the joint you clicked on and the joint beneath it in the hierarchy. It is easiest to do this in an orthographic view (**Figure 9.18**).

4. Press (Enter) to finish, and exit the tool.

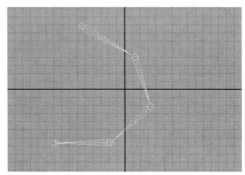

Figure 9.17 A skeleton of several joints is created in an orthographic view.

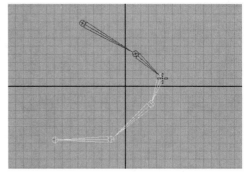

Figure 9.18 A new joint is created between two existing joints. It is positioned between the joints both physically and in the hierarchy.

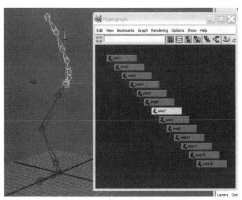

Figure 9.19 You can select a joint by clicking on it in the modeling window, or by clicking the corresponding joint node in the Hypergraph.

Occasionally you may find that you've created more joints than you need. If so, you can select the joint and remove it from the hierarchy without deleting any additional nodes, like simply deleting the joint would do.

To remove a joint from the hierarchy:

1. Select the joint you would like to remove by clicking it (**Figure 9.19**).

2. From the Skeleton menu select Remove Joint (**Figure 9.20**).

   The joint is removed from the hierarchy and deleted from the scene. Now that the selected joint has been removed, the bone from its parent ends at the selected joint's child (**Figure 9.21**).

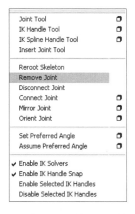

Figure 9.20 Select Remove Joint from the Skeleton menu.

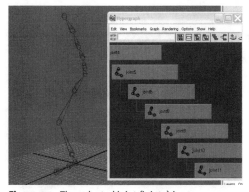

Figure 9.21 The selected joint (joint7) is now completely deleted from the scene and cannot be viewed in the Hypergraph.

ABOUT JOINTS

Sometimes you'll want to disconnect a portion of a previously created skeleton to use it in a new character. Say for a *half-human* character that uses a human joint system—with human-like arms but nonhuman-like legs. By disconnecting the center joint, you could use the upper half of the human skeleton on the human half of the new character.

To disconnect a joint from the hierarchy:

1. Select the joint you would like to disconnect from the hierarchy by clicking it (**Figure 9.22**).

2. From the Skeleton menu, select Disconnect Joint (**Figure 9.23**).

   The selected joint and its children are disconnected from the original hierarchy.

3. From the Window menu select Hypergraph.

   The Hypergraph opens in a new window.

4. Press a to focus all of the joints in the Hypergraph window.

   The skeleton is now split into two hierarchies that can be selected and moved independently of each other (**Figure 9.24**).

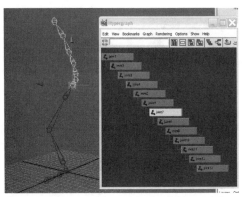

Figure 9.22 You can select a joint by clicking on it in the modeling window, or by clicking the corresponding joint node in the Hypergraph.

Figure 9.23 Select Disconnect Joint from the Skeleton menu.

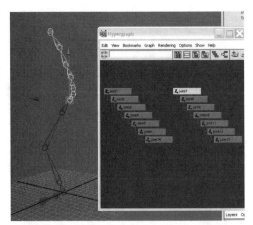

Figure 9.24 Although in the modeling view the skeleton still appears to be one, you can see in the Hypergaph that there are now two separate hierarchies.

Understanding the Hypergraph and Skeletons

When you're creating characters, the Hypergraph plays an important role in hierarchy order and selection. In fact, it's the best tool Maya offers to help you understand the way hierarchies are formed as well as how Maya's various elements relate to one another.

The Hypergraph provides two layout options: Freeform and Automatic, with Automatic being the default. If you choose the Automatic option, Maya lays out the Hypergraph for you, with the root node at the top of the hierarchy and each child indented below its parent with a line connecting child and parent. In addition, nodes are locked in place so that the hierarchies remain visually consistent and organized.

In contrast, if you select Freeform from the Options > Layout menu, you can move the nodes around and organize them to your liking. In addition, you can import an image of your character into the background of the Hypergraph so that you can align its joints to their proper positions on top of the image, making it much easier to select individual joints. In a simple hierarchy this may not be necessary, but when you have hundreds of joints and surfaces, selection can become quite cumbersome without this aid.

The Hypergraph displays each of your joints with the a blue joint icon . When a single joint is selected in the view pane, all of its children are highlighted to indicate their relationship to the selected joint. As children of the joint, they will be affected if the selected joint is rotated. Be aware that although the children are highlighted in the view pane, they haven't been *individually* selected.

Select a joint and open the Hypergraph. The joint you clicked is selected (yellow), but the joints underneath it (its children) are not. Because the parent is selected, the children will follow. If in the Hypergraph you (Shift)-select the children and then rotate the joints, you will see that each joint will rotate. Although you will rarely select the joints in this fashion, it's important to understand what is and is not selected in a hierarchy.

You can move joints from one hierarchy to another or disconnect them from a hierarchy—all from within the Hypergraph. You use the middle mouse button to move joints in and out of hierarchies. To move a joint (and its children) into another hierarchy, simply drag the joint (using the middle mouse button) onto the node you want to serve as its parent. Once you do this, you will see that the selected node (and its children) are connected to the new hierarchy.

To remove a joint (and its children) from a hierarchy, select its node with the middle mouse button and drag it away from the hierarchy (releasing the mouse when the node has been moved away from the hierarchy). This technique also works well for removing objects from a group within the Hypergraph.

About IK Handles and Solvers

Inverse kinematics makes animation easier in many situations. For example, to put a foot in a certain position using forward kinematics, you would need to rotate the hip and the knee. However, by using an IK handle on the ankle, you can simply move the ankle into position, and the hip and knee will rotate accordingly (**Figure 9.25**).

You can also use an IK handle to make a foot or hand stick in one spot. When your character is walking and you want one foot to remain planted on the ground, IK handles make it much easier to keep that foot in place (because multiple rotations in the joints connected to the IK Handle help to keep it that way) (**Figure 9.26**). Once it is keyframed, the foot will do its best to stay where it is even though the joints in the IK chain are rotating. The same goes for arms and hands. If your character is climbing a ladder or leaning against a wall, an IK handle will help keep it in place.

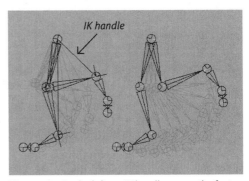

Figure 9.25 On the left, an IK handle moves the foot. On the right, both the hip and ankle are rotated to move the foot.

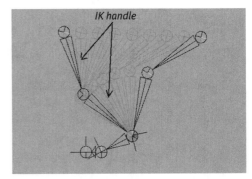

Figure 9.26 The top of the leg is moving, but the ankle is staying put because it has an IK handle, which is keyframed. Note that this foot also has an IK handle going from the ankle to the ball and from the ball to the toe. These IK handles keep the rest of the foot in place.

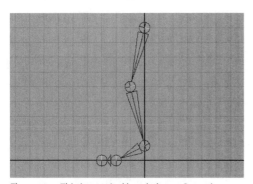

Figure 9.27 This is a typical leg skeleton. Sometimes a heel joint is added, but it is used merely as a placeholder since the ankle joint bends but the foot does not bend at the heel.

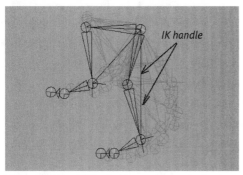

Figure 9.28 The IK handle is moved around, allowing for easy placement of the foot.

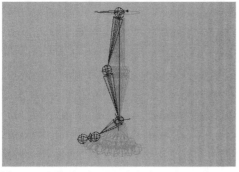

Figure 9.29 The leg is rotated via the Twist attribute.

To add an IK handle:

1. Create a leg out of five joints (**Figure 9.27**).

2. From the Skeleton menu select IK Handle Tool.

3. Click the hip joint.

4. Click the ankle joint.
   An IK handle is created.

5. Move the IK handle around (**Figure 9.28**).

6. Select Twist in the Channel Box.

7. With the middle mouse button, drag from left to right in the Perspective view.
   The leg rotates around the IK chain (**Figure 9.29**).

The Twist attribute only works on a Rotate Plane (RP) type of IK handle. By default, a Rotate Plane solver is created when you make an IK handle. If you move the IK handle too high, however, the leg flips around, and the knee points in the opposite direction (**Figure 9.30**). You can solve this problem by adjusting the Pole Vector attributes, which are in the Channel Box for the IK handle.

Another alternative is to create a Single Chain solver. Although it doesn't permit the Twist attribute like the Rotate Plane solver does, the Single Chain solver doesn't have the same flipping problem that Rotate Plane has. When using a Single Chain solver, you can rotate the limb by rotating the IK handle. However, the Rotate Plane solver is considered more predictable because it's not affected by the rotation of the IK handle.

To create a Single Chain IK handle:

1. Create a leg out of five joints (**Figure 9.31**).

2. From the Skeleton menu select the box next to IK Handle Tool.
   This opens the Options window.

3. Select ikSCsolver from the pop-up menu next to Current Solver (**Figure 9.32**).

4. Click the hip joint.

5. Click the ankle joint. An IK handle is created with a Single Chain solver.

6. Rotate the IK handle.
   The limb rotates.

✔ Tip

■ You can also change the type of solver after you've created the IK handle: Select the IK handle and open the Attribute Editor. If you click IK Solver Attributes, you'll be able to choose the solver type from the pop-up menu (**Figure 9.33**).

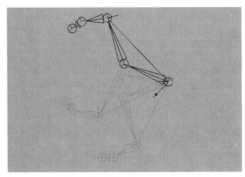

Figure 9.30 When lifted too high, a leg can flip over if you're using an RP IK handle.

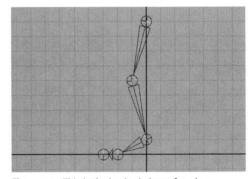

Figure 9.31 This is the basic skeleton for a leg.

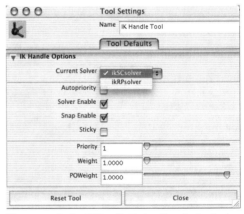

Figure 9.32 In the IK Handle Tool options in the Tool Settings window, ikSCsolver is chosen. This type of IK handle won't cause the flipping problem that an RP handle can cause.

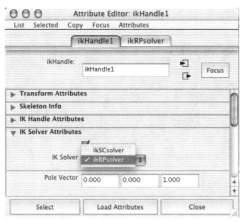

Figure 9.33 In the Attribute Editor for the IK handle, you can change the type of solver after it is created.

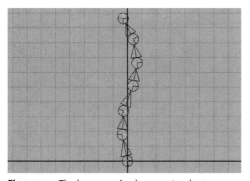

Figure 9.34 By creating an IK spline on these joints, you can animate a spine skeleton by moving just one point. Keyframing the rotation of each joint to achieve the same effect would be much more difficult.

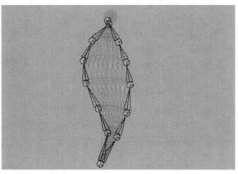

Figure 9.35 The human spine has a natural curve. When creating a spine for a character, it's helpful to match the shape of it's the character's back.

About Spline IK

Spline IK gives you a way of controlling many joints using a curve rather than by rotating them directly. This is especially useful when you have many joints in a continuous chain (such as in a spine or a tail), because you can move the skeleton quickly into the shape you desire without rotating each individual joint (**Figure 9.34**).

To create a Spline IK:

1. Create a spine skeleton, starting from the bottom and working your way up (**Figure 9.35**).

2. From the Skeleton menu select Spline IK (Windows) or IK_Spline Handle Tool (Mac).

3. Click the top joint of the skeleton.

4. Click the second joint from the bottom of the skeleton.

   Two things are created, the Spline IK handle and a curve. By default, the curve is automatically parented to the joints.

5. Select Twist in the Channel Box.

6. With the middle mouse button, drag from left to right.

   The bones rotate around.

   continues on next page

219

7. From the Hypergraph select the curve you just created (**Figure 9.36**).

8. In the Pick mask, select component mode. You can now see the CVs of the curve.

9. Select and move a CV (**Figure 9.37**).

The joints rotate in response and stick to the shape of the control curve.

✔ Tip

■ In general, you don't want to use the root joint of the skeleton as part of your Spline IK chain. If you do, when you move the CVs, the whole skeleton will rotate. To avoid this, choose one joint above the root joint of the skeleton as the base of your Spline IK.

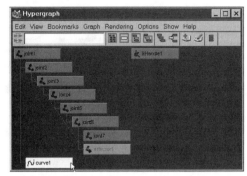

Figure 9.36 It's easier to select the curve in the Hypergraph because the icon can be isolated.

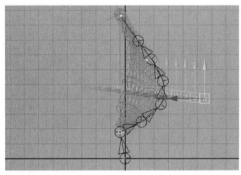

Figure 9.37 When the CV is moved, the spine bends to form the shape of the control curve.

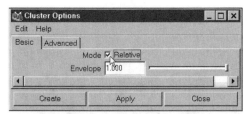

Figure 9.38 In the Cluster Options dialog box, Relative is checked.

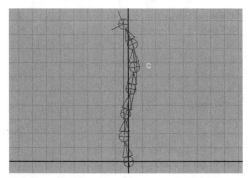

Figure 9.39 A *C* (for *cluster*) appears where the CV is. The cluster controls the CV.

When you are using Spline IK to animate your character, you move and keyframe CVs. However, CVs don't have their own node: Since they're components, they don't show up in the Hypergraph or Outliner as a node that can be animated. It can be helpful to make a cluster for each CV of the curve so that there *is* a node you can keep track of when animating. A cluster can also aid in the selection process since you can move a cluster handle away from the spline curve, making it easier to select.

To create clusters for a Spline IK's CVs:

1. Create a Spline IK as in the previous section.

   Be sure that the root joint of the skeleton is not included in the IK chain.

2. Select one of the CVs of the control curve.

3. From the Deform menu select the box next to Create Cluster. The Cluster Options dialog box opens.

4. Check the box next to Relative (**Figure 9.38**).

   Checking this box will make the cluster move in relation to the curve. If you don't check Relative, the cluster will do a *double transform*, which means it will move twice as much when the root joint is moved.

5. Click Create.

   The cluster is created and is represented as a C (**Figure 9.39**).

   continues on next page

ABOUT SPLINE IK

6. [Shift]-select the root joint of the skeleton.

7. Press [p].

The cluster is now parented to the root joint so that it will move with the whole skeleton.

8. Repeat Steps 2 through 7 for all but the bottom CV of the control curve.

There are now clusters for each of the CVs, which you can easily select and animate (**Figure 9.40**).

✔ Tip

■ When you're making clusters out of the CVs of the curve for an IK spline, don't make a cluster for the bottom CV of the curve. Moving this CV will stretch out the bone—often undesirable because the entire body moves out of place.

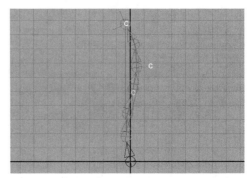

Figure 9.40 The Cs are used as selection tools for the spine's rotation.

Bulldog by O.Martin (www.omartin-design.com)

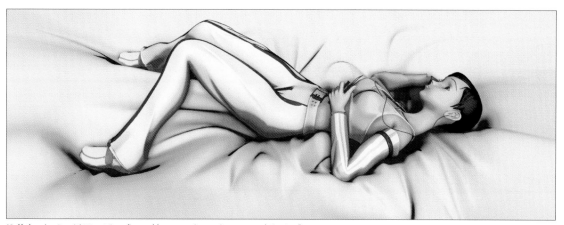

Kelivina by David Wen Ying (http://www.noboundrees.com/yinako/)

Additional gallery images and Maya tutorials can be found at www.upaxis.com.

Pig by Michael Sormann (www.sormann3d.com)

Constructor by Michael Sormann (www.sormann3d.com)

Additional gallery images and Maya tutorials can be found at www.upaxis.com.

Midnight Dragon by Rico Holmes (www.ricoholmes.com)

Additional gallery images and Maya tutorials can be found at www.upaxis.com.

Creation by Meats Meier (www.sketchovision.com)

Additional gallery images and Maya tutorials can be found at www.upaxis.com.

Devil Chrome by Meats Meier (www.sketchovision.com)

Additional gallery images and Maya tutorials can be found at www.upaxis.com.

Dido by Robert Kuczera (www.3dcharacters.de)

Sandra by Robert Kuczera (www.3dcharacters.de)

Additional gallery images and Maya tutorials can be found at www.upaxis.com.

Audi tt by Robert Kuczera (www.3dcharacters.de)

Claude by Robert Kuczera (www.3dcharacters.de)

Additional gallery images and Maya tutorials can be found at www.upaxis.com.

PARENTING AND BINDING TO A SKELETON

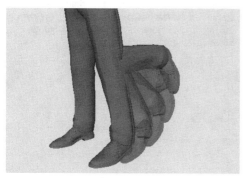

Figure 10.1 For the leg to bend at the knee, it needs to be bound to a skeleton.

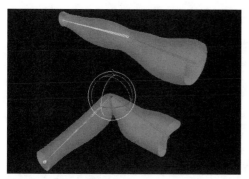

Figure 10.2 When the elbow joint is rotated, only the forearm rotates with it.

Once you've created a skeleton, you need to either parent or bind the surfaces to the joints in order for the surfaces to move with the skeleton. Anything that doesn't need to bend, like a hat, glasses, or eyeballs, can be *parented* to the joints. Anything that does need to bend, like an arm, leg, or torso, must be *bound* to the skeleton (**Figure 10.1**).

Parenting to joints works much like parenting to anything else. The bone is the parent, and the surface is the child, so the surface rotates and moves when the bone is rotated.

Binding, however, is a bit different. When a surface is bound to a skeleton, only a portion of that surface will move with a bone. For example, an arm has a shoulder joint and an elbow joint. However, only the forearm should move when the elbow is rotated; the shoulder and biceps should remain in place (**Figure 10.2**). When you bind the arm geometry to the skeleton, you make the forearm part of the arm (attached at the elbow joint) and the shoulder and biceps part of the arm as well (attached to the shoulder joint).

At the heart of binding are *clusters*. A cluster is like a set of points that have weight. Weight represents the amount of influence a cluster wields over each point in the set. Understanding clusters and weight is an important step in understanding binding. In this chapter, we'll take a close look at clusters and their effect on surfaces.

There are two kinds of binding—*rigid bind* and *smooth bind*. Rigid bind works well for things like arms, legs, and fingers—things that bend clearly at a joint and are rigid in between. Smooth bind works well for things like torsos, tails, and snakes—things that bend gradually along a surface (**Figure 10.3**). Either can be used for any kind of surface, and in some cases it just boils down to a matter of personal preference.

The surface of a simple character, such as a robot, can sometimes be parented, rather than bound, to a skeleton—for example, if all the parts are made out of metal and don't bend. Parenting a character that does not have bending joints is a good way to create your first character since it's easy to set up and quick to animate.

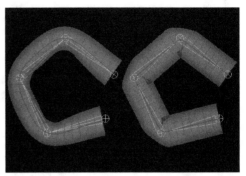

Figure 10.3 These two objects have identical geometry and the same joints, which are rotated equally. However, the one on the left is smooth bound, and the one on the right is rigid bound. The surface on the left bends more smoothly; the one on the right bends more abruptly and is straighter between joints.

Parenting vs. Binding

There are two ways to connect surfaces to geometry, parenting and binding.

If you plan ahead when creating your character, you can save a lot of time by designing a *segmented* character, meaning a character that does not need to bend at the elbows or other major bending joints. A simple example would be a character wearing knee and elbow pads: You can individually parent each surface (the upper leg, bottom leg, and knee pad). Each of these objects can move individually without having to bend or deform, only rotate.

By parenting geometry to a skeleton, you avoid having to create clusters and weigh individual points because the surfaces don't bend and deform with the character.

If, however, your character requires realistic deformations in its joints, you must bind it to the skeleton to create that effect. And this poses all sorts of extra character-setup challenges. Take, for example, a character's armpit: Because the geometry near the outside of the breast and under the arm are so close to one another, Maya must guess which bone each point is to be attached to—and often its choice will differ from yours. This means you'll spend extra time separating the points that are moving with the wrong joint, and moving them onto the correct joints.

Figure 10.4 This character is built from simple shapes. As a robot, he's made of steel and thus does not bend, making him a good candidate for having his surfaces parented (rather than bound) to joints.

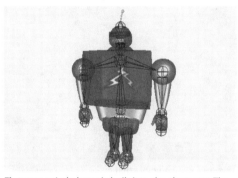

Figure 10.5 A skeleton is built into the character. The root joint, which is at the top of the hierarchy, is at the waist.

Figure 10.6 Once all the surfaces have been parented to the appropriate joints, you can pose or animate the character.

To parent surfaces to joints:

1. Create the surfaces of a character (**Figure 10.4**).

2. Create a skeleton (**Figure 10.5**). (See Chapter 9 for more information.)

3. Select a surface.

4. (Shift)-select the joint to which it will be parented.

5. Press (p).

   Now when you select and rotate that joint, the surface will rotate with it.

6. Repeat Steps 3 through 6 for all of the other surfaces.

   Now when any joint is rotated, the parented surface will move with it (**Figure 10.6**).

About Clusters and Weights

A cluster provides a means of controlling a set of points as a group. The points can be NURBS control vertices (CVs), polygon vertices, or lattice points. (For more information on these elements, see chapter 12.)

Points that are members of a cluster have weight. As mentioned earlier, weight represents the amount of influence the cluster has over the points it contains. Weight is generally set between 0 and 1. A point with a weight of 0 will not move with the cluster. A point with a weight of 1 will move exactly as much as the cluster itself. Anything in between will make the point move a fraction of how much the cluster moves.

For example, suppose a CV in a cluster had a weight of 0.5. If the cluster was moved up two grid units in the y direction, the CV would move only one unit (**Figure 10.7**). Simply multiply the weight by the distance the cluster moves, and you'll get the distance the point moves.

Clusters represent a convenient way of animating portions of a surface. For example, if you wanted to animate the movement of a character's fat belly, you could make a cluster out of the points that form his belly, add different weights to the points on his belly, and then animate that cluster (**Figure 10.8**).

Understanding clusters is also the key to understanding binding. What binding does, in the background, is create clusters of portions of your surface and then parent those clusters to the joints. Once the surface has been bound, you can adjust the weight of the points to get the surface to deform the way you desire. When you understand parenting, clusters, and weight, binding will no longer seem mysterious.

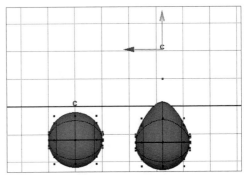

Figure 10.7 A cluster is made with one CV whose weight is set to 0.5—which means the point moves only half the distance of the cluster (right).

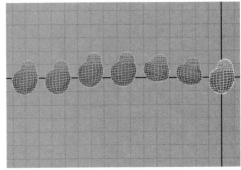

Figure 10.8 The points that make up the belly are included in a cluster. That cluster is parented to the belly and animated to make it bouncy.

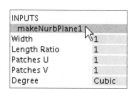

Figure 10.9 When you click makeNurbPlane1 in the Channel Box, it will expand these options.

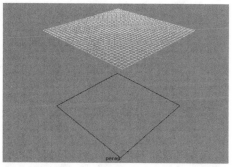

Figure 10.10 At the bottom is the plane before the patches were increased. At the top is the plane after the patches have been increased.

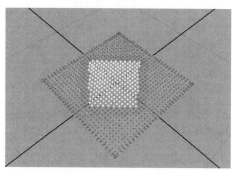

Figure 10.11 The plane is dense, so it has many points. The CVs in the center have been selected so that they can be made into a cluster.

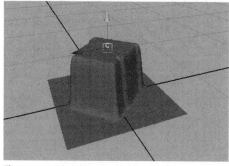

Figure 10.12 The cluster, which is represented by a *C*, has been moved up. The CVs, which are members of the cluster, move with it, forming a plateau.

To create a cluster:

1. From the Create menu select NURBS Primitives > Plane.

2. Select makeNurbPlane1 from the INPUTS section of the Channel Box (**Figure 10.9**).

3. Increase Patches U and Patches V to *30*. The plane becomes denser (**Figure 10.10**).

4. Press F8 to go into component mode.

5. Select some points in the center of the plane (**Figure 10.11**).

6. From the Deform menu select Create Cluster.

   A *C* appears in the middle of the selected points.

7. Press w to go into move mode and then move the cluster.

   The CVs move with it (**Figure 10.12**).

To weight the points of a cluster using the Component Editor:

1. Create a cluster as in the previous section.

2. Select some of the CVs that are included in the cluster (**Figure 10.13**).

3. From the Window menu select General Editors > Component Editor.

   The Component Editor window appears.

4. Select the Weighted Deformers Tab in the Component Editor (**Figure 10.14**).

5. Click on the top numeric field and drag down to highlight all of the weights.

6. Type .5 in the field, and press (Enter).

   All of the weights in that column become 0.5 (**Figure 10.15**).

7. For Windows, click the cluster1 button above the column of weight numbers.

8. (Ctrl)/(Control) -click the top field in the column of weights.

   Now when you use the slider at the bottom of the Component Editor, the CVs move, and the weights change interactively.

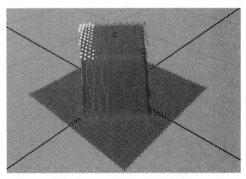

Figure 10.13 Some of the CVs on the side of the cluster have been selected so that their weight can be changed.

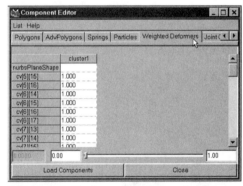

Figure 10.14 In the Component Editor, a cluster is referred to as a Weighted Deformer. The weights of the selected points show up when this tab is selected.

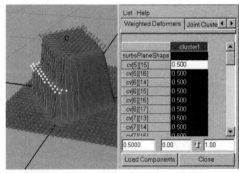

Figure 10.15 On the right, the Component Editor shows that the weights of the selected points have been reduced to 0.5. On the left, the selected points are only moved up half the distance of the cluster because of their lower weight.

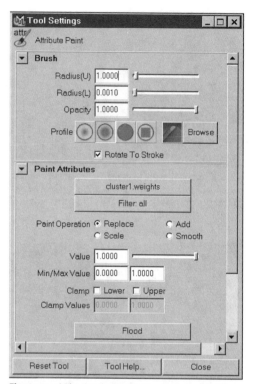

Figure 10.16 The Attribute Paint tool can be used to interactively change the weights of points. The options shown here control how the weight is changed.

About the Attribute Paint tool

Another way of adjusting the weights of a cluster is by using the Attribute Paint tool. Especially handy for working with dense surfaces, this tool includes several options for interactively changing the weight of points (**Figure 10.16**).

There are four settings for Paint Operations:

Replace—When Paint Operation is set to Replace, the current weight of the painted points will change to whatever number is set in the Value field.

Add—When Paint Operation is set to Add, the value will be added to the weight of the painted points. This is useful for incrementally increasing the weights of points.

Scale—When Paint Operation is set to Scale, the current weight of a point will be multiplied by the value when it is painted. If you have a value of 0.9, you can incrementally decrease the weight of a point.

Smooth—This averages the weights of the adjacent points to make the area smoother.

The Flood button can speed work considerably, because rather than have to paint on an effect, you can have the Attribute Paint tool's settings affect all of the points simultaneously by pressing Flood. This is useful when you're setting all points to the same weight or smoothing all points.

ABOUT CLUSTERS AND WEIGHTS

To edit cluster weights using the Attribute Paint tool:

1. Create a cluster, and move it up as in the previous sections.

2. Select the surface.

3. With the right mouse button click the surface. In the Marking Menu that appears, select Paint > cluster > cluster1-weights (**Figure 10.17**).

   This activates the Attribute Paint tool, which should provide color feedback as you're in shaded mode. The area of the surface that includes CVs in the cluster turns white; the rest appears black.

4. Hold down Ⓑ and drag the mouse from right to left to shrink the brush size (**Figure 10.18**).

5. Double-click the Attribute Paint tool in the toolbox. The Tool Settings window for the Attribute Paint tool appears.

6. Change Value to *0.5*.

   Paint Operation should already be set to Replace (**Figure 10.19**).

7. Click and drag on the surface.

   The painted portion moves down because the weight of the points has been changed to 0.5.

8. Change Paint Operation to Smooth.

9. Click Flood several times.

   The lump becomes smooth (**Figure 10.20**).

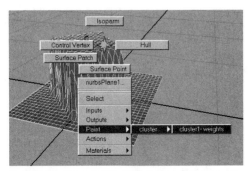

Figure 10.17 Using the Marking Menu, which pops up when you click the surface with your right mouse button, is the most convenient way to access the Attribute Paint tool.

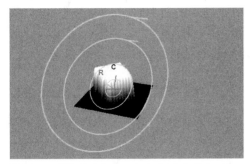

Figure 10.18 The brush size started out much too big for this small surface. Here we see the progression as the brush size gets smaller.

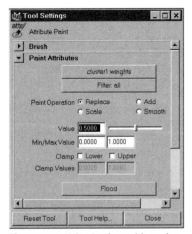

Figure 10.19 Using Replace with a value of 0.5 will bring about the same result as if you had typed it in as the weight in the Component Editor.

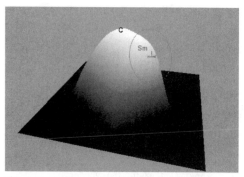

Figure 10.20 Flood will apply the current Paint Operation setting to all members of the cluster. In this case, it's set to Smooth so that all the points are smoothed simultaneously when you click Flood, which is quicker than having to paint the surface.

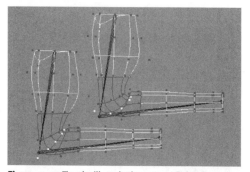

Figure 10.20 Flood will apply the current Paint Operation setting to all members of the cluster. In this case, it's set to Smooth so that all the points are smoothed simultaneously when you click Flood, which is quicker than having to paint the surface.

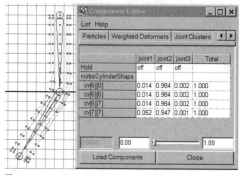

Figure 10.22 The cylinder on the left has been smooth bound. The weights of the selected points show up in the Component Editor. Their weight is spread among the three joints; however, they are primarily influenced by joint2.

About Binding

When you bind skin, you make the surfaces move with the bones. In the beginning the process may seem mysterious; however, it's really little more than a combination of actions you already know.

We've learned that when you parent a surface to a joint, it rotates with that joint. We also know that a cluster is a set of points that have weight. Binding skin creates a cluster composed of the points nearest to a bone, and then parents that cluster to the bone. After this is done, you can adjust the weight to make the points rotate more or less with a specific joint (**Figure 10.21**).

As mentioned earlier, there are two kinds of binding—rigid and smooth. When you use rigid bind, each point can be a member of only one joint. When you use smooth bind, each point is a member of more than one joint. Its weight is spread out among two or more joints, but the total weight always adds up to 1 (**Figure 10.22**).

To bind skin using rigid bind:

1. From the Create menu select NURBS Primitives > Cylinder.

2. Increase Scale Y to *8* (**Figure 10.23**).

3. In the Channel Box select makeNurbCylinder1.

4. Increase Spans to *8* (**Figure 10.24**).

   Bound surfaces require extra detail, particularly in the areas where they bend.

5. Create three joints in the surface (**Figure 10.25**). (See Chapter 9 for more information.)

6. Select the joints, and (Shift)-select the surface.

7. From the Skin menu select the box next to Bind Skin > Rigid Bind.

   The Rigid Bind Skin Options window opens.

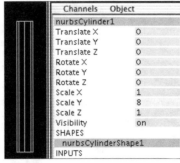

Figure 10.23 On the left is the cylinder with a Y Scale of 8; on the right is the Channel Box, which provides a convenient place to change the scale to a precise number.

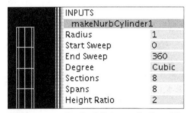

Figure 10.24 On the left is a cylinder with eight spans; on the right is the Channel Box with attributes for this cylinder.

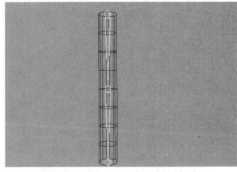

Figure 10.25 Three joints are placed inside the cylinder, which produces two bones.

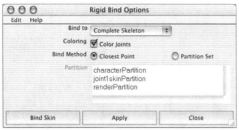

Figure 10.26 The Rigid Bind Skin Options window is set to Bind to Complete Skeleton and Color Joints. Complete Skeleton means that the skin will be bound to every joint in the hierarchy (as opposed to just the selected ones). Color Joints means that the joints and the points that become members of those joints will be color-coded the same once the skin is bound.

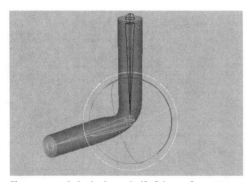

Figure 10.27 Only the lower half of the surface rotates with the middle joint.

8. Select Complete Skeleton in the "Bind to" menu, and check Color Joints next to Coloring (**Figure 10.26**).

9. Click the Bind Skin button.

10. Select the middle joint and rotate it. The lower half of the surface moves with the bone (**Figure 10.27**).

✔ Tips

■ Any kind of surface can be bound to a skeleton—NURBS, polygon, or subdivision. You can also bind a lattice, or just a selection of points.

■ You can bind a whole character with multiple surfaces at once. To do this, select the root joint of the skeleton and all of the surfaces involved, then bind the skin.

ABOUT BINDING

A point becomes a member of a specific joint when you use rigid bind; however, sometimes it can become a member of the *wrong* joint. The Edit Membership tool allows you to change the joint that the point belongs to.

To edit the membership of a point:

1. Create the bound cylinder from the previous section.

2. Select the middle joint.

3. From the Deform menu select Edit Membership Tool.
   The cursor changes.

4. Click the middle joint.
   The points that are members of that joint are selected.

5. [Shift]-select the middle row of points (**Figure 10.28**).
   This adds points to the membership of the middle joint, and they, too, are selected. If you do not hold down [Shift], this will not work.

6. Select and rotate the middle joint.
   The points that were just added now rotate with the joint (**Figure 10.29**).

✔ Tips

■ If you [Ctrl]/[Control]-select points, they will be removed from the joint's membership when you are in the Edit Membership tool. However, if they are not added to a joint, the points will be left behind when the character moves.

■ The Edit Membership tool can be used for any deformer, such as a lattice or a blend shape.

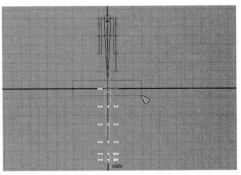

Figure 10.28 The Edit Membership tool allows you to change which joint the points are members of. Here, some of the points that were not members of the middle joint are being added to that joint.

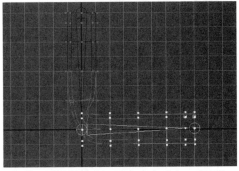

Figure 10.29 When a joint is rotated, all the points that are members of that joint rotate with it. Therefore, the points we just added rotate along with the joint as well.

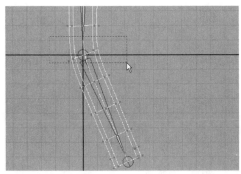

Figure 10.30 Some of the CVs of the surface are being selected so that their weight can be changed. Be sure you're in component mode when you try to select CVs.

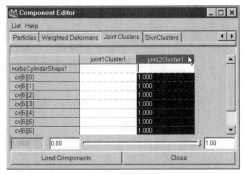

Figure 10.31 In the Component Editor, the entire column of numbers is highlighted when the button above the column is selected. This allows you to conveniently change all of their weights at once.

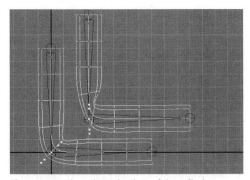

Figure 10.32 The selected points of the cylinder on top have not yet been changed—they still have a weight of 1. On the bottom cylinder, the selected points have a weight of 0.5.

To edit the weights of rigid-bound points:

1. Continue with the bound cylinder from the previous section.

2. Select the row of points at the middle joint (**Figure 10.30**).

3. From the Window menu select General Editors > Component Editor.

4. Click the Joint Clusters tab.

5. Click on the top numeric field and drag down to highlight all of the weights.

   In this case it is labeled joint2Cluster1. The column is highlighted (**Figure 10.31**).

6. Type .5 in the field.

   All of the weights for the selected points become 0.5. The points now rotate half the distance of the joint, creating a smoother shape around the joint (**Figure 10.32**).

Sometimes the area where a surface bends will seem too rounded and you'll want it to be more angular, as with an elbow. A *flexor* provides an easy way to adjust the rounding and creasing that occurs on a surface near a joint.

To create a flexor:

1. Create a rigid-bound cylinder like the one in the previous sections.

2. Make sure that the joint to which you want to add the flexor is straight—that is, its rotations are set to zero.

3. Select the middle joint.

4. From the Skin menu select Edit Rigid Skin > Create Flexor.

5. Click Create.

   A lattice is created around the joint (**Figure 10.33**).

6. Rotate the joint about 90 degrees (**Figure 10.34**).

   When the joint is rotated, the flexor reshapes the surface automatically to prevent creasing.

7. Select the lattice that appeared when the flexor was created.

8. Click Rounding in the Channel Box.

9. With the middle mouse button drag from left to right in the panel until the bent area of the surface is more angular and elbow-shaped (**Figure 10.35**).

✔ Tip

- If you check Position the Flexor in the Create Flexor Options window, it will group the lattice and lattice base together. This allows you to reshape the lattice by moving and scaling the group without having it affect the shape of the surface.

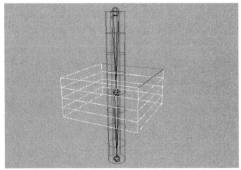

Figure 10.33 Create Flexor makes a lattice appear around the selected joint. It has special attributes that other lattices do not have, such as Creasing and Rounding used to form an elbow or knee. Be sure to add a flexor only when the joint is straight; otherwise, you'll get undesirable results.

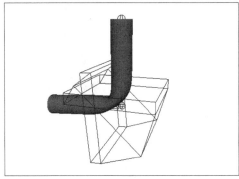

Figure 10.34 A flexor has been put on the middle joint. As the joint is rotated, the flexor improves the shape of the surface where it is bent.

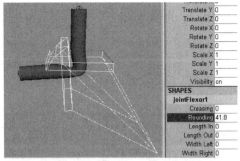

Figure 10.35 By adjusting the Rounding attribute, you can make the bent portion more angular. This is commonly used on things like elbows, knees, and finger joints. When the joint is rotated to straight again, the surface returns to its original shape.

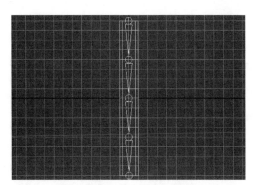

Figure 10.36 Five joints are placed inside the cylinder. Smooth bind lends itself to parts of characters that have many joints and need to bend smoothly.

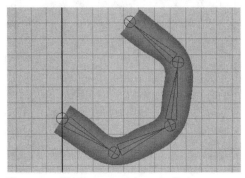

Figure 10.37 This is a smooth bound cylinder.

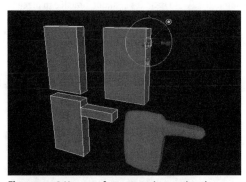

Figure 10.38 Here are four stages in creating the surface. First, create a polygon cube and scale it. Extrude the side face and scale, and move it to the start point of the arm. Extrude again and pull the arm out. Finally, smooth the surface with divisions set to 3 and continuity set to 0.35.

To bind skin using smooth bind:

1. From the Create Menu select NURBS Primitives > Cylinder.

2. Increase Scale Y to *8*.

3. In the Channel Box select makeNurbCylinder1.

4. Increase Spans to *16*.

   Bound surfaces require extra detail, particularly in the area where they bend.

5. Create five joints in the cylinder (**Figure 10.36**).

6. Select the surface, and Shift-select the root joint.

7. From the Skin menu select Bind Skin > Smooth Bind.

8. Select the top joints, and then Shift-select the rest of the joints one by one. Rotate all the joints simultaneously.

   The surface moves with the joints and bends smoothly (**Figure 10.37**).

To paint skin weights on a smooth-bound surface:

1. Create a polygon shape from a cube by scaling it using Extrude Face, and then from the Polygon menu select Smooth (**Figure 10.38**). (See Chapter 8 for more on polygons.)

   The shape roughly represents an arm extending from a torso.

continues on next page

2. Create four joints in the surface (**Figure 10.39**).

3. Select the root joint, and Shift-select the surface.

4. From the Skin menu select Bind Skin > Smooth Bind.

5. Select and rotate the second joint.

It bends too much of the torso portion of the surface (**Figure 10.40**).

6. Select the surface.

7. With the right mouse button click the surface, and select Paint > skinCluster > skinCluster1- paintWeights (**Figure 10.41**).

The Paint Skin Weights Tool is activated.

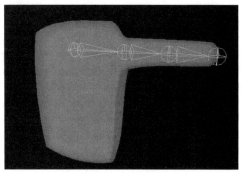

Figure 10.39 Starting from the center of the chest, four joints are placed inside the surface.

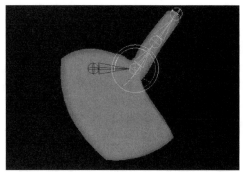

Figure 10.40 When the shoulder is rotated, it affects too much of the torso. Had there been more joints placed in the torso, this would not have been as much of a problem because the points would stick to the joints they were near. It's common practice to place rib joints in a character for this purpose.

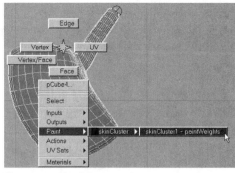

Figure 10.41 The right mouse button makes the Marking Menu appear for easy access to the Paint Skin Weights tool.

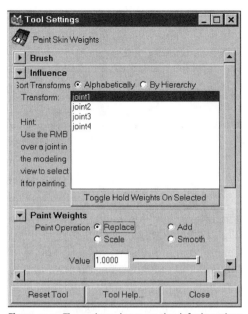

Figure 10.42 The options shown are the default settings for the Paint Skin Weights tool; they also happen to be what we need in this instance.

8. Double-click the Paint Skin Weights tool button in the toolbox .

   This opens the Tool Settings window for Paint Skin Weights. Under Influence, joint1 should be selected; Replace should be the Paint Operation; and Value should be 1.0000 (**Figure 10.42**).

9. Adjust the brush size by holding down ⓑ and dragging from right to left with the middle mouse button.

10. Paint all over the surface of the torso (**Figure 10.43**).

    The torso moves back to its original shape and turns white. This is because all of the weight is being placed on joint1 and taken away from joint2.

11. Change Paint Operation to Smooth.

12. Click Flood several times.

    The area where the surface bends is smoothed (**Figure 10.44**).

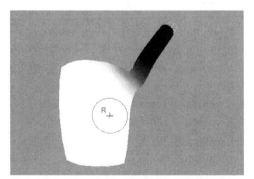

Figure 10.43 When the surface is painted, the points get a weight of 1 with the first joint, so they do not move with the shoulder joint. Be sure to get all around the surface with the brush.

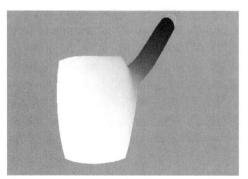

Figure 10.44 Flooding with Smooth creates a smoother connection at the shoulder.

ABOUT BINDING

To detach a surface from joints:

1. To create a bound skeleton, follow the steps outlined earlier in this chapter for binding skin using rigid bind.

2. Select the geometry that you want to detach from the skeleton (**Figure 10.45**).

3. From the Skin menu select Detach Skin (**Figure 10.46**).

   The geometry becomes detached from the skeleton.

4. Select the middle joint and rotate it.

   The joint moves but the surface remains in place (**Figure 10.47**).

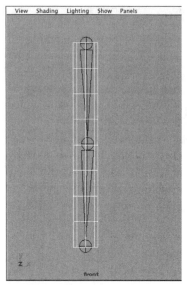

Figure 10.45 Select only the surface, not the joint, for the Detach command to work correctly.

Figure 10.46 Select Detach Skin to separate the surfaces from the bones.

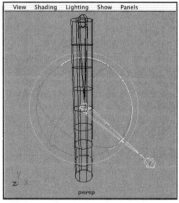

Figure 10.47 Once detached from the surface, joints no longer affect the geometry.

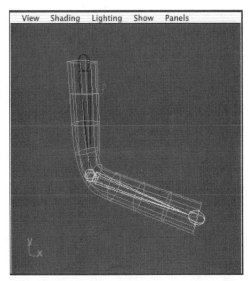

Figure 10.48 Select the joint that you want to reset to its bind pose.

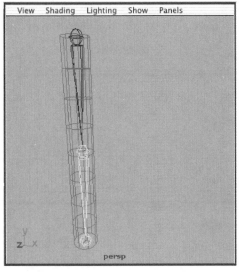

Figure 10.49 The selected joint returns to its original rotation amount.

When you bind geometry to a skeleton, Maya remembers the joints' rotation at the time of binding: This rotation is referred to as the *bind pose*. When animating, there will be times when you want the joints to align with the original rotation—that is, the rotation that existed when you bound the geometry to the skeleton. You can reset joints back to this rotation by setting the joint(s) back to the bind pose.

To set a rotated joint back to its bind pose:

1. Select the joint you want to set to the bind pose (**Figure 10.48**).

2. From the Skin menu select Go to Bind Pose.

   The joint is set to the same rotation as it was when it was bound to the skeleton (**Figure 10.49**).

ANIMATION

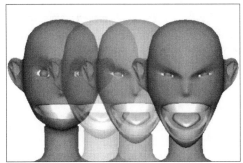

Figure 11.1 Toby Marvin animated the shape of this monkey's face to change his expression from happy to angry.

Maya was built for animation. Almost anything you encounter can be animated, such as a color, an object's shape, or the intensity of a light (**Figure 11.1**).

Most animation is accomplished by setting keyframes. The term *keyframe* stems from traditional hand-drawn animation, in which a lead animator would create *key* poses of a character—drawings at the beginning and end of an action—and an assistant would then draw the in-between frames, making the final result a smooth motion. When using Maya, *you* are the lead animator and the program is your assistant. To animate, you set keyframes—that is, you tell an object or attribute where to be at certain points in time—and the program in-betweens it for you.

Animations are easy to tweak: You can change the timing or distance covered by existing keyframes; you can add or remove keyframes; and you can adjust the acceleration between keyframes by tweaking the animation curve between them.

ANIMATION

Animation Controls

The Time and Range sliders are Maya's primary controls for creating and fine-tuning your animation (**Figure 11.2**).

Time slider—The Time slider determines your position in time. It is the area at the bottom of the screen that includes the playback buttons and timeline. You can click any frame to go to that point in time, or you can click and drag to preview a region of animation. You also use the Time slider to select, move, and scale keyframes (**Figure 11.3**).

Current Time indicator—This shows the present position in time (**Figure 11.4**).

Current Time field—This also shows the current position in time. You can type a number in this field to change the current time (**Figure 11.5**).

Start time/End time—This represents the time span for the entire animation. These numbers establish the length of time within which the Range slider can move (**Figure 11.6**).

Range slider—The Range slider controls the portion of time you're viewing. It has character sets, Auto Keyframe toggle, and Animation preferences adjacent to it. The Range slider allows you to quickly adjust which portion of the animation shows up in the timeline. You can use the buttons on the end to change the playback start and end times, or you can drag the range forward or backward as a whole. This is helpful when you only want to work on small portions of an animation. The smaller the range, the easier it is to pick individual frames (**Figure 11.7**).

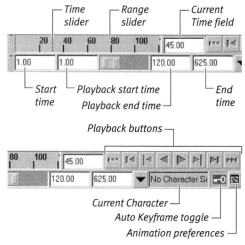

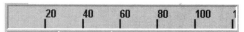

Figure 11.2 The Time and Range sliders allow you to play back animation, control your position in time, and choose the portion of the animation you're looking at.

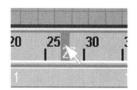

Figure 11.3 Click any point in the timeline to go to that time.

Figure 11.4 The Current Time indicator shows what frame you are on. If you want to cut, copy, or delete a frame in the timeline, the Current Time indicator must be over that frame.

Figure 11.5 The Current Time field also tells you where you are in time. You can type in any time (even one that's not included in the playback range) and go to that time.

Figure 11.6 The number fields on the far left and far right are the Start and End times. You should generally set these to the start and end of your entire animation. They can be changed at any time.

Figure 11.7 The Range slider provides a convenient means of changing which portion of the animation is currently in the timeline.

Figure 11.8 The Playback Start and End times are the fields on the left and right. You can type in the times that will change the beginning and end of your timeline.

Figure 11.9 From left to right, the playback buttons are: go to start of playback range, step back one frame, step back one key, play backward, play forward, step forward one key, step forward one frame, go to end of playback range.

Figure 11.10 The Auto Keyframe function is on when the button looks like this.

Figure 11.11 This is the Animation Preferences button.

Figure 11.12 You can create and choose character sets here.

Playback Start Time/Playback End Time—Controls the range of animation that will play back, much like the Range slider (**Figure 11.8**).

Playback buttons—These are like the buttons on a CD player. The rewind and fast-forward buttons change the current time to the start or end of the playback range. You can step forward one frame at a time, or move to the next or previous keyframe. There is a playback button to go forward or backward; it toggles to a stop button during playback (**Figure 11.9**).

Auto Keyframe toggle—This turns Auto Keyframing on and off. If it is on, any attribute that is already keyframed will be automatically keyframed again when you change its value (**Figure 11.10**).

Animation Preferences button—This opens up a window to set animation preferences. It's also a convenient way to access all general preferences in Maya (**Figure 11.11**).

Current Character—This sets which character in a scene you're currently working on. When working with more than one character, it's helpful to be able to access individual characters' attributes (**Figure 11.12**).

About Setting Keyframes

Keyframes are at the heart of animation in Maya. Setting a keyframe means that you want a certain attribute to have a specific value at a point in time. For example, a ball could begin at -2 along the X-axis at frame 1, and a translate X of 2 at frame 10. Between those frames it would gradually move across the screen (**Figure 11.13**).

There are many ways to set keyframes and adjust them once they've been set. When you set a keyframe, a couple of things happen: The channels that were keyframed are highlighted orange in the Channel Box. In addition, you'll see key ticks in the timeline—thin, red lines indicating where each keyframe is (**Figure 11.14**). Keyframes also show up in the Graph Editor and the Dope Sheet, discussed later in this chapter.

There are many ways to set a keyframe. The following section covers most of them.

To set a keyframe:

1. From the Create menu, select NURBS Primitives > Sphere.

2. Press (Shift)(w).

   This keyframes the translates only. (Shift)(e) keyframes the rotates, and (Shift)(r) keyframes the scales. These correspond to the hotkeys for the Move, Rotate, and Scale tools.

3. In the Channel Box, select Rotate X, and (Shift)-select Rotate Y and Z (**Figure 11.15**).

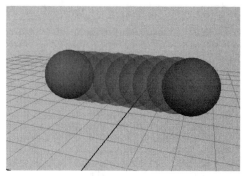

Figure 11.13 As you play back the animation, the sphere moves across the panel.

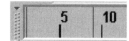

Figure 11.14 The thin, line near the 10 is a key tick. It lets you know there is a keyframe for the selected object at that time.

Channels	Object
nurbsSphere1	
Translate X	0
Translate Y	0
Translate Z	0
Rotate X	0
Rotate Y	0
Rotate Z	0
Scale X	1
Scale Y	1
Scale Z	1
Visibility	on

Figure 11.15 Rotate X, Y, and Z are selected in the Channel Box so that they can be keyframed. You can easily select multiple attributes in the Channel Box by clicking and dragging the names.

Figure 11.16 When you click in the Channel Box with your right mouse button, you can keyframe the selected attributes.

Figure 11.17 The current time is changed to 20 by typing it in the field. When you have a particularly long playback range, typing in a frame number can be easier than clicking it in the timeline.

4. With the right mouse button click in the Channel Box, and select Key Selected from the marking menu that appears (**Figure 11.16**).

   Any channels that are selected (in this case the rotates) are keyframed.

5. Go to Frame 10 by clicking that number in the timeline.

6. Move and rotate the sphere.

7. Press ⓢ.

   All attributes in the Channel Box are keyframed.

8. Turn on Auto Keyframe 🔘.

   The button will look pressed down and become highlighted.

9. Type *20* into the Current Time field to change the time in the timeline, and press Enter (**Figure 11.17**).

10. Move the sphere.

    A new keyframe appears: This is because when Auto Keyframe is turned on, it sets a keyframe any time an attribute is changed.

✔ Tip

- You can only set keyframes on an object when that object is selected. Likewise, you can only see the key ticks in the timeline when the keyframed object is selected.

While much of the advanced editing of keyframes can be done in the Graph Editor and Dope Sheet windows (discussed later in this chapter), you can access the most frequently used editing tools directly from the timeline.

To edit keyframes in the timeline:

1. From the Create menu, select NURBS Primitives > Sphere.

2. Change the playback start time to *1* and the playback end time to *30*.

3. Set keyframes on the sphere every five frames, starting with the first frame. Move the sphere, and then change the current time each time you set a keyframe. If Auto Keyframe is still on, you can press (Shift)(w) in the first frame, and all of the other frames will automatically be keyed (**Figure 11.18**).

4. Click a frame in the timeline where there is a key tick. With your right mouse button click the timeline, and select Delete from the pop-up menu (**Figure 11.19**).

   The keyframe is removed.

5. Hold down (Shift), and click and drag over the range of two key ticks in the timeline.

   A red area should appear with two small arrows near the middle and two small arrows at the edges (**Figure 11.20**).

6. Click and drag from left to right on the two small arrows in the center of the selected area.

   The keyframes move together without being scaled. You can do this with an individual keyframe as well.

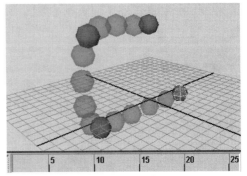

Figure 11.18 This is an example of some simple motion you can put on the object. The sphere is selected and keyframed by pressing (Shift)(w). With Auto Keyframe turned on, Maya will automatically keyframe the sphere every time you move it.

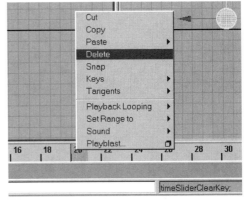

Figure 11.19 Clicking the timeline with your right mouse button gives you access to a variety of convenient commands.

Figure 11.20 The highlighted section of the timeline is selected. The outside arrows allow you to scale the time, and the inside arrows allow you to move several keyframes at once.

Figure 11.21 Double-clicking the timeline is a convenient way to select all of the keyframes in the playback range.

7. Double-click the timeline.

   All of the keyframes in the playback range are selected. However, the arrows used for scaling end up just outside the playback range, so you must change the playback end time to access them.

8. Change the playback end time to 31.

   An arrow appears at the end (**Figure 11.21**).

9. Click and drag the arrow to the left.

   The animation is scaled down, which makes the sphere move faster. Note that the key ticks do not fall on whole-number frames anymore.

10. With the right mouse button click in the timeline, and select Snap from the marking menu that appears.

    The keyframes are moved to the nearest whole-number frame.

✔ Tips

- If you want to ensure that the timeline is sitting on a keyframe, use the back and forward arrows with the red mark on them in the animation controls. This jumps the timeline to the last or the next keyframe, respectively.

- When you're working on the timing of your animation, it's often fastest, and easiest, to select, move, and scale keyframes in the timeline.

Setting Animation Preferences

There are a few animation preferences that are essential to set. They affect the way your animation is played back, and how you see and work with the timeline.

When a scene gets extremely complicated, with many animated surfaces, Maya may not be able to play back every frame of the animation at full speed. This leaves you with two choices: You can either play back at full speed or play every frame. In some cases you'll want to see the detail in the motion; other times you'll want to see the overall pace. For a simple scene, however, you can have your cake and eat it, too—that is, you can play back at full speed and see every frame of animation.

Maya is used to make animations for films, television, games, and the Internet. Films run at 24 frames per second (fps); television runs at 30 fps; and animation on the Internet often runs at 15 fps. It is important to set this option before you start animating: If you don't, the final animation may be incorrectly paced.

To set animation playback speed:

1. Click the Animation Preferences button
   , which is near the lower-right corner of the interface.
   The Preferences window opens (**Figure 11.22**).

2. Select Real-time (Windows) or Normal (24 FPS) (Mac) in the pop-up menu next to Playback Speed.

3. Select Settings from the Categories column.

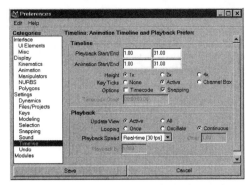

Figure 11.22 It is important to set Playback Speed before you start animating. Choosing the wrong playback speed can cause the audio to go out of sync with the animation when it's rendered.

SETTING ANIMATION PREFERENCES

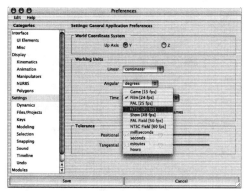

Figure 11.23 Real-time (30 fps) is a fairly standard setting for video.

4. Select your frame rate from the pop-up menu next to Time (**Figure 11.23**).

   NTSC (30 fps) is a standard frame rate for video.

5. Click Save.

   These settings will be recalled the next time you open Maya.

✔ Tip

■ Clicking the Animation Preferences button is a convenient way to access many of Maya's preferences. Once the window is open, try selecting different categories.

Key ticks are the red lines that appear on the timeline when you set a keyframe. You can set the key ticks to appear only for the selected channels, which is helpful if you want to make changes to some attributes and not others in the timeline.

To change key ticks options:

1. Keyframe an object.

2. Click the Animation Preferences button ⊞ , which is near the lower-right corner of the interface.

3. In the Preferences window, for Key Ticks select Channel Box.

   Any key ticks that were currently in the timeline disappear.

continues on next page

SETTING ANIMATION PREFERENCES

4. Select any keyframed channels in the Channel Box.

The key ticks for those channels appear.

5. Open the Preferences window again, and change the Key Ticks setting back to Active. Click Save.

✔ Tip

■ If the Key Ticks options are set to Channel Box, only the attributes selected in the Channel Box will be affected when you edit them. For example, if you were to keyframe both an object's scale and rotate, you could move the keyframes of the scale alone by selecting those attributes in the Channel Box and moving the key ticks. The rotate keyframes would be left behind.

You can import sound by dragging a WAV or AIFF file onto the timeline, and the sound waves will be displayed. You can see the sound waves better if you increase the time-line's height.

To set preferences for timeline height:

1. Click the Animation Preferences button 🖾, which is near the lower-right corner of the interface.

2. Click 2x and 4x next to Height (**Figure 11.24**).

The timeline gets taller (**Figure 11.25**).

3. Click 1x to return it to normal. Click Save to keep these preferences.

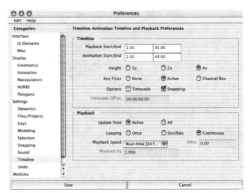

Figure 11.24 You can change the height of the timeline in the animation Preferences window.

Figure 11.25 This is a timeline at the height of 4x. Unless you need it to see the audio more clearly, the extra height takes up valuable real estate.

SETTING ANIMATION PREFERENCES

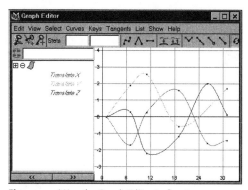

Figure 11.26 Use the Graph Editor to fine-tune your animation once you get the basic timing down.

Figure 11.27 From left to right, these tangent types are spline, linear, and flat.

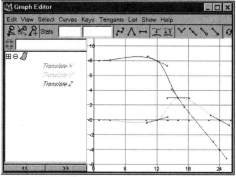

Figure 11.28 These keyframes are set to spline tangent type. Note that while the values at Frames 1 and 12 are the same, there is still a curve between those points because the keyframes are not set flat. This causes drifting, which can be problematic if you want an object to stay still.

About the Graph Editor

The Graph Editor is a window that shows a graphic representation of your animation. It has points that represent the time and position in which a keyframe was set, and curves between the keyframes, which show the acceleration (**Figure 11.26**).

By changing the distance between keyframes, you can change an object's speed. However, you must adjust the curve that represents its motion between keyframes to change its acceleration.

Tangent types in the Graph Editor allow you to quickly change the shapes of the curves (**Figure 11.27**). By default, the keyframes you set will be spline tangents. You can also manually adjust the shapes of the tangents. The Graph Editor is helpful for editing, copying, and looping animation.

Tangent types

There are six tangent types, all of which you can set by selecting a keyframe or an animation curve and choosing from the Tangent menu in the Graph Editor. You can also change which tangent type is automatically assigned to keyframes before they are set, in the Keys section of the Preferences window.

Spline—This is the default tangent type. Keyframes with spline tangents have smooth curves between and through them. When animating a fish through water, you might use a spline tangent (**Figure 11.28**).

continues on next page

Linear—This tangent type simply draws a straight line from one keyframe to the next. It creates jerky movement with sudden changes, which might be good for something mechanical (**Figure 11.29**).

Clamped—This acts just like a spline tangent with one very useful exception: If two keyframes are set at the same value at different points in time, it acts like a linear tangent. It prevents the problem that spline sometimes creates, which is that an object you want to be still will drift slightly (**Figure 11.30**).

Stepped—This tangent type ensures that a value remains the same until it gets to the next keyframe, when it jumps into that position. It makes the curve look like a step, hence the name. One use for this tangent is for producing camera cuts. If you want a camera to hold in one position and then cut to another position, keyframe using stepped tangent (**Figure 11.31**).

Flat—The tangent itself becomes horizontal when using this tangent type. Flat tangents typically create "slow-in slow-out"—which means that the animation gradually accelerates between keyframes, goes quickly in the middle of the curve, then gradually decelerates as it moves to the next keyframe (**Figure 11.32**).

Fixed—With a fixed tangent type, the tangent doesn't change when you edit the keyframe.

Creating a bouncing-ball animation is a good way to learn some of the functions of the Graph Editor.

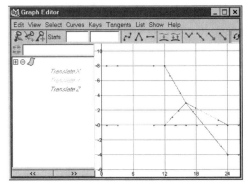

Figure 11.29 These keyframes are set to linear tangent type.

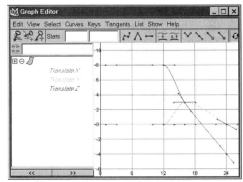

Figure 11.30 These keyframes are set to clamped tangent type. This tangent type is similar to the spline tangent except that the drifting problem between Frames 1 and 12 has been removed.

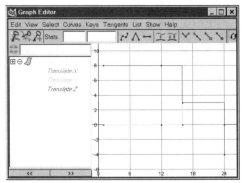

Figure 11.31 The keyframes are set to stepped tangent type.

ABOUT THE GRAPH EDITOR

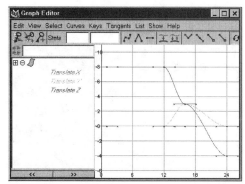

Figure 11.32 The keyframes are set to flat tangent type.

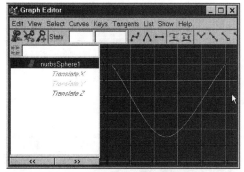

Figure 11.33 The keyframes at the top of the curve are being selected. The ball is at its highest between these points, and it needs to slow down on the way in and out of them—a perfect use for the flat tangent type.

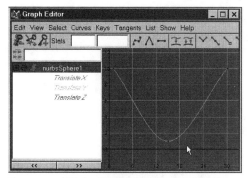

Figure 11.34 This keyframe is at the point when the ball hits the ground. As it is now, the ball doesn't seem to bounce; it just kisses the ground.

To change tangent types:

1. From the Create menu select NURBS Primitives > Sphere.

2. Move the sphere up 10 grid units.

   An easy way to do this is to type *10* in the field next to Translate Y in the Channel Box.

3. Make sure you're at Frame 1 in the timeline and that Auto Keyframe is turned on. The key icon 🔑 should appear red and pressed down.

4. Press (Shift)(w) to keyframe only the translates.

5. Go to Frame 15. Move the sphere's Translate Y down to 1.

   The ball will be keyframed once it is moved, because Auto Keyframe is on.

6. Go to Frame 30. Move the Translate Y of the sphere back up to 10.

   Rewind and play back the animation. The ball's bounce is not convincing.

7. From the Window menu select Animation Editors > Graph Editor.

   The Graph Editor window opens. The curve for the sphere's animation should show up as long as it is still selected.

8. Marquee-select the two keyframes at the top of the graph (**Figure 11.33**).

9. Click the Flat Tangents button ⎯, which is in the Graph Editor window.

10. Select the keyframe at the bottom of the curve (**Figure 11.34**).

    Since you're trying to click on such a small point, it helps if you marquee-select, even when you're only selecting one keyframe.

    continues on next page

11. Click the Break Tangents button 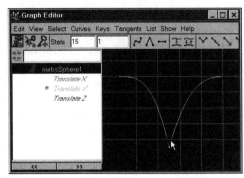. This allows you to move the tangents on either side individually.

12. Select the tangent on the left of the keyframe, then (Shift)-select the tangent on the right.

13. Click the Move Nearest Picked Key Tool button, which is at the top-left corner of the Graph Editor .

14. With the middle mouse button, click and drag on the tangents, and move them up one at a time. They should form a V shape (**Figure 11.35**).

Play back the animation. It should now look more like a real bouncing ball.

Figure 11.35 Now that the tangents have been adjusted, the ball will appear to really bounce.

Perhaps you want your ball to bounce again. One easy way to do this is to copy and paste keyframes in the timeline.

To copy and paste in the timeline:

1. Animate the bouncing ball as described in the previous section.

2. Make sure that the playback end time is set to at least 60.

You can do this by typing *60* in the Playback End Time field.

3. Hold down (Shift) and click and drag in the timeline from 1 to at least 31 (**Figure 11.36**).

4. With your right mouse button, click the timeline, and select Copy from the pop-up menu (**Figure 11.37**).

5. Click Frame 30.

The frame you are on when you paste is the time when the range of keyframes you paste in will begin.

6. With your right mouse button click the timeline, and select Paste > Paste.

7. Rewind and play back the animation. The ball now bounces twice, and there are new key ticks on the timeline.

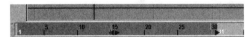

Figure 11.36 (Shift)-click and drag the keyframes you want to copy from. If you stop at Frame 30 in your selection, it will not include the keyframe at 30, so you must go one frame beyond it.

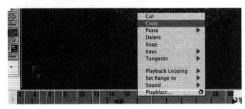

Figure 11.37 Copy the keyframes from the convenient pop-up menu.

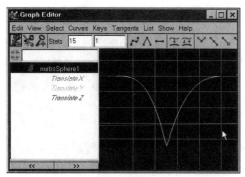

Figure 11.38 Be sure that the current time is at the point where you want to begin the paste. Otherwise, when you paste, the keyframes will end up wherever the current time indicator happens to be and overwrite the frames that were there.

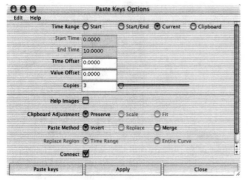

Figure 11.39 Using the Paste Keys options you can conveniently make several copies at once.

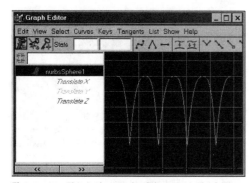

Figure 11.40 This is the result of the paste. The ball bounces four times instead of just once.

Sometimes you want an animation to repeat several times. You can use the Graph Editor to do multiple pastes at once.

To copy and paste in the Graph Editor:

1. Animate a bouncing ball.

2. Make sure that the timeline goes to at least 120.

   You can do this by typing *120* in the Playback End Time field.

3. From the Window menu select Animation Editors > Graph Editor.

   The curve for the sphere's animation should show up. If it does not, select the sphere.

4. From the Edit menu in the Graph Editor select Copy.

5. Hold down k and click and drag in the Graph Editor window until the red line, which is the time indicator, is at the end of the curve (**Figure 11.38**).

6. From the Edit menu in the Graph Editor select the box next to Paste.

   This opens the Paste Keys Options window.

7. In the field next to Copies, type *3* (**Figure 11.39**).

8. While the mouse is over the Graph Editor, press f.

   The entire animation curve is framed. There are now three additional bounces (**Figure 11.40**).

9. Rewind and play back the animation.

   The ball bounces four times.

If you want to speed or slow your animation, you can scale the time in the Graph Editor. A longer time for the same distance means slower movement, and vice versa.

You can also scale value. Perhaps all of your bounces are too high, or none of your arm swings extends far enough. Scaling the value is just as easy as scaling an object's size.

To scale in the Graph Editor:

1. Create a bouncing ball with four bounces, as in the previous section.

2. From the Window menu select Animation Editors > Graph Editor.

3. From the column on the left, select Translate Y. This isolates the Y translate curve.

4. Marquee-select the whole curve.

5. Press [r] to go into scale mode.

6. Move the mouse over the first keyframe on the left side of the curve (**Figure 11.41**).

   The mouse's location when you begin to scale serves as the scale's pivot point.

7. With the middle mouse button drag to the left.

8. Move the mouse over one of the low points of the bounces (**Figure 11.42**).

9. With the middle mouse button drag down. The bounces get shorter (**Figure 11.43**).

✔ Tip

■ You can also scale just a portion of a curve by selecting only those keyframes you want to scale. You can likewise scale multiple animated objects at the same time, which is often desirable so that their actions remain synchronized.

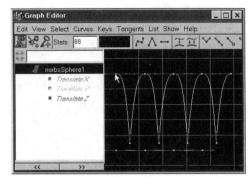

Figure 11.41 It is important to have the mouse at the correct position when you start to scale keyframes in the Graph Editor. Wherever you begin to scale is where the pivot point of the scale will be.

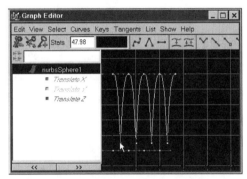

Figure 11.42 Here the time has been scaled down so that the ball bounces faster. The mouse has been carefully placed at the bottom of the bounce, so that position will be the pivot point of the scale.

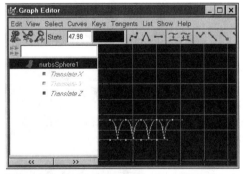

Figure 11.43 Now the value has been scaled down—that is, the bounces don't go as high as they did. Because the pivot point was at the bottom of the curve, the position at which it bounces hasn't changed—which means the ball will still appear to be bouncing on the ground, not above or below it.

Figure 11.44 The Dope Sheet is especially helpful when working on the timing of a large number of objects.

About the Dope Sheet

The Dope Sheet is another window used for editing keyframes. You can move, scale, cut, copy, paste, and delete in it, much as you can in the timeline and the Graph Editor. It has the advantage of being a simple, clear way to move the keyframes of multiple objects in time. For this reason, it's most helpful for adjusting the timing of many objects simultaneously (**Figure 11.44**).

Path Animation

It could be difficult to animate the flight of an airplane just by setting keyframes because of the amount of keyframes that would be required to simulate the detail of the rotation and direction of the plane. Sometimes you'll want to establish the path first and then simply send the object along that path. Maya can even make the object automatically bank around turns and point in the direction of the path.

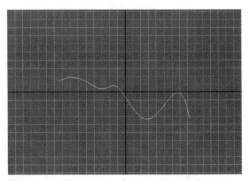

Figure 11.45 This curve is drawn in the Top view.

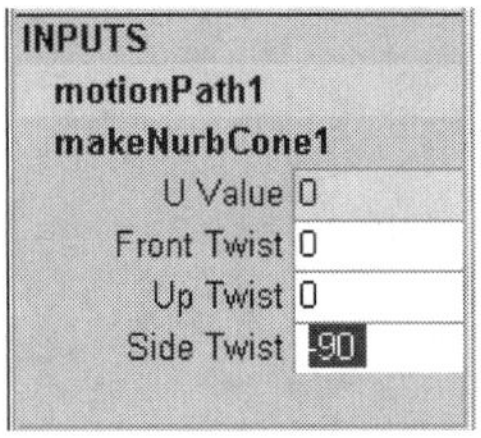

To animate along a path:

1. Create a curve in the Top view (**Figure 11.45**). (See Chapter 7 for more on creating curves.)

2. From the Create menu select NURBS Primitives > Cone.

3. Select the cone, then Shift-select the curve.

4. From the Animate menu select Motion Paths > Attach to Motion Path (Windows) or Paths > Attach to Paths (Mac).

   The cone jumps to the beginning of the curve, and when the animation is played back, it moves along the curve.

5. With the cone still selected, click motionPath1 in the Channel Box.

6. Enter *–90* in the Side Twist field so that the cone points down the path (**Figure 11.46**).

   When the animation is played back now, you can see how the rotation of the cone follows the path (**Figure 11.47**).

Figure 11.46 The different twists are needed to orient the cone. You cannot simply rotate the cone because its rotate attributes are controlled by the path animation.

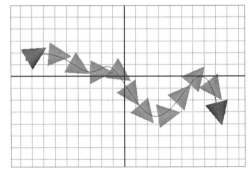

Figure 11.47 This is the resulting path animation.

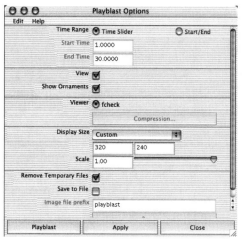

Figure 11.48 The Playblast options are set in this window. If you don't click Save to File and you close your movie player after you watch your animation, you will have to repeat the Playblast procedure on the animation.

Previewing Your Animation

When you want to preview an animation, you can play it back in the timeline. However, a complex scene won't play smoothly at full speed. In addition, you'll often want to output your animations. For this, Maya provides Playblast, which produces screen snapshots of your animation and turns it into an AVI or a series of numbered images.

To make a Playblast:

1. Create an animation.

2. From the Windows menu, select the box next to Playblast to open the Playblast Options window (**Figure 11.48**).

3. Choose the time range you want to make a movie file of.

   The Time slider will use your current playback start and end times. Start/End will allow you to type in your own times.

4. Adjust the resolution for the movie.

   If Display Size is set to From Window, it will use whichever view panel is currently active as the basis for the size. If you change it to Custom, you can type in whatever resolution you want.

5. Check Save to File if you want Playblast to automatically save your series of numbered frames after you create it.

   If Save to File is checked, you can click Browse to choose where you want the files to be saved. On Windows you can make a Movieplayer file instead of a series of numbered frames.

6. Click the Playblast button.

   You will see your animation play back a frame at a time. A moment later the FCheck window, with which you can watch your animation, will pop up.

12

DEFORMERS

Wrinkles, waves, and folds are just a few of the things you can create using Maya's deformer tools and a few simple mouse clicks. You can use these versatile tools to manipulate surfaces with the greatest of precision, as well as to simplify the selection and transformation of complex surfaces. Whether you're creating a twisted logo or a water droplet in a glass, you can find a deformer that fits the bill and makes the task a breeze.

Say, for example, you wanted to create a model of an elderly person: You could use the Wire deformer to create the fine folds and wrinkles of the face, and the Sculpt deformer for the areas of the face that you want to be more rounded.

Deformers can also speed modeling tasks by creating a simplified cage (called a *lattice*) around a complex surface. You use this lattice to select and manipulate the surface with a minimal amount of points—as opposed to selecting all of the fine detail on the surface of a model. You can use a lattice to create the point of an elbow or add emotion to a cartoon character's eye. The following describes Maya's deformers and how to use them.

Nonlinear Deformers

You can use nonlinear deformers to quickly bend, twist, flare, or even squash a surface, greatly speeding tasks that would otherwise require multiple CV selections, rotations, scales, and transformations. Create a spiral staircase out of a cube with the Twist deformer. Bend a steel spoon with ease using a Bend deformer, or create bell-bottom pants using the Flare deformer. Each of the nonlinear deformers performs a specific task related directly to its name. Nonlinear deformers include Bend, Flare, Sine, Squash, Twist, and Wave (**Figure 12.1**).

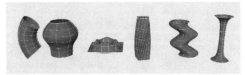

Figure 12.1 The nonlinear deformers (from left): Bend, Flare, Wave, Twist, Sine, and Squash.

The two most common options for the non-linear deformer tools include the following:

◆ **Envelope**—You use this option to specify the scale factor of the deformation. You can *select* values from 0 to 1, and you can *enter* values from -2 to 2. A value of 2 doubles the overall deformation effect; a negative value inverts the effect. The default value is 1.

◆ **Low and High Bound (all nonlinear deformers except Wave)**—Adjust the Low and High Bound when you want part of the surface to remain unaffected by the deformer.

In addition, each of the nonlinear deformer tools has its own distinct options, discussed in the sections that follow.

Figure 12.2 From the Deform menu select Create Nonlinear > Bend.

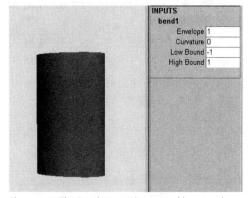

Figure 12.3 The Bend properties control how much an object is deformed.

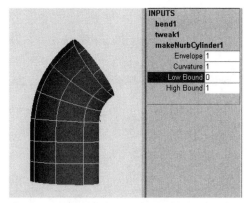

Figure 12.4 Adjusting the curvature adds bend to the object, adjusting the Low Bound controls the start point of the Bend from the bottom of the object. With a Low Bound of 0, half of the cylinder remains undeformed (shown), with a Low Bound of −1, the entire lower half is deformed.

Bend deformer

The Bend deformer can be a great time saver when you need to bend geometry but don't want to take the time to move each CV individually. Once a Bend deformer is added to a surface, the user can control the amount of surface arc, thus making the surface appear to bend. The more isoparms (the lines that define the NURBS geometry) that you add to a surface before adding the Bend deformer, the smoother the arc will appear.

An additional option for the Bend deformer is Curvature, which determines the amount the object bends.

To use the Bend deformer:

1. Select the object to be deformed.

2. From the Deform menu select Create Nonlinear > Bend (**Figure 12.2**).

   The Bend deformer is added to the selected surface.

3. Click the Bend(n) title under the INPUTS section of the Channel Box to view the Bend properties (**Figure 12.3**).

4. Set Curvature to *1*.

   The object is now bent around its center.

5. Set Low Bound to *0*.

   The object's bend still starts at its center, but only the top of the object is bent (**Figure 12.4**).

✔ Tip

- You can translate or rotate deformers through the objects to get different effects.

Flare deformer

You can attach this deformer to a surface to taper or flare selected geometry—useful on surfaces like jugs, bellies, and bell-bottoms.

Additional options for the Flare deformer include the following:

- **Start Flare X and Z**—Determines the amount of flare at the start of the Low Bound along the specified axis.

- **End Flare X and Z**—Determines the amount of flare at the start of the High Bound along the specified axis.

- **Curve**—Determines the amount of curvature between the Low and High Bound.

To use the Flare deformer:

1. Select the object to be deformed.

2. From the Deform menu select Create Nonlinear > Flare.

   A Flare deformer is added to the selected surface (**Figure 12.5**).

3. Click the Flare(n) title under the INPUTS section of the Channel Box to view the Flare properties.

4. Click Start Flare X (**Figure 12.6**).

5. Click and drag with the middle mouse button in the Perspective view to flare the base of the object until Start Flare equals 3.

   The object is flared along the *x* axis (**Figure 12.7**).

✔ Tip

- Have your surface geometry ready with the desired amount of CVs and isoparms before adding a deformer to a surface. Adding geometry after a deformer is applied may cause undesirable results, such as the surface ignoring the deformer or over-emphasizing the deformation.

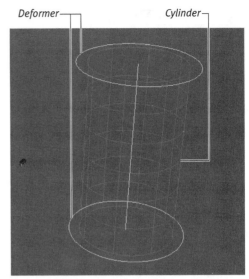

Figure 12.5 When a nonlinear deformer is added to a surface (Flare is shown here), a special manipulator is created to control the look of the deformation. The original cylinder is gray, the deformer is white.

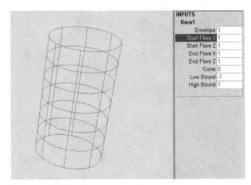

Figure 12.6 The Flare parameters.

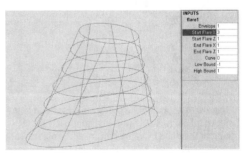

Figure 12.7 The object becomes stretched by the Flare deformer.

Figure 12.8 Select Sine to add the deformer to the geometry.

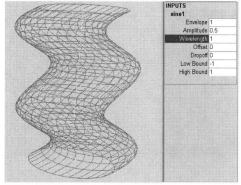

Figure 12.9 The Sine deformer causes the object to appear wavy.

Sine deformer

The Sine deformer changes the shape of an object along a specified sine wave, which is a scribble-like line that looks similar to the way a heart monitor line displays a normal heart beat.

Added Sine options include:

◆ **Amplitude**—Determines the maximum wave amount.

◆ **Wavelength**—Decreasing Wavelength greatens the frequency; increasing it lessens the frequency.

◆ **Offset**—Determines the location of the sine wave relative to the center of the deformer handle.

◆ **Dropoff**—Determines how the amplitude of the sine wave decays. Negative values decay toward the center of the deformer handle; positive values decay away from the center of the deformer handle.

To use the Sine deformer:

1. Select the object to be deformed.

2. From the Deform menu select Create Nonlinear > Sine (**Figure 12.8**).
   A Sine deformer is added to the selected surface.

3. Click the Sine(n) title under the INPUTS section of the Channel Box to view the sine properties.

4. Click on Amplitude.

5. Click and drag with the middle mouse button in the Perspective view until Amplitude equals 0.5.
   The surface begins to have a wavy shape.

6. Click Wavelength.

7. To add more curve to the object's shape, click and drag with the middle mouse button in the Perspective view until Wavelength equals 1 (**Figure 12.9**).

Wave deformer

The Wave deformer is perfect for creating water-droplet rings and small waves over a surface. This deformer works best on highly detailed flat surfaces.

Additional Wave options include:

◆ **Amplitude**—Determines the maximum wave amount.

◆ **Wavelength**—Decreasing Wavelength greatens the frequency; increasing it lessens the frequency.

◆ **Offset**—Determines the location of the sine wave relative to the center of the deformer handle. Animating the Offset will make the surface ripple outward.

◆ **Dropoff**—Determines how the amplitude of the sine wave decays. Negative values decay towards the center of the deformer handle; positive values decay away from the center of the deformer handle.

◆ **Dropoff Position**—Determines the start and end position of the amplitude of the sine wave.

◆ **Min and Max Radius**—Determines the minimum and maximum radius of the circular sine wave.

To use the Wave deformer:

1. Create a Primitive NURBS plane.

2. In the Channel Box change its patches U and patches V to *10*.

3. From the Deform menu select Create Nonlinear > Wave.
   A Wave deformer is added to the selected surface (**Figure 12.10**).

4. Click the Wave(n) title under the INPUTS section of the Channel Box to view Wave properties.

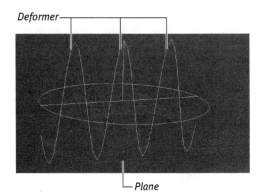

Deformer

Plane

Figure 12.10 The Wave manipulator controls the Wave deformer's parameters. Deformer is white, plane is gray.

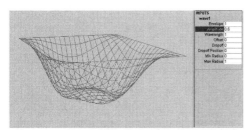

Figure 12.11 The Amplitude setting determines the maximum wave amount.

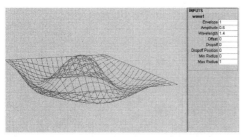

Figures 12.12 By increasing Wavelength to 1.4, we decrease wave frequency.

5. Set Amplitude to *0.6*.

The object becomes wavy (**Figure 12.11**).

6. Set Wavelength to *1.4*.

Fewer waves now define the object's shape (**Figure 12.12**).

The Squash deformer

The Squash deformer gives the user precise control over a surface's volume when it's being squashed. If you scale a surface vertically along one axis without scaling the other axes horizontally, you create a surface with less physical volume, breaking the illusion of real objects, which keep the same volume when they are squashed. If you want your objects to appear realistic, it's important to keep the volume of the object the same when adding squash and stretch.

Additional Squash options include the following:

◆ **Factor**—Determines the amount an object can be squashed or stretched.

◆ **Expand**—Determines how much an object will expand (in volume) outward while squashing, or inward while stretching.

◆ **Start and End Smoothness**—Determines the amount of smoothing (similar to Dropoff) near the low-bound position (Start Smoothness), or near the high-bound (End Smoothness). In a cylinder the high-bound and low-bound position would be the top and bottom of the cylinder, respectively. So if Start Smoothness is altered, the point at the bottom of the cylinder will have a smoother transition into the squash.

To use the Squash deformer:

1. Create a NURBS primitive cylinder to be deformed.

2. From the Deform menu select Create Nonlinear > Squash (**Figure 12.13**).

   A Squash deformer is added to the selected surface.

3. Click the Squash(n) title under the INPUTS section of the Channel Box to view the Squash properties.

4. Set Factor to *-0.7*.

   The object is squashed vertically (**Figure 12.14**).

5. Set Expand to *1.7*.

   The object expands to add volume to the shape (**Figure 12.15**).

✔ Tip

■ The Squash deformer can be keyframed to squash and stretch an object or character.

Figure 12.13 Create Non-Linear > Squash on the Deform menu.

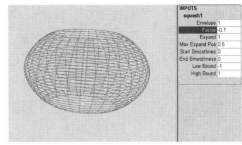

Figure 12.14 A negative Factor setting squashes the object; a positive Factor setting stretches it.

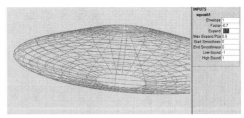

Figure 12.15 If you squash an object, you should expand it to make sure it retains its volume.

NONLINEAR DEFORMERS

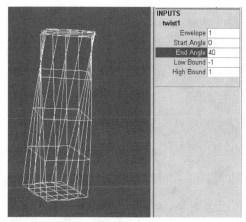

Figure 12.16 Adjusting End Angle twists the surface's shape.

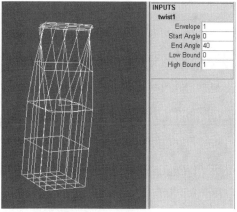

Figure 12.17 Adjusting Low Bound to *0* forces the twisting to begin halfway up the deformed surface.

Twist deformer

The Twist Deformer is often used to twist a cube into a cartoon-style building or to quickly create a twisted metal sculpture. The higher the density of the geometry, the smoother the twist will appear.

The Twist deformer includes one option, the Start and End Angle, which determines the degree of twisting from the Low or High Bound position.

To use the Twist deformer:

1. Create a Primitive Polygonal Cube.

2. From the Deform menu select Create Nonlinear > Twist.

   A Twist deformer is added to the selected surface.

3. Click the Twist(n) title under the INPUTS section of the Channel Box to view the Twist properties.

4. Set End Angle to *40*.

   The entire object twists around the center of the deformer (**Figure 12.16**).

5. Set Low Bound to *0*.

   The twist now starts halfway up the object (**Figure 12.17**).

NONLINEAR DEFORMERS

The Lattice

The Lattice is one of Maya's most-used, and most functional, deformers. You can use it to simplify CV selection on a complex surface, to create the point of a character's elbow, or to provide added control to surface areas prone to creasing (for example, elbows and knees).

Lattice deformers surround deformable objects with a boxlike shape called a *lattice* (**Figure 12.18**). The lattice is then used to select and deform the surface by moving, rotating, or scaling the lattice structure (**Figure 12.19**). Lattices are also deformable objects, which means you can add other deformers to deform the lattice (and the object it's deforming).

An important option of the Lattice deformer is Divisions, found under the Lattice's SHAPE node in the Channel Box; A Lattice is one of the few Maya objects that have options under its SHAPE node. Adding more divisions to a lattice indirectly adds more lattice points for future selection. A lattice point is created at every lattice crossing.

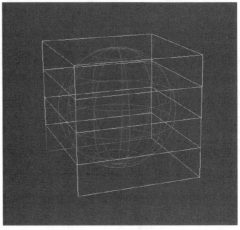

Figure 12.18 A Lattice applied to a primitive NURBS sphere.

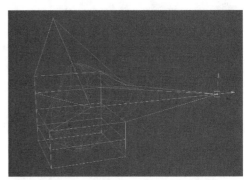

Figure 12.19 By moving Lattice points you deform the surface.

Figure 12.20 Select Create Lattice to apply a lattice to the surface.

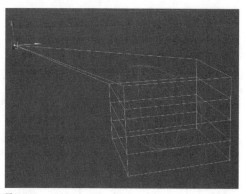

Figure 12.21 Set the Pick Mask selection type to "Select by component type" to show the lattice points.

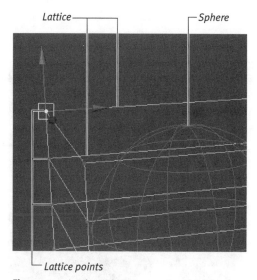

Lattice — Sphere

Lattice points

Figure 12.22 Lattice points appear at each of the lattice cross-sections.

To use a Lattice to deform a surface:

1. Create a NURBS primitive sphere.

2. From the Deform menu select Create Lattice (**Figure 12.20**).

   A Lattice deformer is added to the selected surface.

3. Set the Pick Mask selection type to "Select by component type" (**Figure 12.21**).

   Lattice points appear on the corners of the lattice.

4. Select a corner lattice point (**Figure 12.22**).

5. Move the lattice point away from the surface (**Figure 12.23**).

   The original surface is now deformed by the change in the lattice shape.

Figure 12.23 Moving one lattice point moves multiple CVs on the surface.

THE LATTICE

273

Wire and Sculpt Deformers

The Wire and Sculpt deformers use objects and curves to manipulate and deform a selected surface.

Wire deformers use one or more NURBS curves, called *wires,* to deform the selected surface (**Figure 12.24**). You can use additional curves, called *holders*, to limit the influence of the Wire deformer. This gives you the precise control you need to create subtle surface deformations.

Sculpt deformers use a spherical influence object (a deform manipulator that is shaped like a sphere), called a *sculpt sphere,* to deform a surface (**Figure 12.25**). Sculpt deformers are great for creating rounded surface effects like the tip of a nose or chin. Switching the deformer's mode between flip, project, and stretch can produce different surface effects.

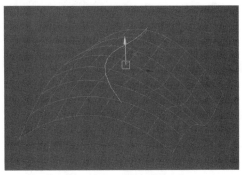

Figure 12.24 One wire is used here to deform a flat plane.

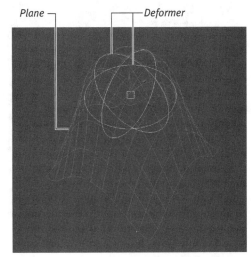

Figure 12.25 A flat plane is deformed by the Sculpt deformer's influence. Deformer is white, plane is gray.

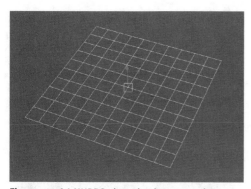

Figure 12.26 A NURBS plane that has 10 patches added in the U and V directions. The more patches you add to a surface, the smoother the deformation will be.

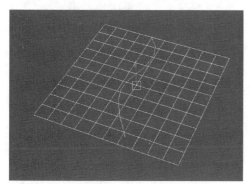

Figure 12.27 Although the wire doesn't need to overlap the deformed surface, it helps clarify the area to be deformed.

Figure 12.28 Select Wire Tool to select the surface to be deformed and the deforming wire.

To create a Wire deformer without a holder:

1. Create a NURBS plane and, in the Channel Box options, set its patches U and patches V to *10* (**Figure 12.26**).

2. Create a NURBS curve that overlaps the plane (**Figure 12.27**).

   This curve will be used as the influence wire (a deform manipulator shaped like a wire; a curve is used for our wire shape).

3. From the Deform menu, select Wire Tool (**Figure 12.28**).

4. Select the plane and press Enter.

5. Select the CV curve and press Enter.

6. Move the CV curve along the *y* axis.

   The plane deforms along the contour of the CV curve (**Figure 12.29**).

✔ Tips

- The curve's CVs can be manipulated along any axis to further control the deformation of the surface.

- If you want the curve to affect less surface area, lower the value of the Dropoff Distance.

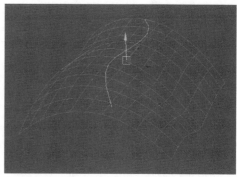

Figure 12.29 The shape of the curve is reflected in the way the surface becomes deformed.

To create a Wire deformer *with* a holder:

1. Create a NURBS primitive plane and, in the options, set its U and V patches to *10* each.

2. Create a NURBS curve that overlaps the plane.

   This curve will be used as the influence wire.

3. Create a NURBS circle that overlaps the plane (**Figure 12.30**).

   The circle will be our holder.

4. From the Deform menu, select the Wire Tool options box.

5. Check Holders to turn it on (**Figure 12.31**).

6. Click Close.

7. Select the plane and press Enter.

8. Select the CV curve and press Enter.

9. Select the NURBS circle and press Enter.

10. Move the CV curve along the *y* axis.

    The plane deforms along the contour of the CV curve but not past the circle object (**Figure 12.32**).

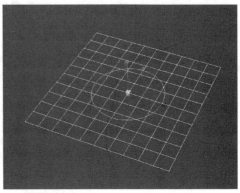

Figure 12.30 Scale the circle until it overlaps most of the plane.

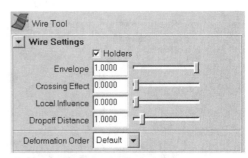

Figure 12.31 If Holders is checked, you can use an additional curve to stop the Wire deformer's influence.

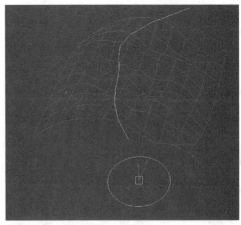

Figure 12.32 The plane deforms along the contour of the CV curve but not past the circle object.

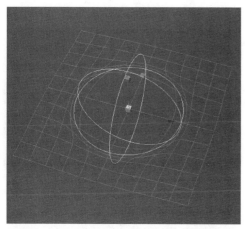

Figure 12.33 The Sculpt deformer pushes the surface geometry around its spherical shape, deforming the plane much like the way mud would look if a heavy ball was dropped onto it.

Figure 12.34 The surface wraps around the Sculpt deformer's influence sphere.

To create a Sculpt deformer:

1. Create a NURBS plane, and in the Channel Box options set its U and V patches to *10*.

2. Set the X, Y, and Z scale to *5*.
   Scaling the plane ensures the deformer will not be larger than the plane.

3. From the Deform menu select Sculpt.
   A Sculpt object is applied to the object (**Figure 12.33**).

4. Select the Sculpt object and move it in the positive *y* direction.
   The Sculpt object causes the original geometry to expand (**Figure 12.34**).

✔ Tip

- You can select and move the locator (crosshairs) to move the geometry over the Sculpt object.

WIRE AND SCULPT DEFORMERS

Hiding, Showing, and Deleting Deformers

To delete a deformer:

1. Select the deformer handle of the deformer you wish to delete (**Figure 12.35**).

2. Select Edit > Delete, or press Backspace.

To delete a deformer but keep the deformations on the surface:

1. Select the object with the deformer you wish to delete (Figure 12.35).

2. Select Edit > Delete by Type > History. The deformer is deleted but the object is locked into its deformed state.

To show all deformers:

◆ From the Display menu select Show > Show Deformers > All (**Figure 12.36**).

To hide all deformers:

◆ From the Display menu select Hide > Hide Deformers > All (**Figure 12.37**).

✔ Tip

■ In addition to showing all of the deformers, you can individually show many object types such as lattices, sculpt objects, cluster handles, and nonlinear deformer handles.

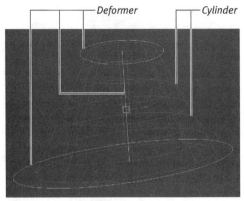

Figure 12.35 The Taper deformer handle connected to a cylinder is selected.

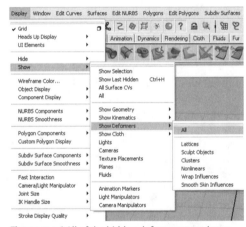

Figure 12.36 All of the hidden deformers are shown.

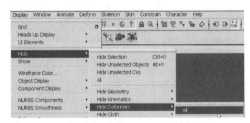

Figure 12.37 All of the deformers are hidden.

HIDING, SHOWING, AND DELETING DEFORMERS

13

CREATING LIGHTS

Figure 13.1 Adding an area of focus strengthens the scene.

Figure 13.2 An object can be accented through the correct use of light.

Light and shadow are essential in creating a three-dimensional, realistic scene. Lighting is a crucial element in setting the mood and feeling of a scene. Too much light can flatten out a scene, leaving the viewer unengaged and uninterested in the imagery. However, the right light intensity and placement can draw the eye around the scene. You can use lights to focus a viewer's attention on a particular place in your scene (**Figure 13.1**) or on an object you don't want the viewer to miss (**Figure 13.2**). Light can be used to draw spectators into the scene, as if they were participants, or to leave them feeling like onlookers, outside the action.

For centuries, artists have used chiaroscuro—the play of light and dark—to invoke emotions and to draw viewers into their paintings. Leonardo da Vinci; Gerrit Van Honthorst; and the master of painting with light, Caravaggio, all experimented with light in their paintings. More recently, we've seen filmmakers use similar techniques in their movies. *Blade Runner, The Godfather,* and *Poltergeist* are all great examples: As these movies unfold, their action is supported with lighting through various colors, intensity, and placement.

Controlling light, however, can be tricky and time-consuming. In this chapter we'll look at some of the attributes and techniques used to control lights in a Maya scene.

Setting the Scene's Mood

One of the first things to consider in lighting your scene is the time of day. A good exercise to demonstrate how much difference lighting can make is to create and light the same scene in three or four different lighting scenarios. You can set up one scene to have a scary and luminous quality (**Figure 13.3**), and then relight the scene for a bright summer day (**Figure 13.4**). You will quickly see how essential lighting is to a well-produced scene.

The following describes the various qualities of light found at different times of the day (from an artistic point of view):

Dawn—Most of the sky is filled with a light glow, soft and diffused, leaving objects in the room dimly lit. Highlights and reflections become visible first, then everything else slowly comes into view. Dawn has a very subtle light, requiring some time for the human eye to adjust.

Sunrise—Light pours into the room as a new day begins. Long shadows and light patterns are projected on the wall through the window, splashing light around the room. As the sunrise progresses, the day's shadows become more transparent and shorter, leading into the sharp midday sun.

Sunset—Orange, red, and pink sunset colors fill the clouds and the sky, bringing a feeling of tranquility and closure to the day. Mountains and trees are silhouetted against the sun at the horizon, and long shadows lay along the ground.

Evening—Peaceful silvery-blue light fills the room, illuminating it softly. The room is lit with candles and ceiling lights that quickly fall off into the darkness. The only light coming in from outside is the moon glowing through the haze around it, creating ominous bluish highlights throughout the scene.

Figure 13.3 You can use light to create specific moods—for example, ominous and scary, as shown here.

Figure 13.4 Light can be used to brighten an entire scene.

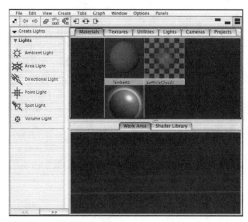

Figure 13.5 The Hypershade.

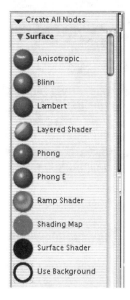

Figure 13.6
The Create bar.

About the Hypershade

The Hypershade is a window where you can create, delete, view, and enhance lights as well as materials, textures, and utilities (**Figure 13.5**).

To open the Hypershade:

◆ Select Panel > Panels > Hypershade.

   or

◆ Click the Hypershade/Persp button right below the toolbar at the left of the layout.

   or

◆ Select Window > Rendering Editors > Hypershade.

When you first open the Hypershade, you'll see a panel on its left side called the Create bar (**Figure 13.6**). This is where the different texture- and light-related nodes are housed. You can create a new node by using the middle mouse button to drag the icon into the work area to the right of the Create bar.

continues on next page

ABOUT THE HYPERSHADE

You can isolate the node types you want to create by clicking Create Textures at the top of the Create bar, and selecting the node type you want to create from the menu. For example, you can select Create Lights to have the Create bar show only the light types (**Figure 13.7**).

The rest of the Hypershade provides tabs for viewing already-created node types: Materials, Textures, Utilities, Lights, Cameras, and Projects. Any created node will be visible under its respective tab or drop-down menu. For instance, if you create a directional light and a point light in your scene, you can view them both by clicking the Lights tab in the Hypershade (**Figure 13.8**).

Under the pane containing the node-type tabs is a pane containing the Work Area and Shader Library tabs. In the Work Area panel you can connect attributes, view all of the connections, and isolate a light or texture for fine-tuning. The Shader Library tab holds all of the pre-made, ready-to-use shaders, including ones for buildings, food, glass, and other common objects. These shaders often provide a good starting point for creating new shaders.

In this chapter we'll explore the lighting section of the Hypershade and Create bar.

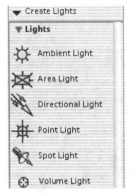

Figure 13.7 The Create bar with Create Lights selected.

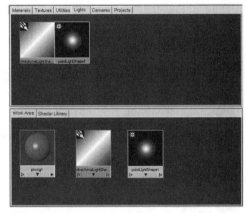

Figure 13.8 The Lights panel shows the two lights created and the work area below them.

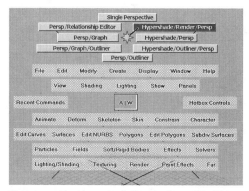

Figure 13.9 The Hypershade/Render/persp Marking Menu.

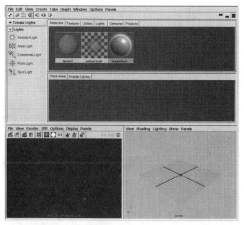

Figure 13.10 The Hypershade on top, the Render View pane on the bottom left, and the Perspective pane on the bottom right.

Setting Up for a Render

Maya provides many ways to create the same result. In this section we'll go over some different setups for streamlining your workflow.

Three essential windows are used to create a final render: the Hypershade, the Render View, and a camera view (front, top, side, perspective, or a camera you create). One way to streamline the render's setup is to use Hypershade/Render/Persp in the Marking Menu in the north region of the Hotbox (**Figure 13.9**). This sets the Layout window to three panes. The top will become a Hypershade; the bottom-left pane will become a Render View; and the bottom-right pane will become a Perspective view (**Figure 13.10**). This is a good way to set up a scene for a render because you can tap the (Spacebar) to enlarge any of the panes, temporarily hiding the other two.

continues on next page

Another way to set up a render is to open each window separately as needed. To open the Hypershade or Render View in its own window, select the window you want in the Window > Rendering Editors menu (**Figure 13.11**). This opens a new window with the view inside it (**Figure 13.12**).

Since most of the light attributes can be edited in the Attribute Editor, you may want to temporarily change the Channel Box (on the right side of the Maya window) to an Attribute Editor (**Figure 13.13**). You do this by clicking in the east region of the Hotbox and selecting Attributes > Attribute Editor or clicking the icon 📐 in the upper-right corner of the Maya window. The Render View holds many of the tools needed to produce an effective render. We'll touch on the Render View throughout this chapter; for a more complete discussion of it, see Chapter 15.

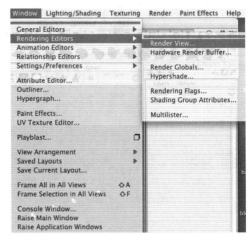

Figure 13.11 The Window > Rendering Editors menu.

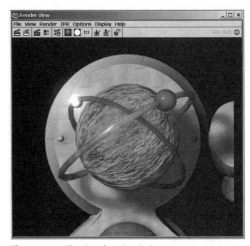

Figure 13.12 The Render View in its own pop-up window.

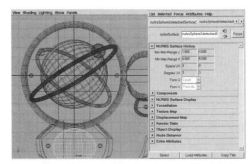

Figure 13.13 The Attribute Editor is docked beside the front view, replacing the Channel Box.

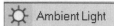

Figure 13.14 The Ambient Light icon.

Figure 13.15 The Area Light icon.

Figure 13.16 The Directional Light icon.

About Lights

There are six light types in Maya: *ambient, area, directional, point, spot,* and *volume.* You can combine these light types to produce just about any lighting scenario. A Maya scene may use one or all of the above light types, depending on the mood and art direction of the scene.

The following describes the different light types and some of their common uses:

Ambient—Produces a uniform light throughout the scene. You should keep this type of light to a minimum, because the more you use it, the flatter and more devoid of contrast the scene will appear (**Figure 13.14**).

Examples of ambient light include the following:

◆ Light that allows you to see in a room or closet without having an actual light on

◆ Light that doesn't originate from an obvious source

Area—Two-dimensional, rectangular light source that emits light from the entire rectangle in the direction of the line perpendicular to the rectangle (see Chapter 8 for more information) (**Figure 13.15**).

Examples of area light include the following:

◆ Illuminated ceiling panels

◆ Rectangular light reflections on walls

Directional—Parallel light rays that wash light across the scene in a specific direction (**Figure 13.16**).

Examples of directional light include sunlight and moonlight.

continues on next page

Point—Radiates light out from its center in all directions. The farther an object is from this light, the less it is illuminated (**Figure 13.17**).

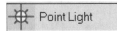

Figure 13.17 The Point Light icon.

Examples of point light include:

♦ Light bulbs

♦ LEDs

♦ Torches

Figure 13.18 The Spotlight icon.

Spot—Lights an area within a cone shape. The light comes from the center point and travels in a specified direction (**Figure 13.18**).

Examples of spotlight include:

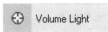

Figure 13.19 The Volume Light icon.

♦ Flashlights

♦ Street lamps

♦ Headlights

♦ Spotlights

Figure 13.20 Common light attributes: type, color, intensity, and decay rate.

Volume—Lights an area within a user-defined volume (**Figure 13.19**).

Examples of volume light include light around a lit candle or torch.

Light types have the following common attributes (**Figure 13.20**):

Type—Sets the kind of light: ambient, area, directional, point, spot, or volume. You can change this attribute at any time—for example, from a point to a spot.

Color—Sets the foundation color of the light. Image maps may be added to vary the color of the light.

ABOUT LIGHTS

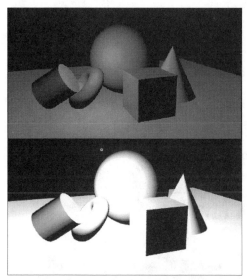

Figure 13.21 The top scene is lit with a light at low intensity; the bottom scene is lit with the same light at a high-intensity setting.

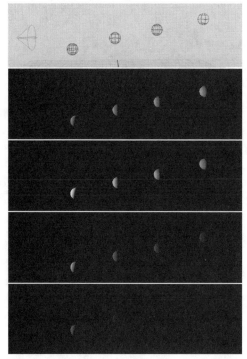

Figure 13.22 Decay rates top to bottom: wireframe, no decay, linear, quadratic, and cubic.

Intensity—Sets the brightness and darkness of the light. For best results, start low and work your way up (**Figure 13.21**).

Decay Rate—Controls how quickly the light's intensity decreases over distance. When you change this setting, you must also raise or lower the intensity of the light to make up for the decay-rate change. This is not an attribute of the ambient or directional lights (**Figure 13.22**).

◆ *No Decay*—Light will have the same intensity regardless of distance.

◆ *Linear Decay*—The light's intensity diminishes with distance less abruptly than with Quadratic and Cubic decay.

◆ *Quadratic Decay*—The light's intensity diminishes at a rate between Linear and Cubic decay. This setting is closest to real-world light decay.

◆ *Cubic Decay*—The light's intensity diminishes most abruptly, substantially more abruptly than with Linear and Quadratic decay.

Ambient light

Ambient light is light that is still present even when you turn the lights out; it's the light your eyes see once they adjust to the darkness, without an obvious light source. Using ambient light gives you a quick way to see how things render without having to set up a bunch of lights. In general, however, you should use ambient light sparingly because it can quickly flatten out a scene.

First, let's create a practice scene.

To create a practice scene:

1. Choose File > New Scene to create a new scene to work on.

2. Create five or six primitives in the scene, and move them around randomly, with the bottom of each sitting on the grid (**Figure 13.23**).

3. From the Create menu select NURBS Primitive > Plane to create a plane at the origin.

4. Scale the plane larger than the objects in your scene (**Figure 13.24**).

5. Save the practice scene as a file called practice.mb.

To create an ambient light:

1. Open the practice.mb file.

2. Choose Create > Lights, and in the submenu select the box next to Ambient Light (**Figure 13.25**).

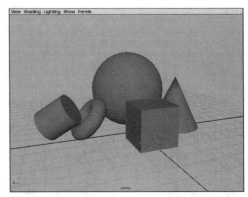

Figure 13.23 Create five or six primitives in the scene, and place them randomly.

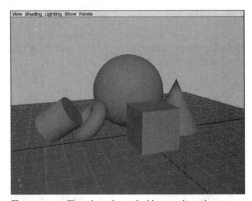

Figure 13.24 The plane is scaled larger than the objects in the scene.

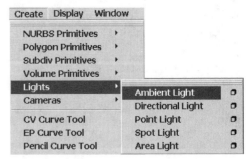

Figure 13.25 Select the box next to Ambient Light.

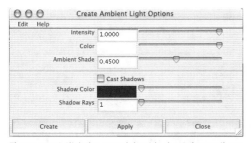

Figure 13.26 Click the swatch beside the Color attribute.

Figure 13.27 Select a color from the color wheel, which in Maya looks more like a color block.

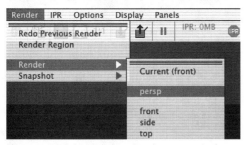

Figure 13.28 Select Render > Render > persp in the Render View to render the scene.

3. In the Options dialog box that opens, click the swatch beside the Color attribute (**Figure 13.26**).

The color wheel opens when you click the swatch.

4. Click in the color wheel to select a color for the light (**Figure 13.27**).

5. Click Apply to lock in the color.

6. Click Create to make the ambient light.

The ambient light is placed at the origin of the scene.

7. In the Hotbox's north-region Marking Menu, select Hypershade/Render/persp to split your window layout into these three panes.

8. In the Render View pane, select Render > Render > persp to render the Perspective view (**Figure 13.28**).

✔ Tip

■ Don't use more than one ambient light per scene unless absolutely necessary. Ambient light can quickly flatten the 3D effect of a scene.

ABOUT LIGHTS

The Ambient Shade attribute affects the direction of the light source. If Ambient Shade is set to 0, light comes from all directions (**Figure 13.29**). If it's set to 1, light comes from the source itself, acting similarly to a point light (**Figure 13.30**). You must be careful when adjusting this attribute because the lower the number, the flatter the image will appear.

To change an ambient light's Ambient Shade attribute:

1. With an ambient light selected, open the Attribute Editor by selecting Window > Attribute Editor, or pressing Ctrl a / Control a.

2. Set the Ambient Shade attribute to *0* (**Figure 13.31**).

   The 0 value sends light evenly over the entire scene.

3. In the Render View pane, select Render > Render > persp to render the Perspective view.

   Because the Ambient Shade attribute is set to 0, the objects in the scene blend together, creating a very flat image, as in Figure 13.29.

4. With the light still selected, go to the Attribute Editor and change the Ambient Shade attribute to *.7*.

   The .7 value makes the ambient light act similarly to a point light, so that its intensity fades slightly as the distance from the light source increases.

5. Click the Redo Previous Render icon in the Render View.

   Because the Ambient Shade value is higher, the scene appears to have more depth, similar to Figure 13.30.

6. In the Attribute Editor set Intensity to *.25* (**Figure 13.32**).

Figure 13.29 The Ambient Shade attribute is set to *0*, flattening the scene.

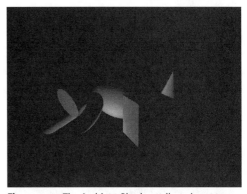

Figure 13.30 The Ambient Shade attribute is set to *1*, making the light similar to a point light.

Figure 13.31 Set the Ambient Shade attribute to *0*.

Figure 13.32 Set the intensity to *.25*.

Figure 13.33 Select Area Light in the Create Lights section of the Create bar.

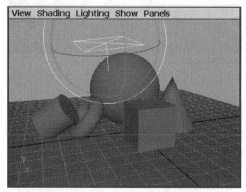

Figure 13.34 Point the surface normal at the area you want to light.

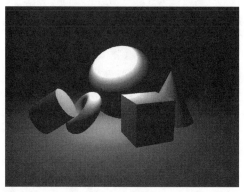

Figure 13.35 Select Render > Render > persp to render the Perspective view.

We use .25 here to bring down the intensity of the ambient light and keep the flattening of the scene to a minimum.

7. Click the Redo Previous Render icon in the Render View.

   The scene will be very dark.

Area lights

Area lights are best for situations that call for rectangular lighting—for example, florescent lighting. Another great use for an area light is to backlight a character. However, using area lights extensively in a scene can slow rendering.

To create an area light:

1. Open the practice.mb file.

2. In the Hypershade select Area Light in the Create Lights section of the Create bar (**Figure 13.33**).

3. Scale the light to the size you want the area light to be.

4. Move and rotate the light around the scene until the surface normal points at the object or area you want to light (**Figure 13.34**).

5. Select the light, and open the Attribute Editor.

6. Click the swatch beside the Color attribute.

7. Click in the color wheel to select a color for the light.

8. Click Accept to lock in the color.

9. Move the Intensity slider in the Attribute Editor to set the light's brightness.

10. Close the Attribute Editor.

11. From the Hotbox's north-region Marking Menu select Hypershade/Render/persp to split your panel layout into these three panes.

12. In the Render pane select Render > Render > persp to render the Perspective view (**Figure 13.35**).

Directional lights

Directional lights work great for representing sunlight and moonlight.

To create a directional light:

1. Open the practice file.

2. From the Create menu select Lights > Directional Light.

   A directional light is created at the origin of the scene. The default direction points down the z axis in the negative direction (**Figure 13.36**). The perpendicular light rays follow a horizontal direction by default (**Figure 13.37**).

3. Select the directional light by clicking it. Rotate the light around the axes until the arrows point in the direction you want the light to follow (**Figure 13.38**).

4. With the light still selected, choose a new intensity setting for the light in the Channel Box.

5. From the Window menu select Rendering Editors > Render View (**Figure 13.39**). The Render View opens in a new window.

6. In the Render window select Render > Render > persp to render the Perspective view.

✔ Tip

■ Translating a directional light has no effect on how it lights the scene; however, it could help you find or select that light later.

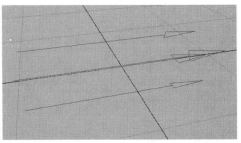

Figure 13.36 The default position of the directional light.

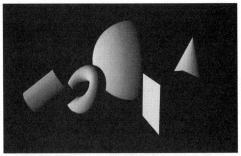

Figure 13.37 The perpendicular light rays of the directional light follow a horizontal direction by default.

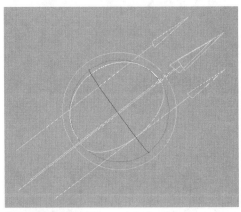

Figure 13.38 Point the arrows in the direction you want the light to follow.

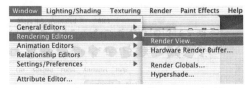

Figure 13.39 Select Rendering Editors > Render View to open the Render View in a new window.

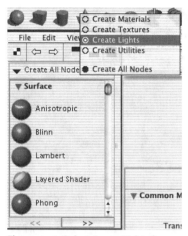

Figure 13.40 Select Create Lights from the pop-up menu in the Hypershade.

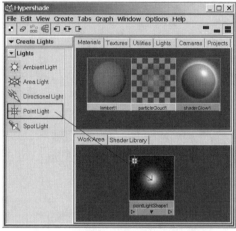

Figure 13.41 With the middle mouse button drag the Point Light icon to the Hypershade's Work Area panel.

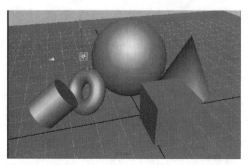

Figure 13.42 Move the light above the ground plane.

Point lights

Point lights are great for lamps and torches. They're also great for adding a little light to a dark corner, removing light from an overlit area, or faking reflected light on an object.

To create a point light:

1. Open the practice.mb file.

2. From the Create bar select Create Lights from the pop-up menu (**Figure 13.40**).

3. Using the middle mouse button, drag the Point Light icon from the Create Lights menu to the Work Area panel inside the Hypershade (**Figure 13.41**).

4. Double-click the Point Light icon in the Work Area to open the Attribute Editor.

5. Set the Color and Intensity attributes, then close the Attribute Editor.

6. Click the light to select it, and move it above the ground plane to keep it from being obstructed by the plane (**Figure 13.42**).

7. From the Hotbox's north-region Marking Menu select Hypershade/Render/persp to split your panel layout into these three panes.

continues on next page

8. In the Render pane select Render > Render > persp to render the Perspective view.

The Perspective view is rendered (**Figure 13.43**).

✔ Tip

■ Setting the intensity attribute to a negative number will subtract light from the area around it.

Spotlights

Spotlights are great for areas where you want to focus light. You can use them as stage or theater spotlights, headlights, or any cone-shaped light source.

To create a spotlight:

1. Open the practice.mb file.

2. Click the Spotlight icon  in the Rendering shelf to create a spotlight at the origin of the scene.

3. Set the Object Pick mask to select lights only, and swipe across the Spotlight icon at the origin to select it (**Figure 13.44**).

If the Object Pick mask is selected correctly, only the light will be selected.

4. Select the Show Manipulator Tool by pressing ⓣ or selecting its icon ▨ in the toolbar.

5. Pull up the *y* axis translation manipulator on the spotlight to raise it above the ground (**Figure 13.45**).

Notice when you're in the Show Manipulator tool that the end of the spotlight stays in its original position, forcing the light to point at it.

6. Select the center square of the end manipulator, and move it to the position where you would like the light to point (**Figure 13.46**).

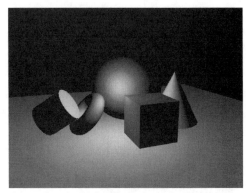

Figure 13.43 The final rendering in the Perspective view.

Figure 13.44 Set the Object Pick mask to select lights only.

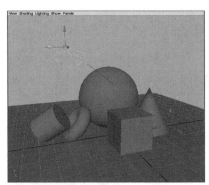

Figure 13.45 Pull up the *y*-axis translation manipulator on the spotlight to raise it above ground.

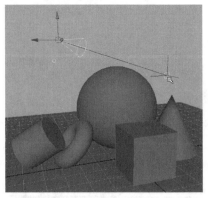

Figure 13.46 Move the end manipulator into a new position.

ABOUT LIGHTS

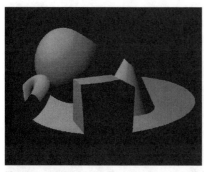

Figure 13.47 Select Render > Render > persp to render the Perspective view.

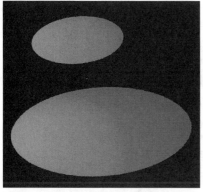

Figure 13.48 The default cone angle on top; the same light position but with a larger cone angle on the bottom.

7. From the Hotbox's north-region Marking Menu select Hypershade/Render/persp to split your panel layout into these three panes.

8. In the Render pane select Render > Render > persp to render the Perspective view (**Figure 13.47**).

A spotlight has a number of attributes that you can change. Below are definitions of some of these attributes.

Spotlight attributes

Cone Angle—The larger the number you input here, the wider the cone (and thus the illuminated area) will be (**Figure 13.48**).

Penumbra Angle—Adjusting the penumbra angle softens the edge of the spotlight by blurring it. A negative number blurs inside the edge of the cone; a positive number blurs outside the edge of the cone (**Figure 13.49**).

Dropoff—Adjusts the intensity of the light from its center out to its edge. Raising the value of this attribute results in a soft gradation from the center to the edge (**Figure 13.50**).

ABOUT LIGHTS

Figure 13.49 Adjusting the penumbra angle blurs the edge of the spotlight. The top light has a setting of 0; the bottom light has a setting of 7.

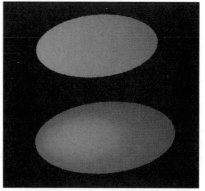

Figure 13.50 Dropoff adjusts the intensity of the light from its center out to its edge. The light at the top has a default setting of 0; the light at the bottom has a setting of 8.

Many light attributes can have an image added to them to affect the light in additional ways. An example would be adding an image into the color attribute of a light. This projects the image through the light—similar to having light filtered through a stained-glass window project a pattern onto the floor (**Figure 13.51**). This technique is also helpful for creating light shapes that aren't round.

Volume light

Volume lights are great for illuminating multiple objects that are placed in the same proximity to each other because you can illuminate all objects within the area of the volume lights icon.

To create a volume light:

1. Open the practice.mb file.

2. From the Create menu select Lights > Volume Light (**Figure 13.52**).

3. Scale the Volume Light icon until it surrounds the objects you want to illuminate (**Figure 13.53**).

4. From the Window menu select Attribute Editor.

   The Attribute Editor opens.

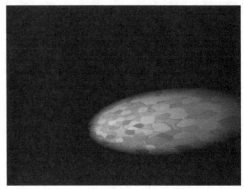

Figure 13.51 A light with an image mapped into it.

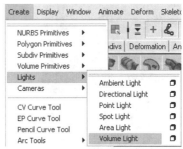

Figure 13.52 Select Lights > Volume Light from the Create menu to create a volume light at the scene's origin.

Figure 13.53 The Volume Light icon is similar to a sphere and should be placed around the objects you want to illuminate.

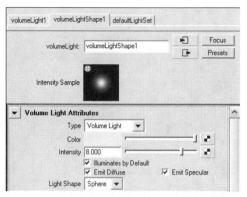

Figure 13.54 Set Color and Intensity to achieve the desired brightness and color for the scene.

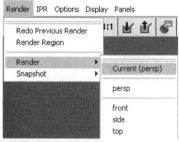

Figure 13.55 The Render drop-down menu allows you to select which view, or camera, you would like rendered.

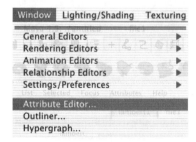

Figure 13.56 Select Window > Attribute Editor.

5. Set the Color and Intensity attributes, then close the Attribute Editor (**Figure 13.54**).

7. From the Hotbox's north-region Marking Menu select Hypershade/Render/persp to split your panel layout into these three panes.

8. In the Render pane select Render > Render > persp to render the Perspective view.

The Perspective view is rendered (**Figure 13.55**).

To add an image map to a light's Color attribute:

1. Click a spotlight to select it.

2. With the light selected, select Window > Attribute Editor (**Figure 13.56**).

3. In the Attribute Editor select the map icon next to the Color slider ▪ to open the Create Render Node panel.

continues on next page

4. In the Create Render Node panel, select File from the 2D Textures section (**Figure 13.57**).

5. In File Attributes select the File icon next to the Image Name attribute.

6. In the Open dialog box, browse to the folder containing the image you want to use, then select it and click Open.

7. From the Hotbox's north-region Marking Menu, select Hypershade/Render/persp to split your panel layout into these three panes.

8. In the Render View pane select Render > Render > persp to render the Perspective view.

The final image is rendered (**Figure 13.58**).

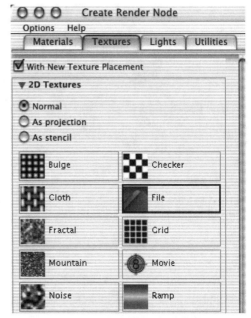

Figure 13.57 From the Create Render Node panel, select Textures, and in the 2D Textures section, select File.

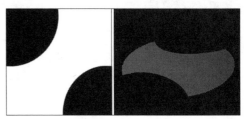

Figure 13.58 The image used is on the left, and the final render of light with the image mapped into it is on the right.

ABOUT LIGHTS

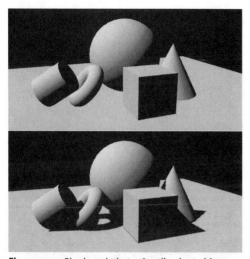

Figure 13.59 Shadows help to visually plant objects on the ground.

Figure 13.60 A real shadow's darkest area is slightly away from the object's edge, near the base of the shadow.

About Shadows

Shadows are an important scene element because they visually plant objects on the ground, as well as make it easier for us to tell how far apart objects are spaced (**Figure 13.59**). Shadows add realism that would often be difficult to achieve in a scene without them.

A real-world shadow is the complementary color of the light source: The sun is yellow; therefore, the shadows it casts are purple—in essence, there are no black shadows in the real world, only very dark representations of a particular color. Keep this in mind as you create both realistic and artistic shadows: If you apply this principle to your 3D work, you'll produce deeper, richer imagery.

A real shadow is darkest close to an object, fading and blurring as it gets farther away. Many times, shadows that people create appear too bold, and are thus unrealistic. You'll do much to bring your scenes to life by remembering that the core, or darkest area, of a shadow is located slightly away from the object's edge, near the base of the shadow (**Figure 13.60**).

Creating shadows

Shadows are turned off on all lights by default. To see shadows in a render, you must turn them on, not only in the light but in the object as well. An individual object will not cast a shadow if shadow casting is turned off on the object, regardless of whether shadow casting is turned on in the light. This gives Maya users an incredible amount of control over each shadow.

There are two types of shadows in Maya: *depth map* (**Figure 13.61**) and *raytraced* (**Figure 13.62**). Both methods can produce realistic shadows; however, raytracing often produces *more* realistic shadow, with less effort and tweaking. However, raytraced shadows can take much longer to render than depth-map shadows, so the choice is really a trade-off. It's a constant battle to produce good-looking shadows while keeping rendering time to a minimum for each scene.

Depth-map shadows attempt to simulate real-world shadows without adding major amounts of rendering time. A depth map is an image file that contains a depth channel (a grayscale representation of how far objects are from the camera, the lights, and each other) rendered from a light's point of view. Maya uses the depth map to determine which surfaces have light hitting them and which surfaces are in shadow. Think of the depth map as a pre-drawn shadow brought into the scene just before it's rendered. This image becomes a replacement for a real shadow in the scene, saving Maya the time it would take to calculate the real shadow. These depth-map image files can be reused, saving even more rendering time.

Figure 13.61 Depth-map shadow.

Figure 13.62 Raytraced shadow.

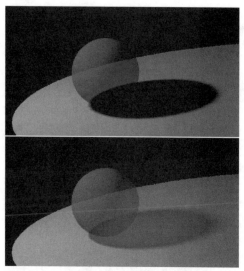

Figure 13.63 A depth-map shadow can't show an object's transparency within the shadow (top); a raytraced shadow, however, can (bottom).

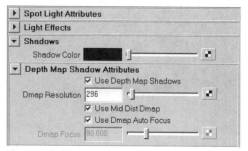

Figure 13.64 Turn on Use Depth Map Shadows.

Figure 13.65 Click the swatch next to the Shadow Color attribute to open the Color Chooser.

In most scenarios, raytraced shadows produce great-looking, realistic images—results you wouldn't be able to achieve with depth-map shadows. One example of this would be a transparent shadow cast from a partially transparent object (**Figure 13.63**).

Raytraced shadows do, however, have some restrictions as well. For one, they won't show up if rendered with interactive photorealistic rendering (IPR) (see Chapter 14)—they only show up through a rendered image. This represents an additional speed cost because you can use IPR to see depth-map shadows, making depth-map shadow adjustment much faster.

Depth-map shadows—which are available in all but ambient light—can produce relatively realistic shadows without greatly affecting rendering time.

To create a depth-map shadow:

1. Select the light from which you want to produce a shadow.

2. Open the Attribute Editor.

3. Click the arrow next to the Shadows heading to expand the shadow options.

4. Select the box next to Use Depth Map Shadows under the Depth Map Shadow Attributes heading (**Figure 13.64**).

5. In the Shadows section (above Depth Map Shadow Attributes), click the swatch next to the Shadow Color attribute to open the Color Chooser (**Figure 13.65**).

continues on next page

6. In the Color Chooser, click in the color wheel to select a shadow color.

7. Click Accept to lock in the color.

8. Select the surface you want to cast shadows.

9. In the Render Stats section of the surface's Attribute Editor, make sure that Casts Shadows is on (the default option) (**Figure 13.66**).

10. From the Hotbox's north-region Marking Menu select Hypershade/Render/persp to split your panel layout into these three panes.

11. Test-render the scene by selecting Render > Render > persp in the Render View pane.

The render shows a depth-map shadow (**Figure 13.67**).

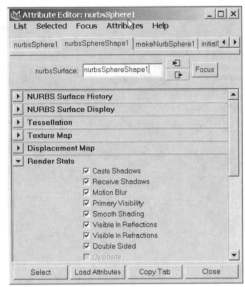

Figure 13.66 Turn on Casts Shadows in the Render Stats section of the Attribute Editor.

Figure 13.67 The final render with a depth-map shadow.

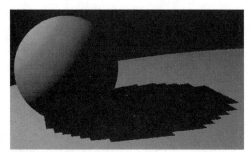

Figure 13.68 Shadow edges appear pixilated if the resolution is too low.

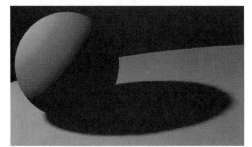

Figure 13.69 Dmap filter size controls the softness of the shadow's edges.

Common depth-map shadow attributes

Dmap Resolution—This is the resolution of the depth-map shadow file. Shadow edges will appear pixilated if the resolution is too low (**Figure 13.68**). However, you will want to use the lowest possible setting that still produces acceptable results, since this attribute is extremely render intensive.

Dmap Filter Size—Works in unison with Dmap resolution to control the softness of the shadow's edges (**Figure 13.69**). Try to maintain a setting of 3 or less to avoid adding excessive render time.

Dmap Bias—Moves the map closer to or away from the light. You will only need to use this attribute in the following circumstances:

◆ If a shadow appears detached from the shadow-casting surface, gradually decrease the Dmap bias value until the shadow looks correct.

◆ If dark spots or streaks appear on illuminated surfaces, gradually increase the Dmap bias value until the spots or streaks disappear.

Raytraced shadows can create highly realistic shadows but also add expensive rendering time.

To produce raytraced shadows, you must check three things:

◆ Use Raytraced Shadows must be selected in the light's Attribute Editor.

◆ Casts Shadows must be selected in the Render Stats section of the Attribute Editor of each object you want to cast a shadow.

◆ Raytracing must be checked in the Raytracing Quality section of the Render Globals window (see Chapter 15).

ABOUT SHADOWS

To create a raytraced shadow:

1. Select the light from which you want to produce a shadow.

2. In the Raytrace Shadow Attributes section of the light's Attribute Editor, select Use Ray Trace Shadows (**Figure 13.70**).

3. Above the Raytrace Shadows Attributes, open the Shadows section and click the swatch beside the Shadow Color attribute to open the Color Chooser.

4. Click in the color wheel to select a shadow color.

5. Click Accept to lock in the color.

6. Select the surface you want to cast shadows.

7. In the Render Stats section of the surface's Attribute Editor, select Casts Shadows.

8. To open the Render Globals panel (**Figure 13.71**), select Window > Rendering Editors > Render Globals (Windows) or Window > Render Globals (Mac), or click the Render Globals icon in the Render View 📇.

9. Select Raytracing in the Raytracing Quality section of the Render Globals panel (**Figure 13.72**).

10. Test-render the scene by selecting Render > Render > persp in the Render View window.

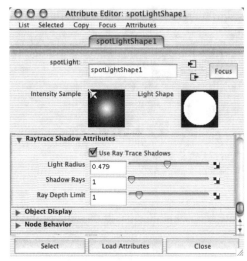

Figure 13.70 Select Use Ray Trace Shadows in the light's Attribute Editor.

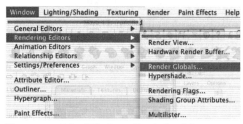

Figure 13.71 Select Window > Rendering Editors > Render Globals to open the Render Globals panel.

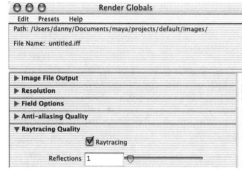

Figure 13.72 Select Raytracing in the Render Globals panel.

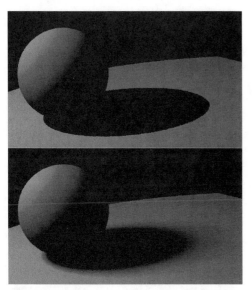

Figure 13.73 A default raytraced shadow (top), and a shadow with the Light Radius attribute turned up (bottom).

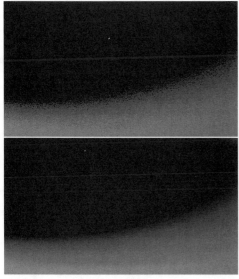

Figure 13.74 Changing the Shadow Rays attribute can cut down on grainy shadows.

Common raytraced shadow attributes

Light Radius—Sets the softness of the shadow's edge relative to the size of the light. For example, smaller light values produce crisper shadows, and greater light values create softer shadows (**Figure 13.73**).

Shadow Rays—Sets the amount of grain visible along soft shadow edges (**Figure 13.74**). Increasing this attribute increases rendering time, so keep it as low as possible.

Ray Depth Limit—If a light bounces off multiple mirrors before it hits your object, the Ray Depth Limit number determines whether that light will still cast a shadow.

ABOUT SHADOWS

SHADERS
AND MATERIALS

Figure 14.1 The objects at left and the objects at right have the same geometry. However, they've been assigned different shaders, which make them look like they're made from different substances.

Objects in Maya start out a drab, gray color. By assigning a *shader* to a surface, you give it a color or a texture map (an image that's mapped onto the surface).

Achieving realistic-looking surfaces, however, is about more than just color. You can make a surface's default gray color look like chrome (if it's shiny and reflective), or you can make it look like rocks (if it's bumpy with a matte finish) (**Figure 14.1**).

Whether a surface is shiny or matte is determined by how it reflects light. A *material* in Maya is the part of a shader that controls an object's shininess and color (in addition to a number of other attributes). There are several Maya material types—all of which deal with reflection differently. One important aspect of how shiny a surface is, is the *specular highlight*, which is the portion of the surface that appears brightest from reflecting the light. By working with the specular highlight, you can achieve the look of different substances. For instance, an eyeball has a tiny, tight, specular highlight, and a plastic surface has a wide, fuzzy specular highlight (**Figure 14.2**).

A light bulb is neither shiny nor reflective, and coloring it yellow is not going to make it look realistic. However, you can add incandescence to a bulb's shader, making it appear to have its own source of light. You can also place glow on an object like a light bulb to surround it with something resembling a halo. By combining incandescence and glow, you can get a realistic-looking light bulb (**Figure 14.3**).

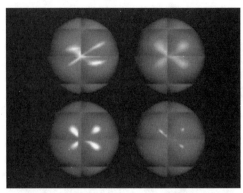

Figure 14.2 Much of what distinguishes different substances is how they reflect light. Light is reflected differently depending on what material you assign to a surface.

Figure 14.3 This light bulb is created when its material is given some incandescence and glow.

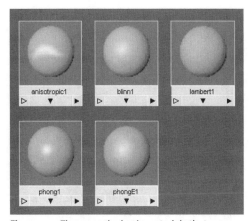

Figure 14.4 These are the basic materials that are available in the Hypershade.

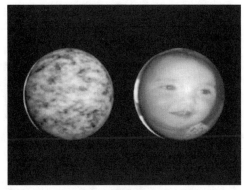

Figure 14.5 The sphere on the left has a fractal texture, which is a procedural texture. The sphere on the right has an image texture.

About the Hypershade

The Hypershade is the window in which you will do much of your work with shaders. In it you will find materials, textures, lights, and utilities.

A *material* is a node that contains most of the controls that determine the look of the object. The kind of material you use also affects the look of the object and which controls are available to it (**Figure 14.4**).

A *texture* is an image, often mapped to the color of an object. However, you can also map a texture to the bump of an object. A bump map makes a surface appear bumpy rather than smooth. The value of the image determines the height of the bumps. A texture can also determine which areas of a surface are transparent or shiny, as well as lighten portions of the surface.

There are two basic texture categories: *image* and *procedural*. An image texture can be something as simple as a scanned photo. A procedural texture is also an image; however, it's calculated based on a mathematical formula. A fractal is one example of a procedural texture (**Figure 14.5**).

Utilities are another kind of node you can find in the Hypershade. Different Maya utilities adjust shaders in various ways. A couple of common utilities are the bump2d utility, which allows for the creation of a bump map, and the 2d placement utility, which allows for the positioning of a texture on a surface.

Using the Hypershade

The Hypershade is split into three areas: the Create bar, the Hypershade tabs, and the work-area tabs.

◆ In the Create bar, click the "Choose which type of node to create" button. It reveals a menu from which you can choose from these selections: Create Materials, Create Textures, Create Lights, Create Utilities, and Create All Nodes. When you make a selection, the buttons beneath change to reveal the types of nodes you chose. For example, if you select Create Lights, a button for each different type of light appears (**Figure 14.6**).

◆ The Hypershade tabs allow you to see all of your materials, textures, utilities, lights, or cameras. If you create any of these nodes, they will show up under the appropriate tab. For example, if you create a material like Blinn by clicking it in the Create Bar, it will show up under the Materials tab (**Figure 14.7**).

◆ The work area is a place to work on your materials and textures. When you make a new node from the Create Bar, it also shows up here. You can middle mouse button–drag nodes from the Hypershade tabs down to the work area. Once they are there, you can make connections. An example of this is assigning a texture to the color of a material. If you middle mouse button–drag a texture onto a material and choose color from the marking menu that appears, the color of the texture will be connected to the color of the material (**Figure 14.8**).

Figure 14.6 The Create bar, which is on the left side of the Hypershade, allows you to easily create a variety of different nodes.

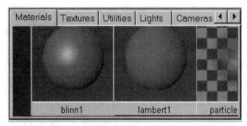

Figure 14.7 The Hypershade tabs allow you to access all of the different nodes, separated by category.

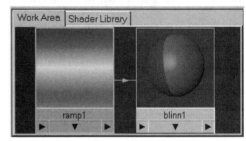

Figure 14.8 The work area is the part of the Hypershade where you can drag other nodes to make connections. Here a ramp texture is connected to the color of a Blinn material.

◆ ▪ The Toggle On/Off Create bar button allows you to hide or show the Create bar. Hiding it will give you more room to work with other nodes.

◆ ✐ The Clear Graph button clears out any nodes in the work area. It doesn't delete them; it just clears the area.

◆ ▦ The Rearrange Graph button cleans up the work area, which tends to get cluttered when you create new nodes.

◆ ▦ The Graph Materials on Selected Objects button provides a quick way to find out what material is assigned to a specific object. Just select the object, then click this button, and the material and everything connected to it will show up in the work area.

◆ ▣ The Show Up and Downstream Connections button shows everything connected to a node. For example, if you select a material and then click this button, the material will show up in the work area with all of its connections.

◆ ▪ ▬ ▤ These buttons let you isolate the Hypershade tabs or the work area. On the left is Show Top Tabs Only. In the middle, Show Bottom Tabs Only. On the right, Show Top and Bottom Tabs.

About Materials

Maya offers several types of materials, including Lambert, Blinn, Phong, Layered, Ocean, Ramp, and Anisotropic. Each material type has its own options and reflects light in a unique fashion. Lambert, for example, has no specular highlight, so it's matte, while Blinn and Phong both look shiny. Anisotropic is also shiny, but unlike Blinn and Phong, it reflects specular light unevenly (**Figure 14.9**). Maya also includes two specialty materials— Ramp and Layered—which we'll cover in this chapter. And finally, the Ocean material, which relates closely to fluid dynamics, is covered in Chapter 16.

There are several controls that are common to the basic materials. They include *color, transparency, ambient color, incandescence,* and *bump mapping.* You can map images to all of these, and most of them can have a color or luminance value assigned to them as well. All are accessible from the Attribute Editor for the corresponding material (**Figure 14.10**).

Common material attributes

◆ Color simply determines the color of an object. You can pick a color using the Color Chooser, or you can map an image to the color.

◆ Transparency allows you to make a surface see-through. You can use the slider to make the surface more or less transparent, or you can map an image to make part of the surface transparent and part of it opaque. This attribute only recognizes luminance—that is, how light or dark an image is. White is transparent; black is opaque (**Figure 14.11**).

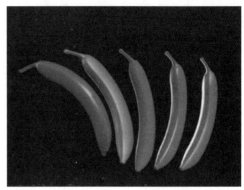

Figure 14.9 Each banana has a different material assigned to it (from left to right): Anisotropic, Blinn, Lambert, Phong, and Phong E.

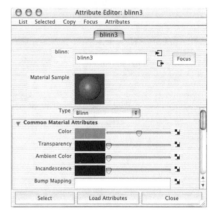

Figure 14.10 This is the Attribute Editor for a Blinn material. It holds most of the controls that determine the look of the surface.

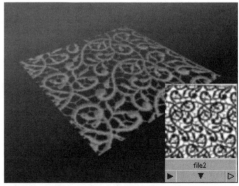

Figure 14.11 The node in the lower-right corner is the texture, which was mapped to the plane as a transparency map. The parts of the image that are white determine the parts of the plane that are transparent.

Figure 14.12 The node in the lower-right corner is the texture, which was mapped to the plane as a bump map. The white areas are higher; the dark areas are lower. You must render to see the results of a bump map.

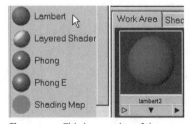

Figure 14.13 This is a portion of the Hypershade. When the Lambert button is clicked, a new material node, called lambert2, appears.

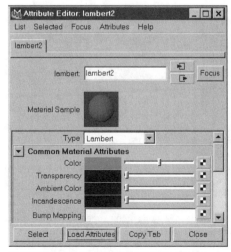

Figure 14.14 This is the Attribute Editor for the material that was just created in the Hypershade.

♦ Ambient color allows you to lighten the color of the material. You can lighten the the whole surface evenly by using the slider, or you can map an image to the ambient color to lighten only certain parts of a surface.

♦ Incandescence gives a material the appearance of having its own light. In general, you need to have a light in a scene for anything to render out. However, if an object has a material on it with the ambient color turned up, it will render out without any lights in the scene.

♦ Bump mapping makes a surface appear bumpy. To work, this attribute must have an image mapped to it. The whitest parts of the image will cause the tallest bumps; the black parts of the image will cause the lowest bumps; 50 percent gray will cause no bumps (**Figure 14.12**).

To change the color of an object:

1. From the Window menu select Rendering Editors > Hypershade.

2. Select Create Materials (if it's not already selected) from the pull-down menu in the Create bar.

3. Click Lambert (**Figure 14.13**).
   A new material appears in the work area (the lower half of the window).

4. Double-click the new material.
   The Attribute Editor for this material appears (**Figure 14.14**).

continues on next page

5. Click the field next to Color.

The Color Chooser opens (**Figure 14.15**).

6. Choose a color by clicking one of the color swatches at the top of the window or by clicking in the color wheel.

7. Click Accept.

The Color Chooser window closes.

8. With the middle mouse button drag the material from the Hypershade onto the surface.

or

Select the surface, and then click the material with the right mouse button. From the Marking Menu that appears, select Assign Material To Selection (**Figure 14.16**).

✔ Tip

■ If you assign a shader to a surface by using the middle mouse button to drag it from the Hypershade, be sure that the view you drag it into is in shaded mode. If it were in wireframe mode, you would need to drag it precisely onto an isoparm or edge of the surface, which is more difficult.

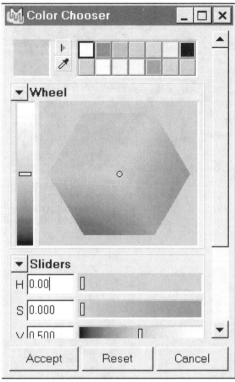

Figure 14.15 The Color Chooser lets you select a color from the swatches at the top or from the color wheel.

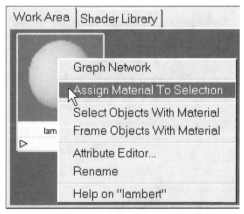

Figure 14.16 When you right-click a material in the Hypershade, a Marking Menu appears that allows you to assign that material to the selected surface. This is a particularly convenient method if you're assigning shaders to multiple surfaces simultaneously.

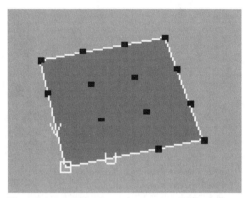

Figure 14.17 On this plane, the CVs are visible, and you can easily see the U and V directions. The square at lower left is the start point; the U is to the right of it, and the V is above it. This means that the U direction goes from left to right, and the V direction runs from bottom to top.

Figure 14.18 The same image is assigned to different NURBS surfaces. It gets wrapped around the surface, and its orientation depends on the U and V directions of the surface.

About texture-mapping NURBS surfaces

A NURBS surface is always four-sided. Even a sphere is four-sided—it's pinched at the top and bottom, and the other two sides meet. NURBS surfaces have U and V directions. In a plane, the U direction extends from left to right, and the V direction extends from bottom to top. This makes the lower-left corner the start point (**Figure 14.17**).

Any image you bring in is also four-sided since image files are square or rectangular. The lower-left corner of the image is placed at the start point of the surface. The bottom of the image is mapped on the surface along the U direction, and the left side of the image is wrapped along the V direction (**Figure 14.18**).

Once the image has been placed on the surface, you can move, rotate, and repeat it. If you want to place one image over two or more surfaces, you must use a *projection map*—which is a bit like pointing a slide projector at a surface.

Maya comes with several textures, but you can also use your own images. Maya can accept many different image formats, including JPEG; TIFF; and Maya's own format, IFF.

ABOUT MATERIALS

To assign an image map from the Shader Library to a NURBS object:

1. From the Create menu select NURBS Primitive > Plane.

2. From the Panel menu in any pane select Panel > Panel > Hypershade.

3. Click Lambert in the Create bar of the Hypershade to create a new material.

   A new Lambert material appears in the Hypershade.

4. Assign the material to the plane by using the middle mouse button to drag it onto the surface.

5. Click the Shader Library tab, in the lower half of the Hypershade window.

6. Click the Textures folder, in the lower half of the Hypershade.

   Several textures appear to the right (**Figure 14.19**).

7. Use the middle mouse button to drag a brick texture onto your new Lambert (probably called lambert2), which is in the top half of the Hypershade .

8. From the Marking Menu that appears, select "color" (**Figure 14.20**).

   The brick texture appears on the Lambert node and is mapped to the Lambert's color channel.

9. Click in the Perspective view, and press ⑥ to go into textured mode.

   The brick texture shows up on the surface to which it was assigned (**Figure 14.21**).

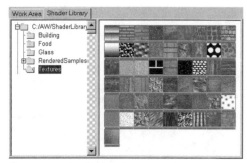

Figure 14.19 The Shader Library provides several textures—all of which are all repeatable, which means that if they're tiled on a surface, there will be no seams.

Figure 14.20 When a texture is dragged onto a material, a Marking Menu appears that allows you to choose which attribute you want to map the texture to.

Figure 14.21 The brick texture appears on the plane. It's only visible when you're in textured mode.

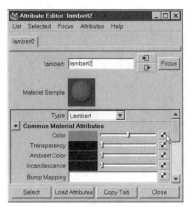

Figure 14.22 By clicking the Map icon, which is little checkerboard to the right of the slider, you can map a texture to the color.

Figure 14.23 In the Create Render Node window, you can choose which texture you want to map to an attribute of a material.

Figure 14.24 An image is mapped to the color of the plane.

To assign your own image map to a NURBS object:

1. From the Create menu select NURBS Primitive > Plane.

2. Open the Hypershade.

3. Click Lambert to create a new material.

   A new Lambert material appears in the Hypershade.

4. Double-click the new Lambert you just created in the Hypershade.

   The Attribute Editor for the Lambert opens.

5. Click the Map icon, which is to the right of the Color slider (**Figure 14.22**).

   The Create Render Node window opens.

6. Make sure the radio button next to Normal is selected, and then click File in the Create Render Node window (**Figure 14.23**).

   The Attribute Editor for the File node opens.

7. Click the Browse button ☐ next to Image Name.

8. Browse for and open your own image file.

9. With the middle mouse button drag the Lambert you created from the Hypershade onto your surface.

10. Click in the Perspective view, and press ⑥ to go into textured mode.

    The image you chose is now color-mapped to your surface (**Figure 14.24**).

continues on next page

ABOUT MATERIALS

✔ Tips

- You can similarly map an image to any of the common material attributes.

- You can also map an image by dragging an existing texture onto the name of an attribute in a material's Attribute Editor (**Figure 14.25**).

When you first map an image on a NURBS surface, it may not be oriented correctly. You can use the "place 2d texture" node to rotate, move, and scale the image on the surface.

To use 'place 2d texture':

1. Map a brick texture to a NURBS plane as you did when assigning an image map to a NURBS object from the Shader Library above.

2. Select the surface.

3. In the Hypershade, click the Graph Materials on Selected Objects icon.

   The entire shading network and its connections show up in the work area of the Hypershade (**Figure 14.26**).

4. Double-click the place2dTexture node, on the left side of the work area.

   The Attribute Editor for the place2dTexture node appears.

5. Click the Interactive Placement button in the Attribute Editor for the place2dTexture node. A red square with a dot in the middle appears on the surface.

6. Drag with the middle mouse button, starting from the center point of the interactive placement icon on the object's surface.

   The texture moves on the surface (**Figure 14.27**).

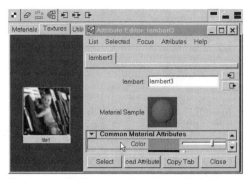

Figure 14.25 The file texture in the Hypershade is being dragged with the middle mouse button to the color in the Attribute Editor of a material. This provides a quick and convenient way to make connections.

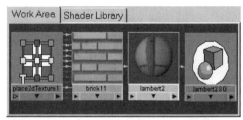

Figure 14.26 In the work area of the Hypershade, we can see all of the nodes that are associated with this material.

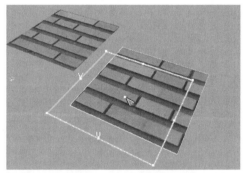

Figure 14.27 The position of the texture is moved via interactive placement. Compare the bricks' position after they've been moved (lower right) with their original position (upper left).

ABOUT MATERIALS

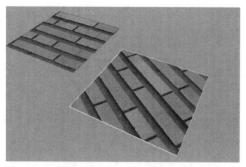

Figure 14.28 The interactive placement was used to rotate the brick texture.

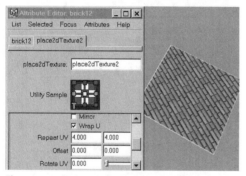

Figure 14.29 By increasing Repeat UV of the place2dTexture to 4 (in the Attribute Editor on the left), you can make the brick texture repeat many times on the surface.

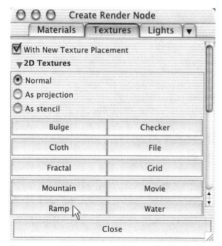

Figure 14.30 When you click Ramp in the Create Render Node window, a new ramp texture is created and mapped to a material.

7. With the middle mouse button drag at the corners of the red square. The texture rotates (**Figure 14.28**).

8. Click in the field next to Repeat UV, and type *4*. Press Enter.

   The bricks are repeated four times in the U direction. The column on the left is for U values; the column on the right is for V values.

9. In the field two columns to the right of Repeat UV, type *4*. Press Enter.

   The bricks are now also repeated four times in the V direction (**Figure 14.29**).

Procedural textures are built into Maya; they do not rely on an image file. Their color and luminance are determined mathematically. One commonly used procedural texture is a ramp, which is like a gradient.

To assign a ramp texture to a surface:

1. From the Create menu select NURBS Primitive > Sphere.

2. In the Channel Box, type *90* in the field next to Rotate X, and press Enter.

3. In the Hypershade, click Phong E.
   A Phong E material shows up in the work area.

4. Double-click the Phong E material in the Hypershade.
   The Attribute Editor for the Phong E material appears.

5. In the Attribute Editor for the Phong E, material, click the Map button next to the Color slider ■.
   The Create Render Node window opens.

6. Click the Ramp button (**Figure 14.30**).
   The Attribute Editor for the ramp appears. A ramp texture node also appears in the Hypershade.

continues on next page

7. With the middle mouse button drag the Phong E from the Hypershade onto the sphere to assign the shader.

If you have trouble finding the Phong E material, click the work area of the Hypershade and press ⓐ. This will frame all of the nodes.

8. Click the Perspective view and press ⑥ to see the texture (**Figure 14.31**).

To make the ramp texture look like an eyeball:

1. Create a material with a ramp texture, and assign it to a sphere as in the previous section.

2. In the work area of the Hypershade, double-click on the ramp texture.

The Attribute Editor for the ramp appears.

3. In the Attribute Editor for the ramp, change the type to U Ramp.

4. Click and drag the top position indicator down slightly (**Figure 14.32**).

5. Change its color to black by dragging the Selected Color slider all the way to the left.

6. Click and drag the middle position indicator, which is green by default, to just below the top one.

7. Click on the ramp about one-fifth of the way down from the top.

A new position indicator appears (**Figure 14.33**).

8. Click and drag the bottom position indicator up to just below the new one.

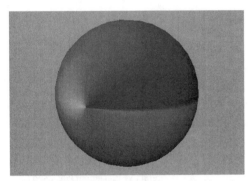

Figure 14.31 This sphere has a ramp textured to its color.

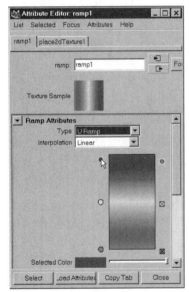

Figure 14.32 The Attribute Editor for the ramp holds the controls for determining the look of the gradient it produces. Position indicators are the circles to the left of the ramp. They determine where a color is positioned within the gradient.

Figure 14.33 When you click in the middle of the ramp, a new position indicator is created. By clicking the square with the X in it to the right of the ramp, you can delete a position indicator.

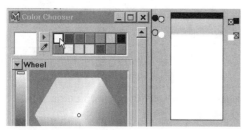

Figure 14.34 The white swatch is selected in the Color Chooser, causing the selected position indicator and the ramp below it to become white.

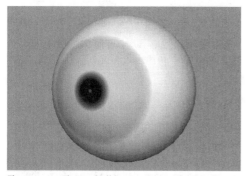

Figure 14.35 The eyeball is complete with a pupil and iris.

Figure 14.36 You can create a ramp shader from the Create Materials drop-down menu.

9. With the bottom position indicator still selected, click the color swatch next to Selected Color.

The Color Chooser opens.

10. Click the white swatch at the top of the Color Chooser (**Figure 14.34**).

The sphere is now textured like an eyeball (**Figure 14.35**).

In addition to the 2D ramp texture available in past versions, Maya 4.5 includes a new shader—called a *Ramp shader*—similar to the 2D ramp texture. Like the 2D ramp texture, the Ramp material shader can be used to create more exotic textures such as cartoon shading, which involves creating a shader that renders like a flat 2d cartoon, instead of rendering with the appearance of 3d surfaces, and advanced gradient effects. You can also use the new Ramp shader to produce the same type of eyeball effect as we created in the steps above, making it a worthy addition to your texturing toolset.

To create a simple cartoon look on a surface:

1. From the Create menu select NURBS Primitives > Sphere.

2. Under the Create Materials menu in the Hypershade, click Ramp Shader to create a ramp shader (**Figure 14.36**).

3. Double-click the Ramp Shader material in the Hypershade.

The Attribute Editor for the Ramp Shader material appears.

4. Click the Selected Color swatch to open the Color Chooser.

5. Select a color for the shadow area of the sphere.

6. Click Accept to close the Color Chooser.

continues on next page

7. Click once in the Color slider beside Selected Color.

A new color is added to the slider (**Figure 14.37**).

8. Click the Selected Color swatch and adjust the Value (V) slider to 1.

9. Click Accept to close the Color Chooser.

10. Set the Color Interpolation drop-down menu to None.

The None setting changes the gradient between the selected colors to two flat colors with no gradient in-between (**Figure 14.38**).

11. Set Color Input to Brightness.

The Brightness setting flattens out the sphere's color to give the surface a flatter, more cartoon-like appearance.

12. Create two colors in the slider beside the Selected Color section of the Incandescence area. Make the left one white and the right one black (**Figure 14.39**).

13. Set Incandescence Interpolation to None.

14. Apply the material to the surface.

The surface now appears to have flat color inside and a white outline (**Figure 14.40**).

✔ Tip

■ For best results, use different shades of the same colors when adding colors to the color sliders. Using shades of color helps to better form the object because when using similar colors, your eye reads those colors as the same surface; whereas using completely different colors makes your eyes jump from color to color.

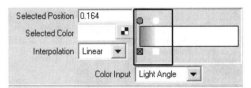

Figure 14.37 Each time you click in the Color slider you create a new color.

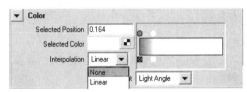

Figure 14.38 The ramp will remain a gradient until you set Interpolation to None.

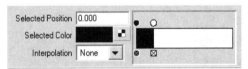

Figure 14.39 Set Interpolation to None to limit the Color slider to only two colors, no gradients.

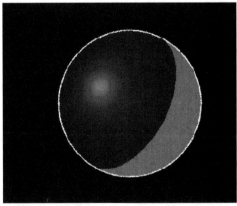

Figure 14.40 A cartoon-style rendering.

Figure 14.41 We're adding a fractal to the Transparency channel so that we can see our red shader through our blue shader.

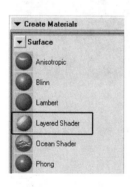

Figure 14.42 You can click Layered Shader once to create it, or you can use the middle mouse button to drag the icon into the Hypershade to create it.

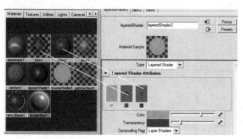

Figure 14.43 You can drag multiple shaders into your layered shader to create layered effects using the transparency of each layer.

To create a layered shader:

1. From the Create menu select NURBS Primitives > Sphere.

2. Create two Blinn materials; color one red and one blue.

3. Double-click the blue Blinn material in the Hypershade.

4. Click the Map icon [·] next to the Transparency slider.

5. Click Fractal in the Textures tab of the Create Render Node window (**Figure 14.41**).

6. Under the Create Materials menu in the Hypershade, click Layered Shader (**Figure 14.42**).

7. Double-click the Layered Shader material in the Hypershade.

   The Attribute Editor for the Layered Shader material appears.

8. With the middle mouse button, drag the red and blue materials from the Hypershade into the red square under Layered Shader Attributes (**Figure 14.43**).

continues on next page

9. Click the *x* under the original green square to delete it (**Figure 14.44**).

You should now have two squares in the red square under Layered Shader Attributes.

10. Apply the layered shader to the sphere.

11. From the Window menu select Rendering Editors > Render View.

12. In the Render view click the Redo Previous Render icon 📽.

The sphere is now red and blue. The red can be seen through the blue because we added a fractal to its transparency channel (**Figure 14.45**).

✔ Tip

■ You must have transparency on the top object in the layered shader if any of the bottom shader is to be visible.

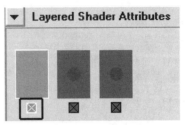

Figure 14.44 The small *x* at the bottom of each square is used to remove shaders from your layered shader.

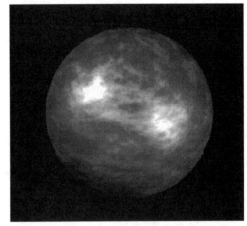

Figure 14.45 The rendered layered shader has both red and blue coloring.

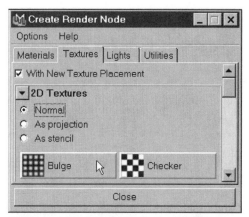

Figure 14.46 Clicking Bulge in the Create Render Node window creates a bulge texture that is mapped to the bump of a material.

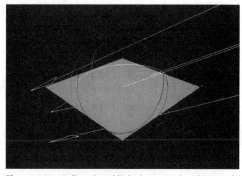

Figure 14.47 A directional light is created and rotated diagonally to the plane. Directional lights make bumps stand out in greater contrast because the light is only coming from one side.

Figure 14.48 This is a rendered image of a plane with a bulge texture mapped to its bump. You must render to see the bump—it does not show up in the Perspective view.

To assign a bump map to a surface:

1. From the Create menu select NURBS Primitives > Plane.

2. In the Hypershade create a Lambert.

3. Assign the Lambert to the plane by using the middle mouse button to drag it from the Hypershade to the plane.

4. Double-click the Lambert in the Hypershade.

   The Attribute Editor for the Lambert appears.

5. Click the Map button next to Bump Mapping ▪.

   The Create Render Node window appears.

6. Click Bulge (**Figure 14.46**).

   The bulge shows up in the work area of the Hypershade. We'll need to render it to see the resulting bump.

7. From the Create menu select Lights > Directional Light.

   Bump maps show up better with a directional source of light than with ambient light.

8. Rotate the light so that it points diagonally at the plane (**Figure 14.47**).

9. Click the Render icon ▦, which is near the top right of the interface.

   The image renders out into a new window. The bulge is visible on the surface (**Figure 14.48**).

To adjust the height of a bump map:

1. Create a plane with a bulge bump map, as in the previous section.

2. Select the plane.

3. Click the Graph Materials on Selected Objects button 📇 in the Hypershade.

   The material with all its connections appears in the work area of the Hypershade (**Figure 14.49**).

4. Double-click the bump2d node.

   The Attribute Editor for the bump2d node appears.

5. Change the bump depth by moving the slider or typing in a number (**Figure 14.50**).

6. Click the Render icon 📷.

   The bumps are smaller than in the previous bump map (**Figure 14.51**).

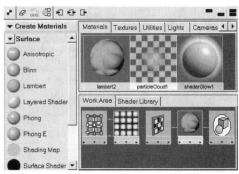

Figure 14.49 All of the nodes associated with the material are visible in the work area of the Hypershade. The utility that controls the height of the bump is in the middle.

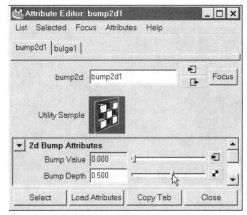

Figure 14.50 The Attribute Editor for the bump2d node contains the Bump Depth attribute. Bump depth controls the overall height of the bump.

Figure 14.51 The plane on the left has a bump depth of 1; the plane the right has a bump depth of 0.5.

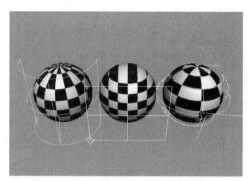

Figure 14.52 A checkered texture is mapped to spheres using three different projection types: (left to right) cylindrical, planar, and spherical.

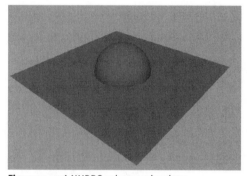

Figure 14.53 A NURBS sphere and a plane.

Figure 14.54 The "As projection" radio button has been selected in the Create Render Node window.

About projection maps

Sometimes you'll want to map one image across two or more surfaces. For that you can use a projection map. The default projection type is *planar,* which acts like a slide projector pointed at a surface. Other projection types include *spherical* and *cylindrical,* which project an image from a shape that surrounds the surface (**Figure 14.52**).

To map a texture as projection:

1. Create a Lambert material in the Hypershade, and assign it to a NURBS plane and a NURBS sphere (**Figure 14.53**).

2. Double-click the Lambert in the Hypershade.

   The Attribute Editor for the Lambert opens.

3. In the Attribute Editor for the Lambert, click the Map button next to the Color slider ▪️.

   The Create Render Node window appears.

4. Click the radio button next to "As projection" (**Figure 14.54**).

5. Click the File button.

   The Attribute Editor for the projection appears. A place3dTexture node appears in the Perspective view.

   continues on next page

6. Click the file1 tab at the top of the Attribute Editor.

The Attribute Editor changes to show the options for the file texture.

7. Click the Folder icon next to Image Name.

The file browser appears.

8. Browse for and open an image of your own.

9. Click the Perspective view, and press ⑥ to go into textured mode.

The place3dtexture node is visible in the Perspective view. The image is visible on the surface, but it is stretched out because it is being projected on from the side (**Figure 14.55**).

✔ Tip

■ If you move a surface with a projection texture mapped to it, the surface will appear to be moving through its texture when it is rendered out. To solve this problem, select the surface, and then from the Texturing menu select Create Texture Reference Object.

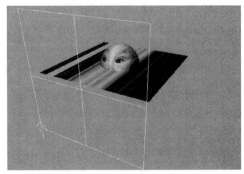

Figure 14.55 The planar projection is projecting the image across the two surfaces from the side. This causes the image to be stretched along the plane.

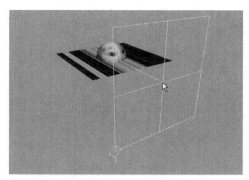

Figure 14.56 The place3dtexture utility has been selected in the Perspective view. You can move, rotate, and scale this node the same way you would for any object.

Figure 14.57 Now that the place3dtexture utility is oriented to the surface, the image is projected across the two surfaces.

Figure 14.58 The place3dtexture utility has been scaled down, rotated, and moved.

To adjust a projection:

1. Projection-map a texture onto a plane as in the previous section.

2. Select the place3dtexture utility in the Perspective view (**Figure 14.56**).

   The line coming out from the center indicates the projection direction—in this case, on the side of the plane—and we want it to project on the top.

3. Rotate the plane -90 degrees in the x axis.

   The image is no longer stretched; however, it doesn't fit precisely on the surface.

4. With the place3dtexture still selected, press [Ctrl]/[Control][a] to open the Attribute Editor.

   The Attribute Editor for the place3dtexture node opens.

5. Click the "Fit to group box" button.

   The place3dtexture is automatically resized to that of the plane, and the image now fits (**Figure 14.57**).

✔ Tip

■ If you move or rotate the place3dtexture, the image on the surface will move or rotate. If you scale it up, the image will scale up. If you scale it down, the image will scale down and be tiled (**Figure 14.58**).

ABOUT MATERIALS

Textures, especially projected ones, often appear blurry in the view even though they render clearly. However, you often need the image to appear sharper in order to place the texture.

To improve the quality of a texture image in a view:

1. Projection-map a checkered texture onto a sphere (**Figure 14.59**).

   The texture on the surface will appear very blurry.

2. Select the sphere.

3. In the Hypershade, click the Graph Materials on Selected Objects icon 🖾.

   The material with all of its connections appears in the work area of the Hypershade.

4. Double-click the material in the Hypershade.

   The Attribute Editor for the material appears.

5. Under Hardware Texturing in the Attribute Editor, click the arrow to expand the options (**Figure 14.60**).

6. Change the "Texture quality" setting to High.

   The blurry checkers on the sphere become sharper (**Figure 14.61**).

✔ Tip

- Making the texture quality high will slow down Maya's interactivity, especially with a high-resolution image. Once you've finished placing the texture, it's a good idea to reset it to low quality.

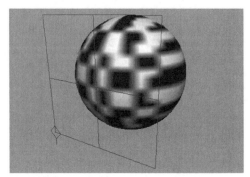

Figure 14.59 A checkered texture is projected onto a sphere. It appears very blurry and does not accurately represent how it will look when it is rendered.

Figure 14.60 Hardware Texturing options are visible in the Attribute Editor for a material. By increasing the "Texture quality" setting to High, the checkers will become clear.

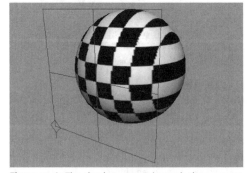

Figure 14.61 The checker texture is much sharper now that the texture quality for Hardware Texturing has been increased.

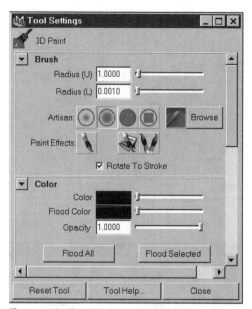

Figure 14.62 The 3D Paint Tool Settings window includes many controls that determine the look of your brush strokes.

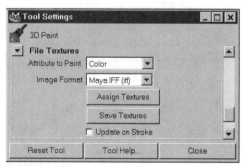

Figure 14.63 Under File Textures in the 3D Paint Tool Settings window, you can assign a texture to the material for a selected object. You cannot paint on a surface that does not have a file mapped to its color.

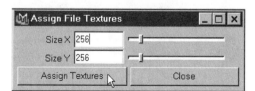

Figure 14.64 Once you click Assign Textures, you can paint, because a file texture has been connected to the material for the object you want to paint.

About the 3D Paint tool

The 3D Paint tool allows you to paint directly on a surface. You can create a new texture image from scratch with this method, and Maya will create a new image file.

It's important to make sure you've set your project (File > Project > Set) before you begin painting, because the current project will determine where this image ends up. When you save the scene after painting, a folder named after your scene is created in the 3dPaintTextures folder of the project you're currently set to. Any images that were created by painting will be put in that folder.

You can also paint on a surface that already has an image file textured on it—for example, to add dirt or other details to an existing image.

To paint directly on a surface:

1. Create a Lambert material in the Hypershade, and assign it to a NURBS sphere.

2. Select the sphere.

3. From the Texturing menu (Windows) or the Lighting/Shading menu (Mac) select the box next to 3D Paint Tool.

    The 3D Paint Tool Settings window opens (**Figure 14.62**).

4. Scroll down until you see File Textures (**Figure 14.63**).

    If necessary, you can change the image format that will be created.

5. Click the Assign Textures button.

    The Assign File Textures window appears. You can increase the resolution of the texture here if you need a highly detailed texture. The default of 256 by 256 will suffice for now (**Figure 14.64**).

continues on next page

6. Click Assign Textures.

A file texture has now been connected to the material so you can paint.

7. Click in the Perspective view, hold down ⬚b⬚, and then using the middle mouse button drag from right to left to get the brush down to size.

The red circle, which represents brush size, should shrink.

8. Click and drag on the surface to paint on it.

A mark appears on the surface (**Figure 14.65**).

To use the 3D Paint tool:

1. Continue with the sphere from the previous section.

If the paintbrush is not visible or the tool options are no longer open, select the sphere, and then from the Texturing menu select the box next to 3D Paint Tool.

2. Click the color swatch next to Flood Color in the 3D Paint Tool Settings window (**Figure 14.66**).

The Color Chooser appears.

3. Choose the yellow swatch at the top of the Color Chooser, and click Accept.

4. Click Flood All.

The sphere turns yellow.

5. Paint a smiley face by clicking and dragging on the surface (**Figure 14.67**).

The following steps only apply to the Windows version of Maya.

6. Click the Get Brush button 🖌, which is to the right of Paint Effects in the 3D Paint Tool Options window.

The Visor window opens.

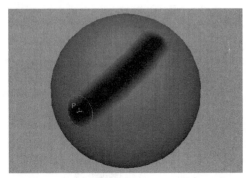

Figure 14.65 The paintbrush has been dragged across the sphere, producing this black mark.

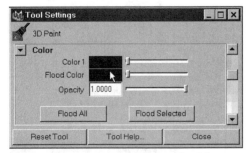

Figure 14.66 You can choose a color to flood the whole object with by clicking the field next to Flood Color.

Figure 14.67 A smiley face has been painted on the sphere with three brush strokes.

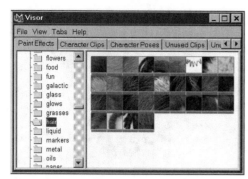

Figure 14.68 You can choose from a variety of brushes to use with the 3D Paint tool in the Visor. Here we see the brushes in the Hair folder.

Figure 14.69 Hair has been painted on the sphere by using one of the Paint Effects brushes.

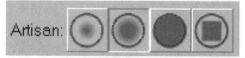

Figure 14.70 To return to a normal brush, choose from one of the profiles of the Artisan brushes.

7. Scroll down in the Visor, and click the Hair folder.

Several hair types appear (**Figure 14.68**).

8. Click on the hair of your choice.

9. Paint some hair on your smiley-face sphere (**Figure 14.69**).

✔ Tips

- After using a Paint Effects brush, you can return to a normal brush by clicking one of the Brush Profile buttons next to Artisan in the 3D Paint Tool Settings window (**Figure 14.70**).

- By decreasing the opacity in the 3D Paint Tool settings, you can paint on a surface but still see the color beneath your brush strokes—helpful if you're trying to make a surface appear dirty.

- You can use this tool to paint areas roughly to mark the different parts of a surface. You can then open the image file (which is created once you save the scene) in Adobe Photoshop and paint the details there.

ABOUT MATERIALS

About Texturing Polygons

All of the techniques covered thus far work on polygon primitives. They will not, however, necessarily work on any polygon surfaces you've modeled. While NURBS surfaces are always four-sided, polygon surfaces are made up of many small faces—which means that applying textures to them is not as simple as it is on NURBS surfaces.

Think of a wrapped present. Imagine carefully removing the wrapping paper and flattening it out. Once the paper has been flattened, you can easily paint a new image on it (**Figure 14.71**).

This is essentially what you need to do to add texture to a polygon surface. Before you can successfully texture-map it, you need to "unwrap" the surface. To do this, you create a UV map, which you can see in the UV Texture Editor (**Figure 14.72**).

The UV maps for complicated characters can be confusing to look at, and require a lot of work to use effectively. However, you don't need to create them for polygon primitives because they come with them.

One distinct advantage of polygons over NURBS is that you can assign multiple materials to a single polygon surface, while a NURBS surface can have only one. You do this by selecting polygon faces and assigning the materials to *them*, not to the object as a whole (**Figure 14.73**).

Figure 14.71 A wrapped-gift texture has been mapped to a cube.

Figure 14.72 The white lines in the UV Texture Editor represent the edges of the cube. You can see how the cube has been "unwrapped." The image beneath these lines is what the actual image file that's mapped to the surface looks like.

Figure 14.73 Four different textures have been mapped to different parts of the same polygon sphere by assigning them to specific faces of the sphere.

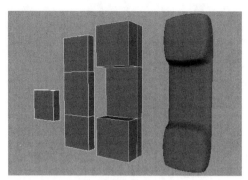

Figure 14.74 By using Extrude Face and Smooth, a phone can be modeled from a cube in a few easy steps.

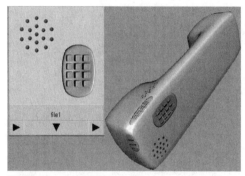

Figure 14.75 On the left is the file texture that is mapped to the phone. On the right, the texture on the phone is stretched out and in the wrong places.

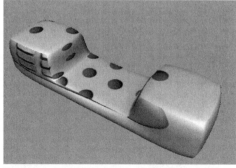

Figure 14.76 Now that a UV map has been created using automatic mapping, the texture is placed on all parts of the surface, but not in the right places.

To create automatic mapping for a polygon texture:

1. Create a polygon telephone (**Figure 14.74**).

   For detailed instruction for how to do this, see "To model a SubD telephone receiver, starting with a polygon" in Chapter 8. However, do not convert it to subdivision surfaces. Instead, smooth the polygon with a subdivision level of 3 and a continuity of 0.35.

2. Create a Blinn material, and assign it to the surface.

3. Double-click the Blinn material in the Hypershade.

   The Attribute Editor for the Blinn material opens.

4. Click the Map button ![icon] next to the Color slider in the Attribute Editor.

   The Create Render Node window appears.

5. Make sure that the radio button next to Normal is selected, and then click File.

   The Attribute Editor for the file node opens.

6. Click the Browse button ![icon] next to Image Name.

7. Browse for and open your own image file.

   I've created one especially for the phone, but any image will do. The image will look messed up and stretched out on the phone in the Perspective view (**Figure 14.75**).

8. Select the surface.

9. From the Edit Polygons menu select Texture > Automatic Mapping.

   Now the image is not stretched out as much, but the different elements are not in place (**Figure 14.76**).

You navigate the UV Texture Editor just as you would any panel. You can track and dolly the same way you do in any view panel. And the Move, Rotate, and Scale tools work just as they do in the rest of the program.

The image that is mapped to the surface is tiled in the UV Texture Editor. This allows you to move up different parts of the surface onto the part of the image you want without a lot of messy overlapping.

To use the UV Texture Editor:

1. Continue using the phone from the previous section.

2. With the right mouse button click the surface, and from the Marking Menu select UV.

3. Choose one UV point from the center of the earpiece of the telephone (**Figure 14.77**).

4. From the Window menu select UV Texture Editor.

   The UV Texture Editor opens. You can see the image that was assigned to the surface, and on top of that is the wireframe of the different parts of the surface (shells) that have been separated. The one point you picked on the surface is visible and is easy to find because of the transform manipulator on it (**Figure 14.78**).

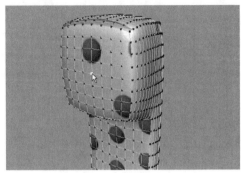

Figure 14.77 One UV point has been selected from the center of the earpiece of the phone.

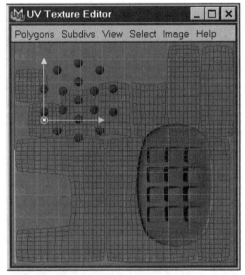

Figure 14.78 In the UV Texture Editor, you can see how the different parts of the surface have been laid out over the image map. The UV point that was selected in the Perspective view is also selected here and is seen with move manipulators on it. This makes it easy to recognize which shell is the phone's earpiece.

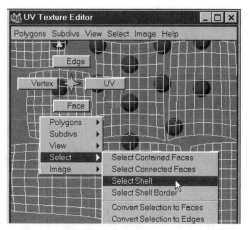

Figure 14.79 Rather than having to carefully select each UV of the shell, you can select the whole shell at once by clicking with the right mouse button and choosing Select Shell from the Marking Menu.

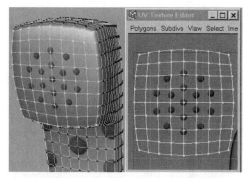

Figure 14.80 While placing the UVs in the Texture view (right), you can see their effect on the surface simultaneously (left).

5. With the right mouse button click the shell, and from the Marking Menu choose Select > Select Shell (**Figure 14.79**).

All the UVs of the shell are selected.

6. Move, scale, and rotate the shell over a recognizable part of the image.

You can watch the image on the selected area of the phone change interactively in the Perspective view (**Figure 14.80**).

7. Repeat Steps 3 through 6 for other parts of the phone.

Because the surface is in many separate pieces (shells) in the UV Texture View, there are seams on the surface. We can combine two shells and get rid of the seam by using Move and Sew UVs (**Figure 14.81**).

To eliminate a seam in a texture using Move and Sew UVs:

1. Continue using the phone from the previous sections.

2. In the Perspective view, carefully select all of the edges along the seam (**Figure 14.82**).

continues on next page

Figure 14.81 A seam in the texture is apparent along the side of the phone.

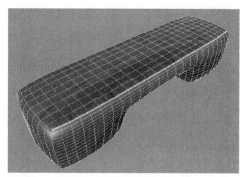

Figure 14.82 All of the polygon edges along the edge of the seam have been carefully selected.

ABOUT TEXTURING POLYGONS

The corresponding edges are automatically selected in the UV Texture Editor when you select them on the object (**Figure 14.83**).

3. From the Edit Polygons menu select Texture > Move and Sew UVs.

The seam on the object disappears in the Perspective view (**Figure 14.84**). In the UV Texture Editor, two shells have been combined along that edge (**Figure 14.85**).

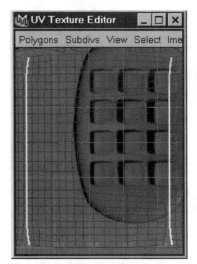

Figure 14.83 The edges of two shells are selected because they are, in fact, one edge shared by both shells.

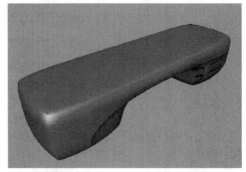

Figure 14.84 The seam is now gone because the edges of the two shells have been sewn together, allowing the texture image to extend across both.

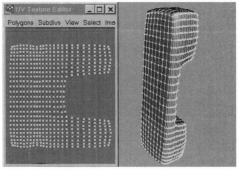

Figure 14.85 What was once two separate shells is now one bigger shell covering a larger portion of the phone.

CAMERAS AND RENDERING

15

Figure 15.1 Compare a hardware render of a tractor (left) with a software render (right). The software render has a bump map that forms the tire treads and a transparency map that creates the grill in the front.

Figure 15.2 A wineglass is rendered using raytracing. Reflections and refractions on the glass are what make it look real.

Creating quality images in Maya, whether for print or video, depends on *rendering*—the process of creating an image (or sequence of images) from a scene. When you render, you create a two-dimensional image from a specified three-dimensional view of your scene. Maya makes intensive mathematical calculations and applies the laws of physics to realistically create lighting, shadows, reflections, and textures. With a few settings, you can take even a very simple scene and make it look realistic by rendering it.

Rendering lights, shadows, and textures is known as *software rendering*. Maya also performs *hardware rendering*, which is essentially what you see in your Perspective view. When you press $\boxed{7}$ for hardware lighting, you are hardware rendering. Maya's Hardware Render Buffer will make a series of screen snapshots and export the images for you. The Hardware Render Buffer also provides a few options for cleaning up your images (**Figure 15.1**).

Maya includes two basic categories of software rendering: the default (known as *A-buffer, or raycasting*) and *raytracing*. The default renderer can create high-quality images with lighting, shadows, texture, and motion blur. However, for added realism, you may need reflections and refractions. This is where raytracing comes in. If you want to make a wineglass look real, you need to raytrace it (**Figure 15.2**).

About Cameras

An essential part of rendering is determining the point of view for your scene. Any time you view a scene in Maya, you're looking through a camera. The four views—Top, Front, Side, and Perspective—are actually four different cameras. Most often you render using the Perspective view; however, you can use the other views as well.

Cameras determine both your view of the scene and the view that is rendered. When you're tumbling and tracking in the Perspective view, you're really just moving and rotating that camera. You can't delete any of the four default cameras, but you can create new ones (**Figure 15.3**).

You can also animate a camera, just as you would any other object. You can simulate camera motion from real films, such as crane, helicopter, and dolly shots. And by animating a camera, you can even do a fly-through, which is often done for architectural visualization. You can also simulate camera cuts—where the camera remains at one view for a while and then jumps to another view.

Cameras include some useful attributes. *Focal length* allows you to adjust the zoom of the lens just as you would on a real camera (this is different from dolly). *Center of interest* allows you to move the point where you want the camera to look. And an *image plane* will place an image in the background of the camera view, regardless of how the camera is moved.

To create and adjust a camera:

1. From the Create menu select Cameras > Camera.

    A new camera appears in the Perspective view (**Figure 15.4**).

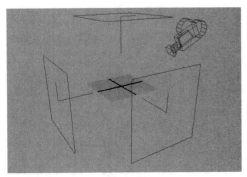

Figure 15.3 The icon that looks like a camera represents the Perspective view. The orthographic views (top, front, and side) are represented by squares with a line extending from the middle.

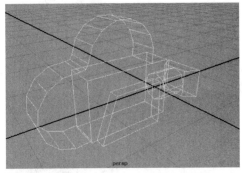

Figure 15.4 When a new camera is created, it appears at the origin.

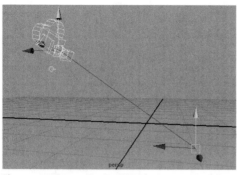

Figure 15.5 The camera itself has been moved, and its center of interest is moved separately; the camera continues to aim at it.

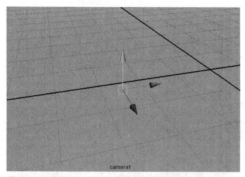

Figure 15.6 This is the view through the camera you just created. The manipulator we see is the camera's own center of interest (still visible because the camera remains selected).

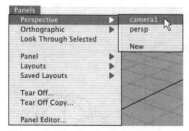

Figure 15.7 The Panels > Perspective menu provides different camera views.

2. With the camera still selected, press [t] for the Show Manipulator tool.

   A move manipulator appears on the camera and another one appears in front of it. The one in front of it is called the center of interest.

3. Move the camera and the center of interest around.

   The camera follows the center of interest—that is, it remains aimed at it (**Figure 15.5**).

4. From the Panels menu in the Perspective view, select Look Through Selected.

   You are now looking through the camera that was just created. Note that the camera name at the bottom of the screen has changed from persp to camera1 (**Figure 15.6**).

✔ Tips

- Another way to choose which camera you are looking through is from the Panels menu in the Perspective view. To find the list of available cameras, select Panels > Perspective (**Figure 15.7**).

- You can rotate a camera—useful when you want to do a camera pan.

- Scaling the camera does not affect its view; however, it could make it easier to select.

There is a subtle but important difference between creating a regular camera and creating a *camera and aim*. The camera-and-aim has an additional node, which can be keyframed or parented to an object.

To create and adjust a camera and aim:

1. From the Create menu select Cameras > Camera and Aim.

   A new camera appears in the Perspective view. The dot in front of the camera is the aim (**Figure 15.8**).

2. From the Window menu select Hypergraph.

   You can see the different nodes associated with the camera group (**Figure 15.9**).

3. From the Hypergraph, select the group node of the camera (probably called camera1_group).

4. Move the camera around.

   The aim and camera move together.

5. In the Perspective view, select and then move the aim.

   The camera remains aimed at it.

6. In the Perspective view, select and then move the camera.

   The camera moves but continues to point at the aim (**Figure 15.10**).

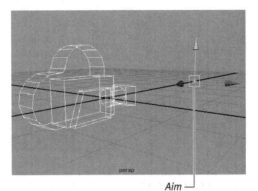

Aim

Figure 15.8 A camera and aim has been created. Note that the aim is represented by a small circle with a dot in the middle.

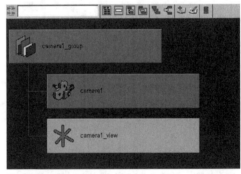

Figure 15.9 This is a camera and aim as represented in the Hypergraph. It has three nodes for added flexibility.

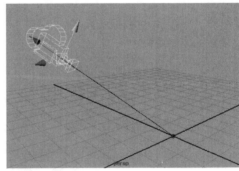

Figure 15.10 The camera has been moved up and away from the origin, but it continues to focus on the aim.

Figure 15.11 If you decide that you want a different camera type after you've created one, you can change the type here, in the Attribute Editor.

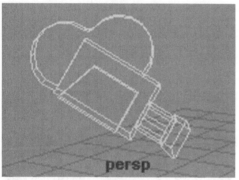

Figure 15.12 At the bottom of the pane, you can see the name of the camera you're looking through—in this case, persp (short for *perspective*). However, note that the camera that's selected is *not* the Perspective (persp) camera.

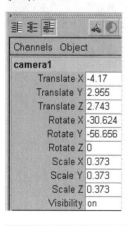

Figure 15.13 In the Channel Box, you can see the name of the camera selected. When you make a new camera, it is named camera1 by default.

✔ Tips

- You can also create a *camera, aim and up*. Similar to the camera and aim, it includes an additional node that controls the tilt of the camera.

- You can change whether the camera has an aim and up after it's been created. In the Attribute Editor for the camera, there is an option under Camera Attributes called Controls where you can choose among the three types of cameras (**Figure 15.11**).

Animating the camera

Animating a camera is, in essence, the same as animating anything else: You select it, keyframe it, change the current time, move it, and keyframe it again. However, there are a number of things you do differently when animating a camera.

You may, for example, want to do camera cuts, where the camera remains still, then jumps to the next position. Or you might want the aim of the camera to follow an object as it passes through a scene. Cameras can also be animated along a path—useful for creating a fly-through of a scene.

One thing you need to understand before you begin animating is that the selected camera isn't necessarily the one you're looking through. At the bottom of the view, you can see the name of the camera you're currently looking through (**Figure 15.12**). In the Channel Box you can see the name of the currently selected camera (**Figure 15.13**). One common mistake is to move the view and set keyframes without having that camera selected. If you make this mistake, you won't end up with any camera animation.

ABOUT CAMERAS

An easy way to animate the camera is to use tumble, track, and dolly, which you've been using all along to see different parts of your scene.

To animate the camera using tumble, track, and dolly:

1. Create some objects and move them around the scene so you have something to look at.

2. From the View menu in the Perspective view, choose Select Camera (**Figure 15.14**).

   You can see that the camera is selected because the name of the camera, persp, appears at the top of the Channel Box.

3. Press $\boxed{s}$ to keyframe the camera.

4. In the Time slider, change the current time to 30 by clicking the number 30.

5. Tumble, track, and dolly the camera to change the point of view.

   (See Chapter 2 for more on how to tumble, track, and dolly.)

6. Press $\boxed{s}$ to keyframe the camera again.

7. Rewind and play back the animation by using the playback control buttons in the timeline (**Figure 15.15**).

   Because the camera's motion is animated, the view changes as you play back the animation (**Figure 15.16**).

Figure 15.14 From the View menu in the Perspective view, choose Select Camera. This selects the camera you're currently looking through.

Figure 15.15 These are the playback controls. On the far left is the Rewind button. The large triangle pointing to the right is the Play button.

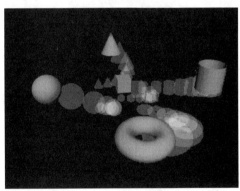

Figure 15.16 This image represents what you would see through the camera once it's animated.

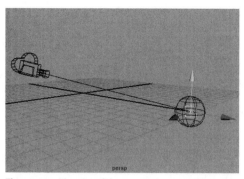

Figure 15.17 The aim of the camera is put at the center of an animated sphere and then parented to it.

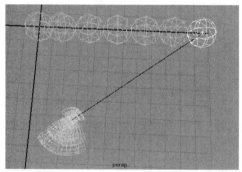

Figure 15.18 The camera follows the sphere as it is animated across the screen.

To make the aim of the camera follow an object:

1. From the Create menu select NURBS Primitives > Sphere.

2. With the sphere still selected, press ⓢ to keyframe the sphere.

3. Change the current time in the timeline to 30.

4. Move the sphere, then press ⓢ to keyframe it again.

   The sphere is now animated.

5. From the Create menu select Cameras > Camera and Aim.

6. Select and move the aim of the camera to the center of the sphere (**Figure 15.17**).

7. With the aim still selected, Shift-select the sphere. Press ⓟ to parent the aim to the sphere.

8. Rewind and play back the animation.

   The camera follows the sphere (**Figure 15.18**).

9. Select the camera, and from the Panels menu in the Perspective view choose Look Through Selected.

   The view changes to the camera you just created.

10. Rewind and play back the animation.

    You can see the camera following the sphere from the point of view of the camera.

ABOUT CAMERAS

When modelers want to show off their models, they often do a turntable animation. One way to create this is to place the model at the center of the scene and rotate the camera around it.

To rotate the camera around an object:

1. Place any object at the origin.

2. From the Create menu select Cameras > Camera.

   A new camera appears in the Perspective view.

3. Move the camera back from the origin.

4. Press w, then press Insert/Home to go into Pivot Move mode.

5. Move the pivot point to the origin (**Figure 15.19**). Press Insert/Home again to get out of Pivot Move mode.

6. Select the camera, and press s to keyframe it.

7. Change the current time in the timeline to 30.

8. In the Channel Box, type *360* in the field next to Rotate Y. Press Enter.

9. Press s to keyframe the camera again.

   If you play back the animation now, you will see the camera rotating around the object (**Figure 15.20**).

10. Select the camera, and from the Panels menu in the Perspective view choose Panels > Look Through Selected.

    You are now seeing through the view of the camera. When the animation is played back, it will look like a turntable animation.

✔ Tip

■ To move the pivot point to the exact origin of the scene, hold down x to snap the pivot point to the grid.

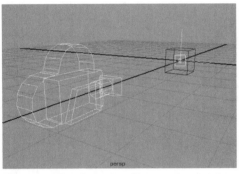

Figure 15.19 The pivot point of a camera is put at the center of an object so it can rotate around that object.

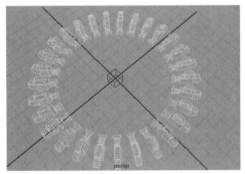

Figure 15.20 The camera is animated to rotate around the object.

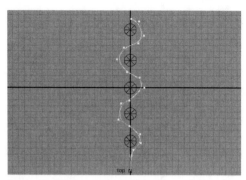

Figure 15.21 A curve is created that weaves through some cones, seen from the Top view.

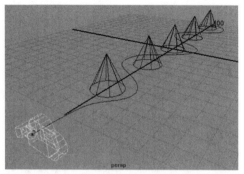

Figure 15.22 The camera has been attached to a motion path, so it jumps to the beginning of the curve. However, it is facing the wrong way.

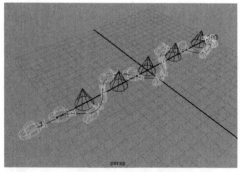

Figure 15.23 The camera, now oriented correctly, follows the curve as the animation is played back.

To animate a camera along a path:

1. Create a row of cones.

2. In the top view, create a NURBS curve that weaves through the cones (**Figure 15.21**).

3. From the Create menu select Cameras > Camera.

   A new camera appears in the Perspective view.

4. With the camera still selected, (Shift)-select the curve.

5. From the Animate menu select Motion Paths > Attach to Motion Path.

   The camera jumps to the beginning of the path, but it might not be pointing in the right direction (**Figure 15.22**).

6. With the camera still selected, click motionPath1 in the Channel Box.

   Four attributes of the motionPath appear.

7. If the camera is not pointing in the right direction, click Up Twist in the Channel Box, and then using the middle mouse button, drag in the Perspective view until the camera is pointing down the path correctly.

8. Rewind and play back the animation.

   The camera travels down the path (**Figure 15.23**).

ABOUT CAMERAS

Focal length

The Focal Length attribute is similar to the zoom on a real camera. When you increase the focal length, you zoom in. An object appears closer, but zooming in also has the effect of flattening distance. When you decrease focal length, you zoom out. Distances seem exaggerated with a short focal length, and you get a fisheye lens effect.

To adjust the focal length of the camera:

1. Place any surface at the origin (**Figure 15.24**).

2. From the View menu in the Perspective view choose Select Camera.

   The Perspective camera becomes selected.

3. In the Channel Box, change Focal Length to *6*.

   The object seems farther away (**Figure 15.25**).

4. Dolly the camera in close to the object (for more information on dollying, see Chapter 2).

   The object is distorted, as it would be with a fisheye lens on a real camera (**Figure 15.26**).

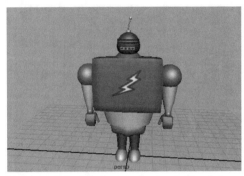

Figure 15.24 A robot character has been placed at the origin. The camera's focal length is set to the default of 35.

Figure 15.25 With the focal length set to 6, the robot seems very far away, even though the camera hasn't moved.

Figure 15.26 The camera has been moved close to the robot with the focal length still set to 6. The effect is similar to that provided by a fisheye lens—distances are exaggerated.

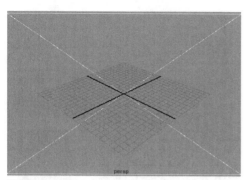

Figure 15.27 When you create an image plane, a big square with an *X* through it shows up in the view. This is where the image will be placed once you choose it.

Figure 15.28 The sunrise image appears in the background of the scene. This image will stay in the same place relative to the camera even if you tumble, track, or dolly.

■ A quick way to hide an image plane is to uncheck Cameras from the Show menu of the view pane you're in. Since the image plane is a component of the camera and you're hiding the camera, the image plane is also hidden.

Image planes

An image plane is a component of the camera that remains in the background of the view regardless of where the camera is moved. Since it's always oriented to the camera and can have an attached image, an image plane can come in handy when you want to use an image as a template for modeling a character. You can also use an image plane as a backdrop to a scene; it renders out with the rest of the scene.

To create an image plane:

1. From the View menu of the Perspective view select Camera Attribute Editor.

   The Attribute Editor for the camera appears.

2. Scroll down the Attribute Editor, and click the triangle next to Environment. This expands the options related to the camera environment.

3. Click Create next to Image Plane.

   The image plane appears in the Perspective view (**Figure 15.27**), and the Attribute Editor changes to show the options for it.

4. Click the folder icon next to Image Name.

5. Browse for and open your image, then close the Attribute Editor.

6. The image now appears on the image plane (**Figure 15.28**).

✔ Tips

■ To select the image plane, you must set the Pick Mask to "Select by component type" by clicking that icon ▦ . You must also select the Miscellaneous icon ？ .

■ Once the image plane is selected, you can move it by changing the Center X, Y, and Z settings in the Channel Box. You can delete it by pressing ⟨Backspace⟩/⟨Delete⟩.

ABOUT CAMERAS

About Rendering

Rendering is how you output images once you finish modeling, animating, lighting, and texturing your scene. There are many options to set—all of which you'll find in the Render Globals window.

First, you must decide what your output will be. The resolution of an image is its size in pixels. The size you choose depends on what medium your images will end up on.

If you're creating a small image for a Web site, you might use the default resolution of 320 by 240. If you plan to put the images on NTSC video, you'll probably use 720 by 486 (**Figure 15.29**).

For decent-quality printing, you need a much higher resolution. Printing at 300 dots per inch (dpi) will produce a sharp image. If you want to print an 8-by-10-inch image, you will need a resolution of 2,400 by 3,300 pixels—which will take a long time to render.

You can set resolution quality in the Render Globals window. Lower-quality images will render faster, making them good for tests. Higher-quality settings will make for a cleaner, better-looking image and should be used for final output (**Figure 15.30**).

Figure 15.29 The same scene has been rendered out in a variety of resolutions.

Figure 15.30 Compare production quality (left) with preview quality (right). The one on the right renders out much more quickly but looks worse.

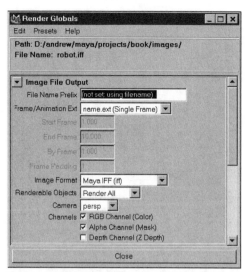

Figure 15.31 In the Render Globals window you can set options such as quality, resolution, image file format, and more.

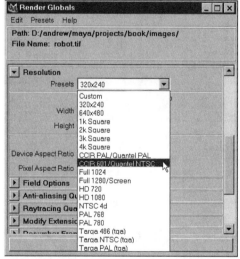

Figure 15.32 Choose a resolution from the list of presets. Resolution determines the size of your image in pixels.

Before you render your scene, you need to save it and set your project. Taking these steps will help you avoid losing images when you render because if the project is set, the renders will automatically be sent to the correct folder.

To render out a single image:

1. In the Render View click the Render Globals button 🖫, or from the Options menu select Render Globals.

   The Render Globals window appears (**Figure 15.31**).

2. Choose an image format.

   Maya IFF is the default, but it won't necessarily open in other programs. You might want to choose something more common, like TIFF or Targa.

3. Choose the camera view you want to render from.

   Even if you've created new cameras, Perspective is still the default camera in the Render Globals window. It's a common mistake to overlook this and render out the wrong camera view.

4. Click the triangle next to Resolution.

   The Resolution options are expanded.

5. From the Presets menu choose CCIR 601/Quantel NTSC (**Figure 15.32**).

   This is a good choice if your image is going to end up on NTSC video.

6. Click the triangle next to Anti-Aliasing Quality.

   The Anti-Aliasing options are expanded.

   continues on next page

7. From the Presets menu choose Production Quality (**Figure 15.33**).

This will automatically set several of the options below and is a good choice for most renders.

8. Click the Render button 📷.

The Render View window appears. The image will take some time to render, depending on the scene's complexity (**Figure 15.34**).

9. From the File menu in the Render View window select Save Image.

You can save the image to any folder and in any format you desire.

To render out a series of images:

1. In the Render View click the Render Globals button 📷, or from the Options menu select Render Globals.

The Render Globals window appears.

2. Set the camera, anti-aliasing quality, resolution, and image-format options as in the previous section.

3. Change the file name if you want the images to be named something other than the name of the scene file.

When a new name is typed in, the example file name at the top of the window reflects this change (**Figure 15.35**).

4. Choose name.#.ext from the Frame/Animation Ext menu.

The example name changes to reflect this update. You must choose an option that includes the pound sign (#) to be able to render animation as opposed to rendering single frames.

name.#.ext is a good choice for the Windows operating system, but for Macintosh or Irix, you may want to use either name.# or name.ext.#. The choice mostly depends on the software into which you plan to bring the images.

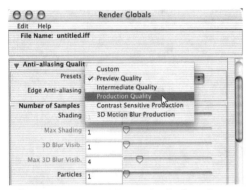

Figure 15.33 Choose Production Quality from the Presets menu. This is the setting you will typically want to use when creating your final image.

Figure 15.34 This image is in the process of rendering in the Render View window. It doesn't appear all at once. The image is broken down into little rectangles that appear gradually.

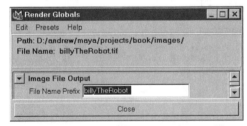

Figure 15.35 The example file name at the top of the Render Globals window changes when a different file name is typed in.

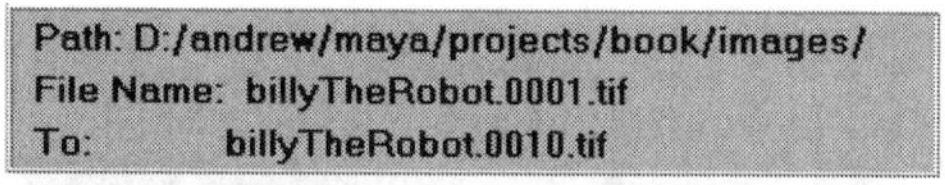

```
Path: D:/andrew/maya/projects/book/images/
File Name:  billyTheRobot.0001.tif
To:         billyTheRobot.0010.tif
```

Figure 15.36 When Frame Padding is changed to 4, the image number becomes four digits long.

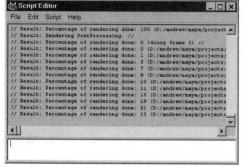

Figure 15.37 You can watch the progress of your render in the Script Editor, which also shows you where it's placing the images (using their full paths) and what the images are named.

5. Set the Start and End frames of your animation.

These should be set to the range of time you want to render out.

6. Change Frame Padding to 4 and close the Render Globals window.

This will put zeros in front of the numbers in the image name so that they are four digits long. This is helpful because your images will be listed in order when sorted by name (**Figure 15.36**).

7. From the Render menu select Batch Render.

The render begins.

8. Click the Script Editor icon ▤ in the lower right corner of the interface.

The Script Editor opens. You can watch the progress of the render here (**Figure 15.37**).

✔ Tips

- If you choose AVI from the image format, it will just render out a single movie file rather than a series of individual numbered images.

- In Render Globals you can turn on Motion Blur, which causes moving surfaces to blur slightly. This makes them look better because they more closely resemble moving objects captured by a real camera.

Maya comes with FCheck, a program that provides an easy way to view images and animations.

To view a render:

1. From the Render menu select Show Batch Render.

   If it's still rendering, the progress of the current frame opens in FCheck (**Figure 15.38**). If it is finished rendering, the last frame opens FCheck.

2. From the File menu in the FCheck window, select Open Animation (Windows) or Open Sequence (Mac) (**Figure 15.39**). A file-browsing window opens.

3. Browse for your rendered image files. They should be in the images folder of the project folder you are currently set to.

4. Open the first image in the series.

   The animation will load slowly and play back at full speed. However, the animation may never get to full speed if it includes lots of images or the resolution is high. Animation speed will also depend on your computer's hardware.

Click and drag from left to right to scroll through the animation.

✔ Tip

■ FCheck includes the following hotkeys to make it easier to use:

   (Spacebar) starts and stops the animation's playback.

   (←) goes back one frame.

   (→) goes forward one frame.

Figure 15.38 Since the batch render is still in process, the progress of the current frame shows up in FCheck. This view will not be updated as the render continues.

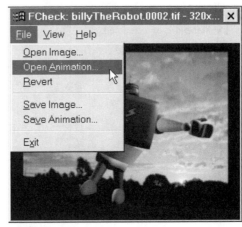

Figure 15.39 You can open an animation in the FCheck window, which can play back all of the frames you've rendered out.

Figure 15.40 The robot was rendered using the Hardware Render Buffer with motion blur turned on. In the bottom, you can see the alpha channel created for this image; you can use it for compositing.

Figure 15.41 This robot was software-rendered. Note the bump map on the arms, the glow on the visor, and the reflectivity of his chest.

Using the Hardware Render Buffer

Software rendering can take a long time. If you want to make a preview of your animation without having to software-render it, you can hardware-render it instead. This provides a kind of a middle ground between a playblast and a software render. Hardware rendering is essentially a series of screen snapshots of your scene.

Hardware rendering does a few things that playblast cannot. It can anti-alias the edges of your surfaces and create motion blur so that the animation looks smoother. It can also create an alpha channel, so that you can easily composite with other images (**Figure 15.40**). One technique is to hardware-render some elements of your scene and composite them with a software-rendered background.

There are also a number of things that hardware rendering *doesn't* do that software rendering does. It cannot create shadows, reflections, or refractions. And it doesn't do as good a job with textures and lights. Special effects like glow don't work, and you can't see bump maps. In general, hardware renders are great for scenes that have minimal textures, and/or have hardware rendered particle effects that you would like to layer into a high-res file later (**Figure 15.41**).

To use the Hardware Render Buffer:

1. Open or create a scene that includes animation.

2. From the Window menu select Rendering Editors > Hardware Render Buffer.

   The Hardware Render Buffer appears.

3. From the Cameras menu in the Hardware Render Buffer select the camera view you want to render out (**Figure 15.42**).

   To adjust the view, you can tumble, track, and dolly inside the Hardware Render Buffer.

4. From the Render menu in the Hardware Render Buffer select Attributes.

   The Attribute Editor for Hardware Render Globals opens (**Figure 15.43**). Hardware Render Globals is a collection of settings for outputting your image files using the Hardware Render Buffer. Note that this is not the same as Render Globals, which is for software rendering only.

5. Set the file name, extension, start frame, end frame, image format, and resolution as desired.

   See "To render out a single image" and "To render out a series of images" earlier in this chapter for more information on these. All the same issues apply for hardware rendering.

6. From the Render menu in the Hardware Render Buffer select Render Sequence.

   The sequence quickly renders out. The image files are put in the Images folder of the project you are currently set to.

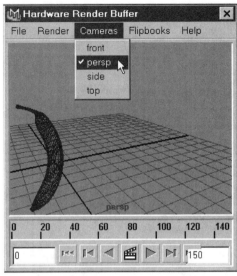

Figure 15.42 Choose a camera view from the Cameras menu in the Hardware Render Buffer.

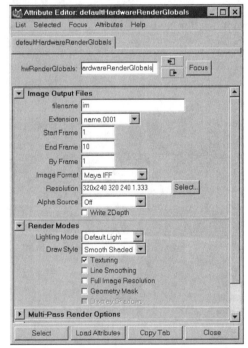

Figure 15.43 The Hardware Render Globals window is where you indicate the file name, resolution, range of frames, and numerous other attributes of the render.

ABOUT RENDERING

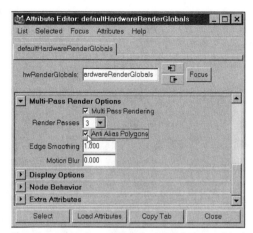

Figure 15.44 Turning on Multi Pass Rendering and Anti Alias Polygons will improve the look of your render by smoothing aliased (stair-stepped) edges.

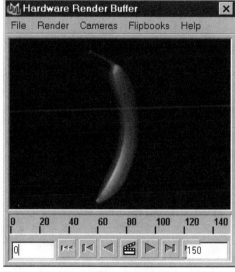

Figure 15.45 Since the banana was animated and Motion Blur was turned on in Hardware Render Globals, you can see some blur in the resulting image.

To adjust hardware-render quality:

1. From the Window menu select Rendering Editors > Hardware Render Buffer.

   The Hardware Render Buffer appears.

2. Set up the hardware-render attributes as in the previous section.

3. Scroll down to Multi-Pass Render Options. Select Multi Pass Rendering and Anti Alias Polygons (**Figure 15.44**).

4. Click the Test Render button in the Hardware Render Buffer to see the result 🎬.

   Three passes of the image are done and then composited together automatically. The edges of the surfaces are anti-aliased.

5. Change Render Passes to 5 and Motion Blur to 1.

6. Click the Test Render button in the Hardware Render Buffer to see the result.

7. Five passes of the image are completed. With Motion Blur set to 1, the passes occur over the duration of one frame (**Figure 15.45**).

ABOUT RENDERING

About Raytracing

Achieving realistic renders often requires reflections and refractions. To achieve these effects, you must turn on raytracing. Although renders can take significantly longer with raytracing on, they look much more realistic.

When you can see other objects in an object's reflection, the light rays are bouncing off one surface and then bouncing off another surface and into your eyes or a camera lens. You need other objects in the scene in order to see a reflection of them; the object has to have something to reflect (**Figure 15.46**).

Refraction is the bending of light as it travels through a dense, transparent material such as glass or liquid. Without it, glass doesn't look real. You can set a refraction index, which controls how much the light bends as it passes through the surface (**Figure 15.47**).

A good example of refraction would be when you're standing in a lake and see a fish under water: If you were to reach in the water and try to grab that fish, you would miss it because refraction has bent the image of the fish into a new position from your point of view. You must compensate for the bending of light to catch the fish.

To create reflections:

1. Create a scene with a large plane, a sphere, many cubes, and some lights (**Figure 15.48**).

2. Assign a Phong material that is red to the cubes, a Phong material with a checker color to the plane, and a Phong material to the sphere.

3. In the Render View click the Render Globals button 🖼, or from the Options menu select Render Globals.

   The Render Globals window appears.

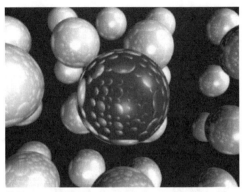

Figure 15.46 This is a scene made up exclusively of spheres. The spheres reflect one another because raytracing is turned on.

Figure 15.47 Each transparent sphere has a different refraction index: left, 1.0; middle, 1.333; right, 2.0.

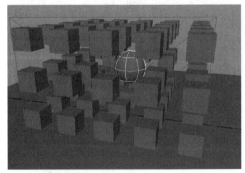

Figure 15.48 This scene has a plane, a sphere surrounded by many cubes, a directional light, and an area light.

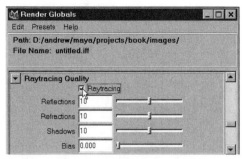

Figure 15.49 Raytracing is turned on in Render Globals. Reflections and refractions do not render out unless this is selected.

Figure 15.50 When the scene is rendered, you can see the cubes reflected in the sphere.

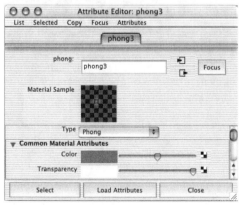

Figure 15.51 The Transparency slider is dragged to the right, which makes the color field white. White is transparent, and black is opaque in Maya.

4. Change the Anti-Aliasing Quality Preset to Production Quality.

5. Scroll down and click the triangle next to Raytracing Quality.

The Raytracing Quality options are expanded.

6. Select Raytracing (**Figure 15.49**).

7. Frame the sphere in the Perspective view, then click the Render button.

8. The Render View appears, and the image renders with reflections (**Figure 15.50**).

To create refraction:

1. Continue with the scene from the previous section.

2. Select the sphere.

3. Click the Graph Materials on Selected Items button in the Hypershade.

The material for the sphere appears in the work area of the Hypershade.

4. Double-click the Phong material assigned to the sphere.

The Attribute Editor for the Phong material opens.

5. Drag the Transparency slider all the way to the right.

The color field next to Transparency becomes white (**Figure 15.51**).

continues on next page

ABOUT RAYTRACING

6. Scroll down in the Attribute Editor, and click the arrow next to Raytrace Options. The Raytrace Options are expanded.

7. Select Refractions.

8. Change Refractive Index to 1.333 (**Figure 15.52**).

9. Click the Render button ![render icon].

The Render View window appears, and the scene renders out. The sphere refracts the light, which causes the objects seen through it to appear warped (**Figure 15.53**).

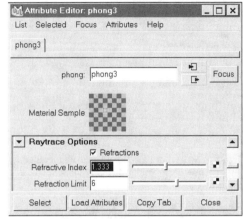

Figure 15.52 Refractions are turned on, and the Refractive Index is set to 1.333. If you do not do this, reflections will render but refractions will not.

Figure 15.53 The transparent sphere is rendered out and refracts light. It is dark because the scene surrounding it is dark.

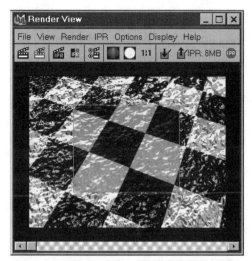

Figure 15.54 A bump map is tweaked in IPR. The selected area updates when the bump depth for this surface is changed from 1.0 to 0.1.

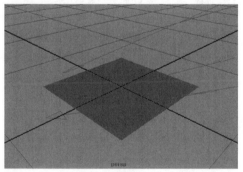

Figure 15.55 A plane is created with a bump map and a directional light pointed at it.

About Interactive Photorealistic Rendering

Every time you make a change to a material or a light you need to render it out again. This makes tweaking things like lights or bump maps time-consuming because of the wait for render time.

To address this problem, Maya offers Interactive Photorealistic Rendering, or IPR. If you render out using IPR, you can select a region of the render, and the changes you make will update interactively (**Figure 15.54**).

IPR, however, has some limits. It won't update the positions of objects or changes to the camera. It won't update the position of a shadow. It doesn't do any raytracing, which means no reflections or refractions. And it always performs low-quality anti-aliasing.

However, IPR will update most changes to materials and lights—and that capability alone can save you a great deal of time. A good workflow is to use IPR rendering while you're setting up and tweaking your objects' color and lighting, and then use software rendering for your final images and tweaks.

To use IPR:

1. Create a plane, assign a material with a bump map to it, and create a directional light pointed diagonally to the plane (**Figure 15.55**).

   See "To assign a bump map to a surface" in Chapter 14 for more on bump maps.

2. Click the IPR button 📷.

   The Render View appears, and the scene renders out. You will see the prompt "Select a region to begin tuning" at the bottom of the Render View.

continues on next page

ABOUT INTERACTIVE PHOTOREALISTIC RENDERING

3. Select a region in the Render View (**Figure 15.56**).

4. Select the plane.

5. Click the Graph Materials on Selected Items button in the Hypershade.

The nodes for the shader appear in the work area of the Hypershade.

6. Double-click the bump2d utility in the Hypershade.

The Attribute Editor for bump2d opens.

7. Change Bump Depth to 2.

The selected region of the Render view updates the change quickly (**Figure 15.57**). Try updating other things, such as the intensity and color of lights, or the color or type of material.

✔ Tip

■ If IPR is not updating, it may be because Raytracing is on. Turn Raytracing off in Render Globals and try IPR again.

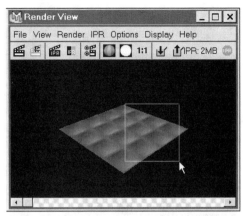

Figure 15.56 After being prompted in the Render View, select a region. Only this region will update when you make changes, but you can select the whole image as the region if you want.

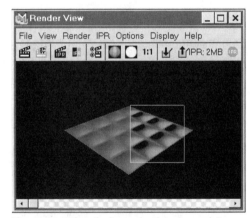

Figure 15.57 When the bump depth is changed, it updates interactively in the Render View.

16

DYNAMICS

As you build your scenes in Maya, you'll likely encounter effects or situations that would be difficult to create or animate using traditional keyframing. Leaves blowing across the landscape, for example, or a glass shattering as it hits the ground can take hours to animate by hand—and they still may not end up looking realistic.

You can use Maya's Dynamics menu set to simplify these tasks by simulating the motion of an object being affected by different physical forces (see **Figure 16.1** on the next page). For example, with just a few mouse-clicks (and without setting a single keyframe), you can make a leaf appear to be pushed along by the wind as it simultaneously collides with and rolls along the ground.

While using the Dynamics menu set can be fun, it can also be frustrating: Hundreds of options are available for most dynamic simulations. In this chapter, we'll concentrate on only the basics so that you can get up and running quickly.

Particles

Particle dynamics can be used to create myriad effects, including fire, fog, dust, explosions, mud, and even a swarm of bees.

A particle is a point in 3D space that can be affected by simulated physical forces, which are displayed as a number of items, including spheres, clouds, images, and blobby surfaces—even specified objects like leaves or spaceships.

You can draw particles into the scene by using the Particle tool, or you can create them with an emitter, which emits particles automatically in a number of ways depending on the effect desired.

Let's begin by creating a simple particle object and changing the size in the Attribute Editor.

To create a particle object:

1. Switch to the Dynamics menu set by choosing Dynamics from the pop-up menu in the top left corner of Maya's interface.

2. From the Particles menu select Particle Tool (**Figure 16.2**).

3. Click in the Top view to place particles in the scene. Each click creates one particle (**Figure 16.3**).

    You can use any view you want, and the particles will be placed on the grid. As you place the particles, they will be displayed as crosshairs.

Figure 16.1 Rocket trails created using particle effects.

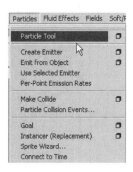

Figure 16.2 From the Particles menu select Particle Tool.

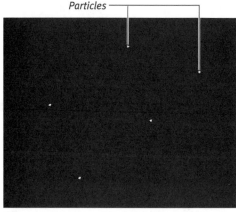

Figure 16.3 Create particles by clicking in the Top view.

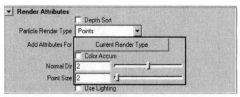

Figure 16.4 The Render Attributes section is used to change the look of the particle.

4. You can place as many particles as you like. When you have finished, press Enter to complete the particle object.

A particle object is a group of individual particles. Each individual particle is a component of the particle object.

5. With the particle object selected, open the Attribute Editor by pressing Ctrl a / Control a .

6. Scroll down to the Render Attributes section of the Attribute Editor.

7. Click Add Attributes for Current Render Type.

Extra attributes are now available for you to adjust (**Figure 16.4**).

8. Change the value of Point Size to make the particles bigger or smaller.

This will change the size in the display as well as in the render.

✔ Tip

■ By default, you create particles by clicking in the View pane. In the options for the Particle tool, you can turn on the Sketch option to draw particles on the grid.

Particles can also be produced by an *emitter*, which emits particles in a particular speed and direction. There are three types of emitters:

◆ **Omni**—Emits particles in all directions (**Figure 16.5**).

◆ **Directional**—Emits particles in one user-specified direction (**Figure 16.6**).

◆ **Volume**—Emits particles from a primitive shape such as a cube or cone (**Figure 16.7**).

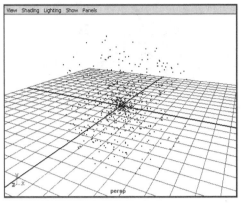

Figure 16.5 An Omni emitter.

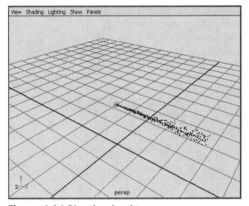

Figure 16.6 A Directional emitter.

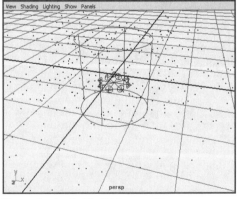

Figure 16.7 A cylindrical Volume emitter.

Emitter ─┐

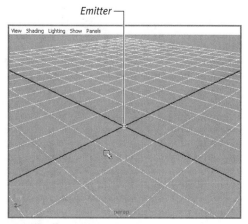

Figure 16.8 An emitter is created at the center of the grid.

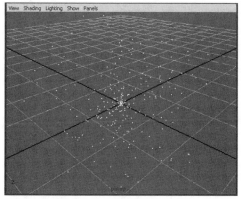

Figure 16.9 Particles emit in all directions from an Omni emitter.

You can select what type of emitter you want to use when you create the object (in its Options window), or you can change the emitter type in the Attribute Editor.

To create an emitter:

1. From the Particles menu select Create Emitter.

   By default an Omni emitter is created, and its icon appears at the center of the grid. This is where the particles will be emitted. (**Figure 16.8**).

2. Press Play ▷ in the playback controls.

   You will see particles emitting from the center of the grid (**Figure 16.9**).

3. With the particles selected, open the Attribute Editor by pressing Ctrl a /Control a.

4. In the Attribute Editor select the particleShape1 tab.

5. Scroll down and open the Lifespan Attributes section.

6. From the pop-up menu, select Constant.

   You can now change the duration of the particles once they've been emitted. With a Constant value of 1, they will last for just one second, then disappear.

7. Press Play again to see the results.

Render Types

You determine the appearance of your particles by assigning to each a *render type*, which include *Points, MultiPoint, Streak, MultiStreak, Sprites, Spheres, Tube [s/w], Blobby Surface [s/w], Cloud [s/w],* and *Numeric.* Most of these types are rendered through the Hardware Render Buffer. The types whose names include "[s/w]" are rendered through software. (See Chapter 15 for more information on hardware and software rendering.)

To change a particle's render type:

1. Select a particle object (**Figure 16.10**).

2. Open the Attribute Editor by pressing Ctrl a/Control a.

3. Under particleShape1 tab, open the Render Attributes sectionand select the pop-up menu for Particle Render Type.

4. Select Cloud [s/w] from the list.
   The particles now look like circles in the Perspective view (**Figure 16.11**).

5. Click Add Attributes For Current Render Type (**Figure 16.12**).

6. Change the Radius from 1 to 3 by adjusting the slider.
   This allows you to interactively change the size of the cloud particle for the display as well as the render.

7. To render the cloud particle, click the Render Current Frame button 🎬.
   or
   From the Window menu, select Rendering Editors > Render View (**Figure 16.13**).

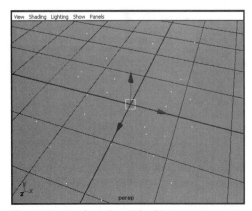

Figure 16.10 A selected particle object.

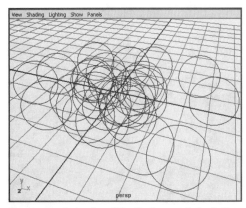

Figure 16.11 A cloud particle displays as circles in the Perspective view.

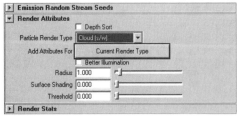

Figure 16.12 Each render type has a number of different attributes to adjust.

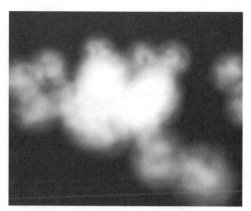

Figure 16.13 A rendered cloud particle effect.

Figure 16.14 Points render as dots.

Figure 16.15 MultiPoint renders as clusters of dots.

Hardware render

The following are the render methods for the hardware render type:

Points—Points render as dots on the screen (**Figure 16.14**). The radius is adjustable, but the particles will look like squares at larger sizes.

MultiPoint—Renders as a cluster of dots on the screen (**Figure 16.15**). Extra attributes include Multi Radius, which controls the size of each cluster, and Multi Count, which controls the number of dots in each cluster.

Streak—Streaks render as lines on the screen (**Figure 16.16**). Extra attributes include Size, Line Width, Tail Size, and Tail Fade.

continues on next page

Figure 16.16 Streaks render as straight lines.

369

MultiStreak—Like Streaks, MultiStreak renders as lines on the screen (**Figure 16.17**). Multi Streak has the same attributes as Streak, plus Multi Count, and Multi Radius.

Sprites—Sprites have an image file attached to them (**Figure 16.18**). From the Particles menu select Sprite Wizard to choose the image file you want to use.

Spheres—Spheres render as opaque spheres (**Figure 16.19**). You can assign any shader you want to a Sphere particle. Transparency is not supported.

Numeric—Numeric particles have a number value associated with them (**Figure 16.20**). These number values can represent static, dynamic, or per-particle attributes.

Figure 16.17 MultiStreak renders as clusters of lines.

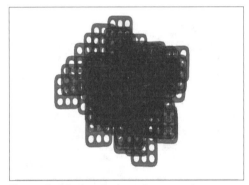

Figure 16.18 Sprites display as images and support opacity and alpha channels.

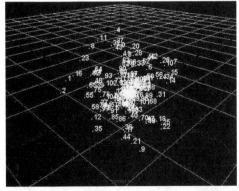

Figure 16.20 Numeric particles display with specified information pertaining to the particle. Numeric particles render as dots.

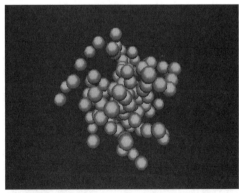

Figure 16.19 Spheres render as polygonal spheres that can be textured.

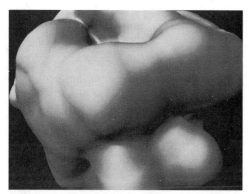

Figure 16.21 Blobby Surfaces render as spheres but look as though they're melting or blending together.

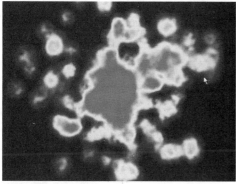

Figure 16.22 Clouds render as a foggy or cloudy surface that is partially transparent.

Figure 16.23 Tubes render as cylindrical surfaces and look a bit like Streak particles; the difference is that you can render them via the Software Render window.

Software render

The following are the render methods for the software render type:

Blobby Surface—Blobby Surface particles render as spheres that can appear to melt into one surface (**Figure 16.21**). Attributes include Radius and Threshold:

◆ **Radius.** Determines the initial size of the particle.

◆ **Threshold.** Determines how much the particles blend together. As the Threshold attribute is increased, the radius of the particle diminishes and begins to blend with other particles.

Cloud—Clouds render as spheres that grow more transparent as you move farther from the center (**Figure 16.22**). Clouds behave like Blobby Surfaces but render with a Particle Cloud shader. You can adjust the shader's density, color, and other attributes in the Hypershade. (See Chapter 13 for more information on shaders).

Tube—Tubes render as cylinders that grow as the animation progresses (**Figure 16.23**). You can adjust when the cylinder begins and stops expanding using Radius0 and Radius1. Tail Size determines the length of the tube.

Fields

Fields are used in conjunction with particle objects to give them a specific behavior. There are nine types of fields in Maya: *Air, Drag, Gravity, Newton, Radial, Turbulence, Uniform, Vortex*, and *Volume Axis*. You can use more than one field on any particle object to achieve the desired motion for your animation.

The following is a list of field types and their effect on particle objects.

Air—The Air field produces the effect of a moving volume of air (**Figure 16.24**). The following are the three default Air field types:

◆ **Wind**. This type of Air field blows particles in a specified direction until they catch up to the speed of the Air field.

◆ **Wake.** As the Air field moves through a particle object, it disturbs the particles and drags them along, creating a wake effect.

◆ **Fan.** This type of Air field pushes particles in a 45-degree spread, simulating a fan.

Drag—The Drag field helps slow down, or add friction to, a moving particle.

Gravity—The Gravity field simulates a real-world gravity effect on the selected particle; you can apply it in any direction you specify.

Newton—A Newton field will attract particles.

Radial—A Radial field will attract or repel particles in a spherical manner.

Turbulence—A Turbulence field will disrupt the position of the particles. You can use this to randomize the movement slightly for your particle animation.

Uniform—This field's effect is similar to that of the Air field: It pushes the particles in a specified direction.

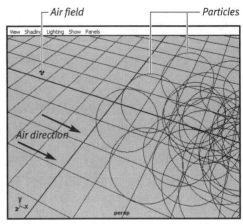

Figure 16.24 An Air field is used to push particles in a specific direction.

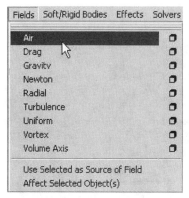

Figure 16.25 From the Fields menu, select Air.

Vortex—A Vortex field exerts a spiraling force on the particles. You can use it to create a tornado effect.

Volume Axis—A Volume Axis field is defined by a volume shape. This lets you affect particles with a shape, such as a sphere or cube.

Common attributes

The following are the attributes that are common to all fields:

Magnitude—Sets how much force is exerted from the field.

Attenuation—Sets how much the force drops off as the affected object moves away from the field.

Direction—Usually in X, Y, Z, determines the direction of the force.

Use Max Distance—Allows you to set a maximum distance to define the area of effect.

Max Distance—The value in units that the field will affect.

To attach a field to a particle object:

1. Create an emitter.

2. Press Play ▷ once to emit the particles; press it again to halt playback.

3. Select the particles.

4. From the Fields menu select Air (**Figure 16.25**).

   This will attach the field to the selected object.

   continues on next page

FIELDS

5. Play back the animation to see the effect of the Air field on the particles (**Figure 16.26**).

6. Select the Air field.

If you have trouble selecting the Air Field, try selecting Window > Hypergraph, and then clicking on the Air field.

7. Open the Attribute Editor by pressing [Ctrl][a]/[Control][a].

8. Under the Air Field Attributes tab, change Magnitude to *20* (**Figure 16.27**).

9. Play back the animation again to see the effect of the magnitude change.

The Air field pushes with more force as the magnitude increases.

✔ Tip

■ You can animate Air field attributes. Try setting keyframes on the Magnitude attribute to make its value change over time.

Air field ⎯⎯⎯ ⎯⎯ Affected particles

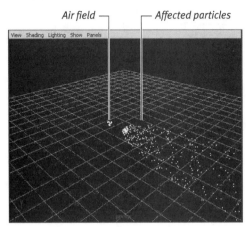

Figure 16.26 The particles are blown in the *X* direction by the Air field.

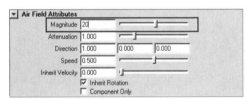

Figure 16.27 Increasing the Magnitude attribute of an Air field will make the particles blow away from it faster.

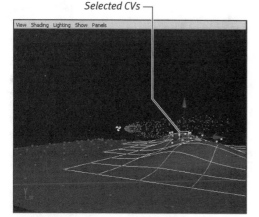

Selected CVs

Figure 16.28 Create a small hill for the particles to collide with.

Collisions

If we had added a Gravity field to our particle object it would have simply fallen out of view because there was nothing in the scene to stop it. You can use the Make Collide command to tell Maya to make the particles collide with certain geometry.

For example, for a scene in which you wanted fog to roll along the ground, you could create a particle object, attach Air and Gravity fields, and have the particles collide with the ground. Now the particles will fall to the ground and be pushed along by the Air field.

To create a particle collision:

1. Create the particle object and attach an Air field (see previous example).

2. Select the particle and from the Fields menu select Gravity.

3. From the Create menu select the box beside NURBS Primitive > Plane.

   In the Options dialog box, give the plane 10 patches in U and V.

4. Click Create.

5. Scale the plane so that it's large enough to represent the ground. Select a few CVs around the center of the plane and translate them in the positive *Y* direction to create a hill (**Figure 16.28**).

continues on next page

COLLISIONS

6. Translate the plane in object mode in the negative *Y* direction so that the plane is below the particles.

7. Select the particle object and select the ground plane (**Figure 16.29**).

8. From the Particles menu select Make Collide.

9. Rewind the animation by pressing the Rewind button ⟦⟧ and press Play ▶ to see the effect.

   The particles now fall to the ground and are pushed along the surface by the Air field (**Figure 16.30**).

✔ Tip

■ Change the render type to Cloud by selecting the particle and opening the Attribute Editor by pressing ⟦Ctrl⟧⟦a⟧/ ⟦Control⟧⟦a⟧. This will make it easier to select and see the particles.

Ground plane ⌐   ⌐*Particle object*

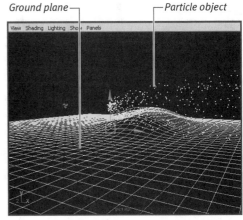

Figure 16.29 Select the ground plane and the particle object to make them collide.

Figure 16.30 Particles collide with the ground geometry and flow over the hill.

COLLISIONS

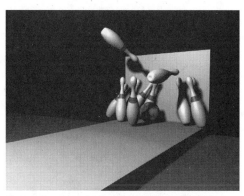

Figure 16.31 A render from a Rigid Body simulation. The ball collides with the pins, which in turn collide with the back wall, floor, and each other.

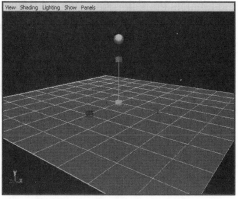

Figure 16.32 A plane is used as a rigid surface for the ball to bounce off of.

Rigid Body Dynamics

Both rigid and soft bodies connect dynamic properties to geometry. Define an object as a rigid body when you want it to collide with another object without yielding; if you want your object to behave with flexibility or elasticity, make it a soft body.

By using Maya's Rigid Body dynamics, you simulate what occurs when one or more objects collide.

Imagine trying to animate a bowling ball crashing into ten pins at the end of the alley—it would take a lot of time and talent to make that action appear realistic. Maya solves this problem by letting us define objects that are going to interact with (or hit) each other so that it can simulate what will happen when they made contact (**Figure 16.31**).

You can create *active rigid bodies,* which react to collisions and fields (Gravity, Air, and so on), or you can create *passive rigid bodies,* which are unaffected by collisions or fields. You use passive rigid bodies for things like floors and walls—basically any unmovable object.

To create a Rigid Body simulation:

1. Create a NURBS sphere.

2. Translate the sphere in the positive *Y* direction.

3. Create a NURBS plane and scale it up to create the floor (**Figure 16.32**).

4. Select the sphere.

continues on next page

5. From the Soft/Rigid Bodies menu select Create Active Rigid Body (**Figure 16.33**).

6. Select the plane.

7. From the Soft/Rigid Bodies menu select Create Passive Rigid Body.

8. Select the sphere.

9. From the Fields menu select Gravity. This attaches a Gravity field to the sphere to make it fall to the ground.

10. Play back the animation to see the result (**Figure 16.34**).

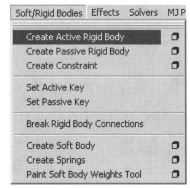

Figure 16.33 From the Soft/Rigid Bodies menu select Create Active Rigid Body.

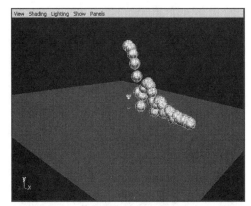

Figure 16.34 A rigid sphere bouncing off of a slightly rotated plane (to make the motion more visible).

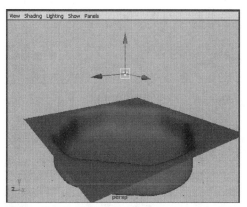

Figure 16.35 An Air field pushing part of a soft body plane down in the negative Y direction.

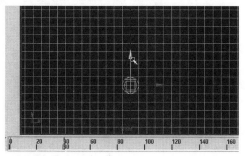

Figure 16.36 Setting a keyframe at Frame 40 in the timeline.

Soft Body Dynamics

Unlike rigid bodies, Maya's soft bodies have elasticity. Each CV, or vertex, has an associated particle, which can be affected by other dynamics (such as fields) or by particle collisions, thereby deforming the object (**Figure 16.35**).

With particles affecting the surface, we can make flags wave in the wind, gelatin cubes wiggle when they hit the ground, or a belly jiggle as a character walks.

Soft bodies can also use nonsoft objects as goal shapes. A *goal shape* represents a target shape for the soft body to settle into. The particles affecting the soft body are attracted to the CVs, or vertices, of the goal object—almost as if they were attached by springs. This means that you can animate the original geometry, and the soft body will lag behind it, overshooting the original geometry before finally settling into that shape. An overweight man with a double chin that jiggles and lags behind the chin bone's movement is one example of this.

To create a soft body:

1. Create a NURBS sphere.

   In the timeline at Frame 1, set a keyframe on the sphere by pressing ⓢ.

2. Move to Frame 40 in the timeline.

3. Translate the sphere 10 units in the negative *Y* direction (**Figure 16.36**). Set another keyframe by pressing ⓢ.

4. Move back to Frame 1 and select the sphere.

5. From the Soft/Rigid Bodies menu select the box next to Create Soft Body to open the options.

continues on next page

6. From the pop-up menu select Duplicate, Make Copy Soft.

7. Check the boxes next to Make Non-Soft a Goal and Hide Non-Soft Object (**Figure 16.37**).

This will duplicate and hide the original geometry and make the duplicate a soft body. The goal then will be the original animated geometry that is hidden.

8. Click Create.

If you play back the animation now, the soft body will simply follow the original animation of the sphere. This is because goal weights on the soft body are all set to 1.

Goal weights can be adjusted, even painted, on a soft body so that you can get just the right amount of movement from your object. In the next section, we'll make the top of the sphere lag behind and wiggle as the sphere stops.

To adjust goal weights for a soft body:

1. Select the Soft Body sphere.

2. From the Soft/Rigid Bodies menu, select the box beside Paint Soft Body Weights Tool.

The Artisan tool opens, and our soft body turns white (**Figure 16.38**).

3. In the Artisan window (which looks like the Attribute Editor), click the Reset Tool button at the top.

4. In the Paint Attributes section change Value to .5

5. Paint the top of the sphere by clicking and dragging. The color on the top should turn gray (**Figure 16.39**).

6. Play back the animation. You should see the top jiggle as the sphere stops at Frame 40 (Figure **16.40**).

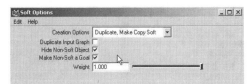

Figure 16.37 The options for creating a soft body.

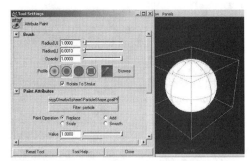

Figure 16.38 You use the Artisan tool to paint soft-body goal weights.

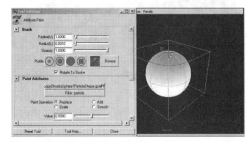

Figure 16.39 The Attribute paint tool lets you interactively paint weight values onto your objects.

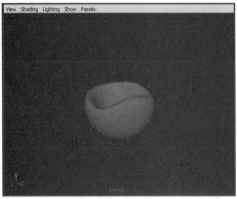

Figure 16.40 As the original sphere stops at Frame 40, the soft body will jiggle on the top until it comes to rest in its original shape.

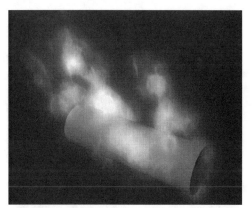

Figure 16.41 The Fire effect.

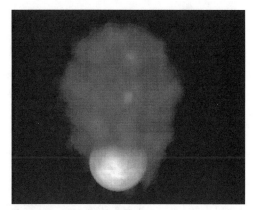

Figure 16.42 The Smoke effect.

Expressions

Expressions are small written commands and mathematical functions that connect the attributes of different nodes. An example would be:

```
nurbsSphere2.rotateX =
nurbsSphere1.rotateX*3
```

The above lines of code would automatically make nurbsSphere2 rotate three times as fast as nurbsSphere1 on the *x* axis.

Effects

Maya provides all sorts of premade particle effects. You can use them to set objects on fire, emit smoke, produce lightning, even make a river flow through a valley. Typically these pre-made effects act as a starting point for something more complex, which means you'll need to adjust them to get the desired effect.

By using a premade effect from the Effects menu, you can take advantage of a particle system with extra attributes that directly affect the way the particles react, or render. These attributes are made up of premade expressions and connections. When you make fire using the Create Fire effect, for example, Maya automatically connects Turbulence, Gravity, and Drag fields to the particles, as well as a premade shader and special expressions to give you added control.

The following provides a brief description of each of the seven premade effects available on the Effects menu:

Create Fire—Produces an emitter that has Gravity, Drag, and Turbulence fields attached to a cloud particle. You can set Density, Radius, Direction, and Intensity in the Options menu. Fire can be emitted from a surface, curve or a directional point. A directional point will emit fire particles in a specified direction from any point in space (**Figure 16.41**).

Create Smoke—Produces an emitter that uses sprite images instead of clouds or points. To use a particular set of images, select Sprite Wizard from the Particles menu. A default set of images and directions are included with the program. You can set Lifespan, Opacity, Direction, Spread, and Speed in the Options menu (**Figure 16.42**).

continues on next page

Create Fireworks—Produces a cluster of rockets and explosions depending on the options you set (**Figure 16.43**).

Create Lightning—Creates an animated electric bolt between two or more objects. Thickness, Spread, Jagged Sections, and Glow and Light Intensity can be adjusted in the Options menu (**Figure 16.44**).

Create Shatter—Lets you break apart an object into a specified number of pieces. There are three types of Shatter: Surface, Solid, and Crack (**Figure 16.45**).

Figure 16.43 The Fireworks effect.

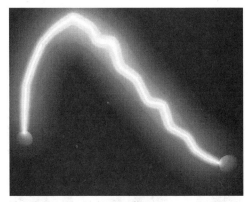

Figure 16.44 The Lightning effect.

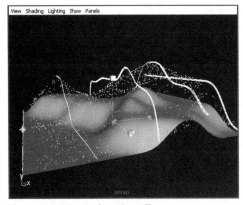

Figure 16.46 The Surface Flow effect.

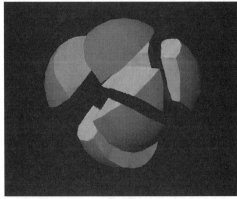

Figure 16.45 The Shatter effect.

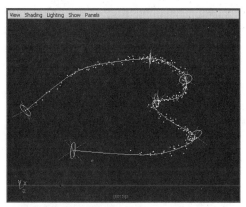

Figure 16.47 The Curve Flow effect.

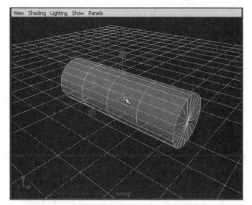

Figure 16.48 A cylinder used to represent a log.

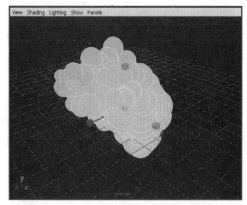

Figure 16.49 A render of a log on fire.

Surface Flow—Creates manipulators that will direct particles to flow along a NURBS surface (**Figure 16.46**).

Create Curve Flow—Produces manipulators to control the flow of particles along a curve's path (**Figure 16.47**).

To make an object emit fire:

1. Create a polygon cylinder. Rotate and scale it to represent a log (**Figure 16.48**).

2. Select the cylinder and from the Effects menu select Create Fire.

3. Press Play ▶ to start the fire simulation (**Figure 16.49**).

4. Press Stop ■ at any point in the time-line and render the Perspective view to see the results.

5. Select the particles and open the Attribute Editor.

6. Under Extra Attributes, adjust Fire Density to *20*, Fire Lifespan to *.2*, and Fire Speed to *10*, and then play back the animation to see the effect (**Figure 16.50**).

   Try changing these and other attributes to get a different type of fire effect.

7. Rewind, play, stop, and render to see the changes.

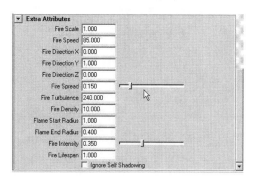

Figure 16.50 Extra attributes to affect the fire particles.

EFFECTS

To create lightning:

1. Create two spheres and translate them so that they aren't overlapping (**Figure 16.51**).

2. Select both spheres.

3. From the Effects menu select Create Lightning.

   A zigzag appears between the two spheres. Also created are two locators, a light, and a selection handle.

4. Select one of the locators and translate it away from the objects. The lightning will now have a curve in its trajectory (**Figure 16.52**).

5. Select the selection handle in the middle of the lightning object (**Figure 16.53**).

6. In the Channel Box adjust the attributes for Thickness, Start and End, and Color to get the desired effect.

   You can also find these attributes in the Attribute Editor under the Lighning1 tab in the Extra Attributes section.

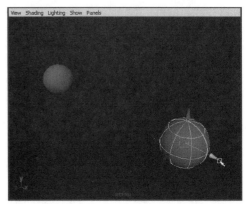

Figure 16.51 Two spheres used to create a lightning effect.

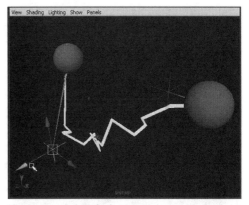

Figure 16.52 Select the locator and move it to put an arc in the lightning bolt.

Selection handle

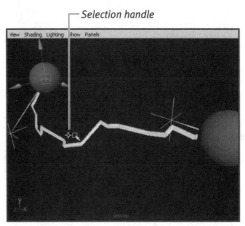

Figure 16.53 The selection handle for the lightning effect.

EFFECTS

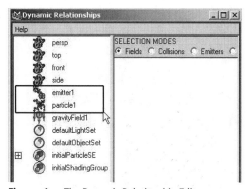

Figure 16.54 The Dynamic Relationship Editor.

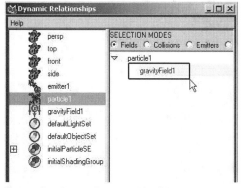

Figure 16.55 Connecting a particle object to a gravity field in the Dynamic Relationship Editor.

The Dynamic Relationship Editor

Sometimes you'll want to attach a particle object or a rigid or soft body to an existing field or collision object. The Dynamic Relationship Editor lets you see a list of a scene's nodes as well as the existing fields, collisions, and emitters—all of which you can then connect.

To connect a field to a particle using the Dynamic Relationship Editor:

1. From the Particles menu select Create Emitter.

2. From the Fields menu select Gravity.

   If you play the animation at this point, the particles won't fall because the particle object wasn't selected when you created the Gravity field—which means the two aren't connected.

3. From the Window menu select Relationship Editors > Dynamic Relationships.

   On the left side of the editor is a list of the scene's nodes.

   You should see emitter1, particle1, and gravityField1 in this column (**Figure 16.54**).

4. Select particle1 from the left column.

   Now, on the right side of the editor, gravityField1 should appear in the list. It's not highlighted at this point because the two nodes have not been connected.

5. Click gravityField1 on the right side of the editor (**Figure 16.55**).

   Particle1 is now connected to gravityField1.

6. Play back the animation to make sure the Gravity field has caused the particles to fall.

Fluid Effects

Fluid Effects are used to create a realistic simulation of a particles movement depending on its surrounding environment, for example if the temperature of the air is higher in a certain area, a particle will rise more quickly through that area.

At the time of this writing, Fluid Effects, a new dynamic system in Maya, is only available in Maya Unlimited. And Maya Unlimited, unfortunately, is only available on Windows. The word *fluid* actually refers to motion (rather than a simulation of actual fluid), which means you can use the system to create such effects as explosions, smoke, flames, oceans, clouds, and thick liquids.

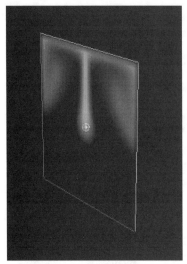

Figure 16.56 A 2D fluid container.

About containers

At the heart of Fluid Effects is the *container*. All Fluid Effects take place inside of a container; in fact, they can't exist outside a container. Containers are 2D or 3D rectangular objects.

2D containers are useful for any effect where the camera is not moving around the effect. The container can be translated, rotated, and animated but has no thickness or depth (**Figure 16.56**).

3D containers have depth, which you can set in the Options window when you create the container. These containers are useful for creating clouds, explosions, or any other effect that requires depth (**Figure 16.57**).

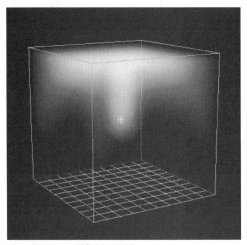

Figure 16.57 A 3D fluid container.

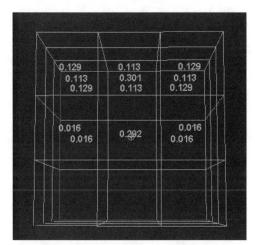

Figure 16.58 The Density grid values are displayed here for a 3D container.

A container uses *voxels* (short for *volume pixels*) arranged in a grid to display the fluid effect. Each voxel has multiple associated attributes and values that determine the way the fluid effect behaves and displays (**Figure 16.58**).

Grids are used for multiple attributes of fluid objects, and each attribute can use a different type of grid. The attributes for fluid effects are as follows:

Density—The Density grid determines where the fluid will be visible as well as its opacity.

Velocity—The Velocity grid determines which direction, or flow, the fluid will have.

Temperature—The Temperature grid determines the amount of heat emitted by a particular voxel. (Heat rises and dissipates as time passes—parameters that you can control.)

Fuel—The Fuel grid determines where a reaction will take place within the grid. Temperature will ignite fuel to start the reaction. Thus, density is affected as the fuel burns off.

Color Method—The Color Method grid determines whether the color will be a shaded color, dynamic grid, or static grid.

You can use three grid types for the above-described attributes:

Static Grid—This type of grid lets you define the values of each voxel in the grid. These values will remain static throughout the simulation.

Dynamic Grid—With this type of grid, you can assign a value to each voxel it includes. As the simulation plays, the value of each voxel will dynamically change depending on the forces acting on it.

Gradient—A gradient will assign a linear value of 0 to 1 across the grid in any direction or out from the center. These values do not change over time.

There are a number of ways to get a fluid into a container: You can create an emitter, paint fluids, or use gradients. We're going to create a 2D container with an attached emitter.

To create a 2D Container:

1. From the Fluid Effects menu select the box next to Create 2D Container with Emitter (**Figure 16.59**).

   In the options that appear you can define the container's size (units) and resolution (number of voxels).

2. Rewind the animation and press Play ▶.

   As the simulation runs, you should see a white stream of particles being emitted from the center of the container (**Figure 16.60**).

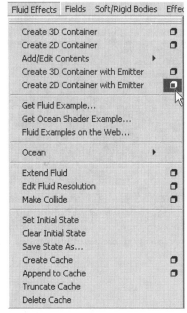

Figure 16.59 From the Fluid Effects menu, select the box beside Create 2D Container with Emitter.

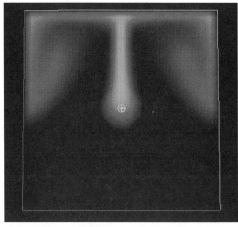

Figure 16.60 The fluid is emitted upward from the center of the container.

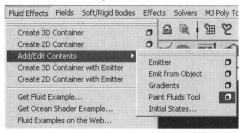

Figure 16.61 From the Fluid Effects menu, select the box beside Add/Edit Contents > Paint Fluids Tool.

Figure 16.62 Setting the Density and Fuel grid to Dynamic.

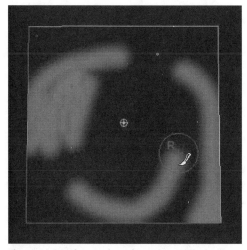

Figure 16.63 A few strokes of Density and Fuel will change the behavior of the fluid effect.

Now that you've emitted a fluid, you can change the value of each attribute by using the Artisan Paint tool.

To edit the contents of a container using paint fluids:

1. Select the fluid container.

2. Rewind the animation.

3. From the Fluid Effects menu select Add/Edit Contents > Paint Fluids Tool > Options box (**Figure 16.61**).

   This opens the Artisan Paint tool.

4. From the Paintable Attributes pop-up menu, select Density and Fuel.

   A dialog box appears to inform you that you must set the attribute to Dynamic Grid; click Set to Dynamic (**Figure 16.62**).

5. Paint a few strokes into the container (**Figure 16.63**).

6. Press Play to see how Density and Fuel affect the results.

The same principles guide the creation of 3D containers. You get an extra manipulator to provide control over where you're painting in the *z* axis, or Depth. To create a 3D container, follow the steps you used to create the 2D container.

About fluid container attributes

Fluid containers contain many unique attributes, which you can adjust from within the Attribute Editor. The following describes each section of the Attribute Editor and its contents.

Container Properties—Determines the resolution (number of voxels) and size of the grid.

Contents Method—Determines the grid type for each fluid property.

Display—Determines how the fluid displays in the View pane.

Dynamic Simulation—Determines the gravity, viscosity (thickness), and friction of the fluid.

Contents Details—Determines multiple parameters for each fluid property: Density, Velocity, Turbulence, Temperature, Fuel, and Color.

Grids Cache—Determines the options for saving the simulation to a file.

Surface—Defines how the surface renders. For various fluids, you can choose between Volume Render and Surface Render. A Volume Render can be used for voluminous things like smoke or steam. A Surface Render can be used for surfaces that need to look as though they have thickness, such as mud.

Shading—Determines the fluid's color, incandescence, and opacity.

Shading Quality—Displays options for how the fluid is depicted.

Textures—Provides options for color, incandescence, and opacity texture types.

Lighting—Lets you choose to use Self Shadowing, which will make the effect cast shadows on itself. Also lets you choose to use the lights in the scene by checking the Real Lights box, or to set your own direction for lighting.

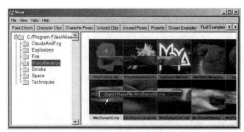

Figure 16.64 Importing a fluid example from the Visor.

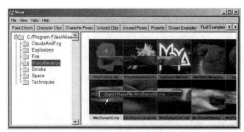

Figure 16.65 The attributes for a fluid effect.

Sample fluid effects

Sometimes the best way to learn a new effects procedure is to look at already-created systems. A great place to start is Maya's library of example fluid effects. If you import one of these example effects into your scene, you can then use the Attribute Editor to view the settings used to create it.

In addition, the Attribute Editor in Maya 4.5 includes a new section at its bottom, called the Notes section. This area may also include an explanation of the procedure used to create certain effects. You can also use the Notes section to add your own comments about an effect. The comments are then saved with that specific node for later viewing.

To import a fluid example:

From the Fluid Effects menu, select Get Fluid Example.

1. This opens the Visor, which contains the different examples (**Figure 16.64**).

2. In the left column of the Visor, select the folder for the type of effect you would like to import.

3. In the right hand column right-click the effect you desire, and select Import Maya File (your file.ma).

   The effect is imported into the scene at the center of the grid.

4. Experiment with the settings in the Attribute Editor by pressing Ctrl/a/ Control a to change the way the fluid is displayed and evaluated (**Figure 16.65**).

Maya Ocean and Ocean shader

New to version 4.5 of Maya is the Ocean effect, which uses fluid dynamics to simulate an effect that was previously very difficult to achieve: With just one click, you can now create a photo-realistic ocean and control how calm or stormy the seas are (**Figure 16.66**). And by creating a locator and connecting it to the fluid simulation, you can even make objects appear to float in your ocean.

As with the other fluid effects, Maya provides ocean examples that you can import into your scenes.

To create a default Maya ocean:

1. From the Fluid Effects menu, select Ocean > Create Ocean (**Figure 16.67**). A NURBS Plane is created on the grid in the scene.

2. Open the Attribute Editor and select the OceanShader tab.

3. Open the Ocean Attributes section and adjust Wave Height, Turbulence, Peaking, Speed, Frequency, Direction, and so on.

   Most of the adjustments for the Ocean effect are available in the Ocean shader, which uses the output to displace the NURBS surface.

Figure 16.66 A render of the Maya Ocean effect.

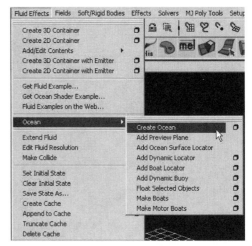

Figure 16.67 From the Fluid Effects menu, select Ocean > Create Ocean.

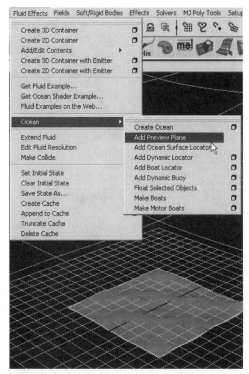

Figure 16.68 Adding a preview plane to the ocean will help you interactively view the adjustments you make to the ocean.

✔ Tips

■ Maya won't shade the ocean plane because it would slow playback too much. You can create a preview plane when you create the ocean by opening the Option dialog box and checking Create Preview Plane. You can add a preview plane to an existing ocean by selecting Ocean > Add Preview Plane from the Fluid Effects menu. (**Figure 16.68**). The preview plane is a small patch with the Ocean shader attached to it so that you can see the results as you make adjustments.

■ You may want to attach the ocean to the Perspective camera in the Create Ocean options. This will move and scale the ocean with the camera to give you an acceptable resolution wherever the camera is positioned.

FLUID EFFECTS

Now that your scene includes an ocean, let's add an object that floats. We can use the Make Boat command to float objects, or groups of objects, and control their buoyancy and other attributes.

To make a boat:

1. Create an ocean by following the steps outlined in the previous task.

2. From the Create menu, select Polygons > Cube.

3. Scale the cube to represent the size of a boat.

4. With the cube selected, choose Fluid Effects > Ocean > Make Boats (**Figure 16.69**).

   The cube is now parented under a locator, which is controlled by the ocean and in turn controls the movement of the cube (**Figure 16.70**).

5. Select the locator and open the Attribute Editor by pressing Ctrl a / Control a .

6. In the Attribute Editor open the Extra Attributes tab.

7. Press Play in the playback controls.

8. Interactively adjust Buoyancy, Water Damping, Air Damping, Roll, and Pitch to adjust how the boat reacts.

   You will want to have at least 500 frames in the range slider to allow you enough time to adjust and see the effect.

✔ Tip

■ Now that you've made a boat and familiarized yourself with the attributes, try creating a motor boat (following the steps outlined above, but in Step 2 select Fluid Effects > Ocean > Make Motor Boat). The motor boat includes Throttle and Rudder controls so you can interactively drive the boat through your scene!

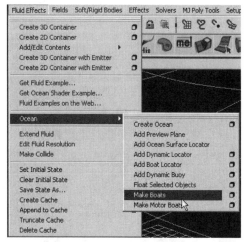

Figure 16.69 From the Fluid Effects menu, select Ocean > Make Boats.

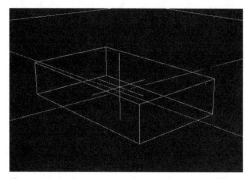

Figure 16.70 A locator controls how the ocean affects the boat.

INDEX

INDEX

W

Wake Air field type, 373
Wave deformer, 268–269
wave effects, 267–268
wave frequency, 268–269
Wave manipulator, 268
Wavelength option, 267–268
Wedge Face tool, 185–186
wedges, creating, 185–186
weights
    clusters, 224, 228–230
    described, 224
    points, 228–230, 235
    skin, 237–239
Width attribute, 74
Wind Air field type, 373
Windows computers, 352
    Macintosh and, ix
Wire deformers, 274–276
wire shapes, 274–276
Wire Tool, 275
wireframe mode, 51–52, 172
wires, 274
world coordinates, 3

X

x-y-z axes, 100
XYZ coordinate system, 3

Z

zooming
    with camera, 44
    objects, 44, 89
    scenes, 32

WWW.PEACHPIT.COM

Quality How-to Computer Books

Visit Peachpit Press on the Web at www.peachpit.com

- Check out new feature articles each Monday: excerpts, interviews, tips, and plenty of how-tos

- Find any Peachpit book by title, series, author, or topic on the Books page

- See what our authors are up to on the News page: signings, chats, appearances, and more

- Meet the Peachpit staff and authors in the About section: bios, profiles, and candid shots

- Use Resources to reach our academic, sales, customer service, and tech support areas and find out how to become a Peachpit author

About

News

Books

Features

Resources

Order

Find

Welcome!

Peachpit.com is also the place to:

- Chat with our authors online
- Take advantage of special Web-only offers
- Get the latest info on new books